JULIA MORGAN
ARCHITECT

JULIA MORGAN
ARCHITECT

SARA HOLMES BOUTELLE

COLOR PHOTOGRAPHY BY RICHARD BARNES

ABBEVILLE PRESS PUBLISHERS NEW YORK

For Christopher, Jonathan, Will and Ann—and Mary

EDITOR: NANCY GRUBB

DESIGNER: JOEL AVIROM

PRODUCTION SUPERVISOR: HOPE KOTURO

Front cover: View from the north tower of the Main Building, San Simeon
Back cover and frontispiece: Roman pool, San Simeon

Unless otherwise indicated, captions and pictures read left to right and top to bottom. All buildings are located in California, except as noted. Dates are for plans and construction (as closely as could be determined); preliminary drawings for some structures may have occurred earlier.

First edition, third printing

LIBRARY OF CONGRESS
Library of Congress Cataloging-in-Publication Data

Boutelle, Sara Holmes.
Julia Morgan, architect/Sara Holmes Boutelle.
p. cm.
Bibliography: p.
Includes index.
ISBN 0-89659-792-X
1. Morgan, Julia, 1872–1957.   2. Architects—California—
Biography.   3. Architecture, Modern—20th century—California.
4. Architecture—California.   I. Morgan, Julia, 1872–1957.
II. Title.
NA737.M68B68   1988
720′.92′4—dc19
[B]
87-29008
CIP

C O N T E N T S

INTRODUCTION

The eye-dazzling theatricality of Hearst's famous castle, perched on a hilltop midway between San Francisco and Los Angeles, attracts a million or so curious visitors each year. The saga of this glamorous estate has become a familiar part of American lore, along with countless anecdotes about the mercurial man who commissioned it. But among the crowds of marveling visitors, only a handful can identify Julia Morgan as the architect who designed and built this extravagantly beautiful showplace. That she continued to work on it for more than twenty years, making the four-hundred-mile round trip by train and taxi nearly every weekend while maintaining a thriving practice in San Francisco, exemplifies her dauntless commitment to the project, to her career, and to architecture.

Julia Morgan (1872–1957) stood just five feet tall and weighed about one hundred pounds. Her frail appearance belied her inexhaustible strength and iron will. Wearing tailored suits and French silk blouses, she clambered over scaffolds and descended into trenches to make sure that the walls and drains met her high standards. The head of a busy, prosperous practice, she worked quietly and alone, with no sounding board in the form of a close colleague or mate. Devoted to her career, she seems never even to have considered marriage, although she had many friends among her fellow students, clients, and colleagues and is remembered with affectionate respect by the surviving members of her staff.

Over the course of her forty-seven-year career, Morgan designed upwards of seven hundred buildings, of which all but a small minority were built. She worked for institutions and individuals with equal ease, creating schools, churches, stores, YWCAs, hospitals, houses, apartments, and a hay barn or two—not to mention the theaters, bowling alley, billiard rooms, and zoo she built for William Randolph Hearst. Morgan had a special knack for swimming pools, using color, light, and shape to create sumptuous designs that flaunted a hedonism startling for so modest an architect.

Opposite: Bear House, Wyntoon, on the McCloud River, 1932–33

Julia Morgan, 1926

7

Two opposing forces determined Morgan's approach to architecture. One was the stately classicism she learned at the Ecole des Beaux-Arts in Paris, the other was the environment (both natural and man-made) of her native California. Having earned a degree in engineering from the University of California, Berkeley—the closest thing to architectural training then available on the West Coast—she became the first woman admitted into the architectural program at the Ecole des Beaux-Arts, long regarded as the world's foremost architectural school. Yet unlike most of her fellow students, even those who were later her colleagues and competitors on the West Coast, Morgan adhered to the Beaux-Arts style only when it suited her. The extensive range of historical styles she mastered at the Ecole enriched her design vocabulary so she could refer to the past with authority but without feeling bound to precedent. This was the heart of academic eclecticism, but the decision about how faithful to remain to the past was a difficult one that tripped up many other architects of the period. What held Morgan steady throughout her career was the balance she established between historicism on the one hand and the demands of client and site on the other.

Julia Morgan was born in San Francisco, and her affection for the California landscape infused her work, influencing her choice of styles, materials, and colors. Her mother's letters to her in Paris refer frequently to Morgan's love of the rocks, trees, fruits, and flowers of the California countryside. Having established her office in San Francisco, Morgan worked throughout the state, with occasional forays as far afield as Illinois, Utah, and Hawaii. She chose her styles carefully to relate to the site at hand: the light-filled, woodsy comfort of the Arts and Crafts style seemed well suited to the rolling hills of the Bay Area; the simplicity of the California missions offered inspiration for dwellings and courtyards in more arid landscapes; buildings in the Bavarian style provided an apt choice for the snowy mountains of Tahoe and Shasta.

It is difficult to trace any clear-cut development in Morgan's work. A strict chronology offers little help since some of her commissions stretched out over ten or more years and were designed concurrently with other buildings of very different types. Classifying her buildings by the materials and methods of their construction is equally unilluminating since those elements were interpreted differently from project to project. Morgan used reinforced concrete early and often, producing the first house ever built of that material in Berkeley, in 1906.[1] Redwood was the cheapest and most readily available material during her early years of practice, but it lost favor after serious fires such as the one in Berkeley in 1923 (she nevertheless continued to use wood as late as 1939). Stucco and half-timber was a combination popular during the 1920s, and brick was also favored, especially by clients eager to create an impressive appearance and willing to risk brick's instability in an earthquake.

The Arts and Crafts movement exerted a deep influence on Morgan. Begun by John Ruskin and William Morris as a reaction against the blight of industrialization in England, it quickly spread to America and soon made its way to the West Coast. The emphasis was on recapturing a simpler way of life, lived in harmony with nature. A building's materials were to come, if possible, from its own environment; simplicity and utility were the goals. Details were to be based on local traditions and natural sources, not pattern books. Architects associated with the movement worked with craftsmen, sculptors, and painters in a return to the collaborative ideals of the Middle Ages. They did not copy past styles but worked out "free" versions of them. No meaningless ornamentation was permitted, and unpainted, unadorned materials were preferred, with construction elements left visible to reveal the highly skilled workmanship.

The Arts and Crafts movement was brought to northern California by Joseph Worcester, a Swedenborgian minister and amateur builder who was influenced by Ruskin. In 1876 Worcester built a house of redwood shingles in Piedmont, across the bay from San Francisco. His use of unpainted redwood board for the interior and other radical departures from prevailing styles aroused the curiosity and enthusiasm of architects and artists throughout the Bay Area. Charles Keeler and Bernard Maybeck of Berkeley and Louis Christian Mullgardt, Willis Polk, and A.C. Schweinfurth of San Francisco formed the nucleus of a group that met during the late 1880s to discuss Crafts-related theories of design. For a short time in 1890 Polk put out a monthly journal, *Architectural News*, which propagated their ideas.

In 1898 Keeler organized the Ruskin Club, which met in Schweinfurth's newly completed Unitarian Church in Berkeley. This small shingled structure with broad pitched roof has porches on two sides supported by unpeeled redwood trunks. A landmark example of Crafts architecture, it was the perfect setting for Keeler's club. That same year women activists founded the Hillside Club to protect the natural environment of the north Berkeley hills; members met at the Schweinfurth church and in various homes. Only women were allowed to belong until 1902, when the membership was opened to men, the most enthusiastic being Keeler and Maybeck, who designed a permanent clubhouse in 1906. Keeler's book *The Simple Home*

Top: Clifton Price apartments, Berkeley, 1907–8

Center: Lodge, Asilomar, 1914–15

Bottom: Stairway, Lodge, Asilomar

(1904) apparently became a sort of bible for the group. The Hillside Club's most frequently quoted maxim was that a house was "landscape gardening with a few rooms for use in case of rain." Unpainted wood was the material of choice for houses, inside and out (Maybeck's wife, Annie, called the few white-painted neighboring houses the "beached ships" of Berkeley).

The moral fervor relating to nature extended to near fanaticism about health. Raising vegetables at home, maintaining a vegetarian diet, drinking coffee substitutes, taking ice-cold showers, sleeping in the open air (hence the need for "sleeping porches"), and pursuing fitness through jogging, swimming, hiking, and dress reform—all became part of the crusade. Julia Morgan knew the Maybecks and other members of the Hillside Club and shared many of their aesthetic ideas, if not the related moral commitments (she was reported by her wood-carver Jules Suppo to prefer lamb chops for dinner and to drink coffee morning and night).

Morgan was the only prominent member of the group of architects interested in the Crafts movement who was born in California; the others all arrived as adults: Mullgardt from Saint Louis, Maybeck from New York, Ernest Coxhead from England, Polk from Kansas City, and the Greene brothers from Ohio. Her own deep response to nature and to the local environment reinforced her interest in the Crafts principles of building simply and in harmony with the site. While she was in Paris, from 1896 to 1902, she had a subscription to *The Architect* magazine and also had access to British architectural periodicals, which must have familiarized her with what Morris's followers were doing. At the same time, her interest in medieval guilds, the Italian hill towns, and Eugène-Emmanuel Viollet-le-Duc's medievalism was as important a part of her education as the rational theory of the Beaux-Arts course. Thus, she was not unprepared for building in the Crafts tradition, although her engineering background and classical training made her aware how difficult it was to achieve a "simple" building.

Much of Morgan's early domestic architecture reflected Crafts principles, as did such important structures as Saint John's Presbyterian Church in Berkeley (1908–1910) and the Asilomar YWCA Conference Center

Cast-stone frieze, Chapel of the Chimes, Oakland, 1926–30

Opposite: Gothic Study, Main Building, San Simeon, 1922–26. The barrel vaulting was painted with medieval tales by Camille Solon. At the far end of the room can be seen the only portrait Hearst ever sat for, by his friend Orrin Peck.

Guests' library, Main Building, San Simeon, 1922–26. The deeply coffered ceiling from sixteenth-century Spain is complemented by bookshelves carved at San Simeon under Theodore Van der Loo's supervision.

Opposite, top: Roofs of San Simeon

Opposite, center: Tile and ironwork, tower walkway, Main Building, San Simeon

Opposite, bottom: Drawing for Desert House, c. 1930

(1913–1928). Morgan's buildings made a considerable contribution to the style, and it remained important to her philosophically long after a shortage of inexpensive wood and a change in fashion meant that she was generally building with concrete in Tudor, Mediterranean, or Bavarian styles.

Morgan did not hesitate to apply Crafts principles to the interiors of Mediterranean buildings, large and small. She carried out those principles most dramatically in her work on the Hearst estate at San Simeon. There she presided over a kind of brotherhood of highly qualified artisans, including workers skilled in stone casting, ornamental plastering, wood carving (including John Klang, a specialist in creating wormholes and in matching new and old woods), and elaborate ironworking, as well as painters, weavers, tapestry workers, and tile designers. At San Simeon and in workshops in Los Angeles, San Francisco, Alameda, and Carmel, these specialists toiled for union wages (then two dollars an hour) to repair, copy, and add to the works of antiquity that Hearst kept buying so voraciously. They also improvised and designed, working from books and magazines borrowed from Morgan's library and from photographs or sketches of buildings she had admired in Europe. Ed Trinkeller, an Alsatian ironworker, did caricatures and likenesses in iron. Camille Solon painted scenes and figures on the stone arches of the Gothic Study. Austro-Hungarian Frank Gyorgy did antiquing in wood and metal. All followed Morgan's direction of "careful carelessness." The ceilings, doors, windows, and furniture they created stand as significant

Crafts work produced during a period when the movement was increasingly disregarded. Morgan brought many of these workers to Berkeley, to San Francisco, and to Wyntoon, and they all looked up to her, proud to be part of such a highly skilled group.

The demand for such luxury diminished with the Depression, and although the years following the war brought a building boom, there was a new emphasis on technology and a loss of interest in human scale, while escalating labor costs made craftsmanship prohibitively expensive. The predominant International Style of architecture, with its denigration of ornament, had little sympathy for Crafts ideals or accomplishments, and interest in the movement was not revived until the mid-1960s, nearly a decade after Morgan's death.

In striking contrast to the dark wood and rough shingles of Morgan's Crafts buildings are the smooth white walls and sculptured mass of her structures in a style loosely identified as Mediterranean. More a polyglot compilation of styles, often called Spanish Colonial Revival, it was derived from the Mediterranean world at large. Californian missions, based on memories of Rome, provided Morgan with a local source of typical Mediterranean elements such as courtyards, arches, tile floors and tile roofs, and quatrefoil or trefoil windows. She used all of these in both pure and hybrid ways, and the predominance of any one aspect of the style would shift from commission to commission. Some Islamic details such as elaborate wrought-iron balconies and stairways, tiles with abstract polychrome patterns, ornately decorated arched entrances, the use of water as central to the plan, and even domes, crenellated arches, and columns became part of the Mediterranean style as well. Even Pueblo and Hopi Indian adobes, similar to Greek vernacular buildings, were absorbed; indeed, Morgan made some watercolor designs marked "Desert House" that clearly reveal this influence.

The popularity of the Mediterranean style in California reflected a new awareness of local history and tradition, stimulated by the romanticizing of California as a "new Eden"—a view reflected in paintings by William Keith and in the widely successful novel of mission life, *Ramona* (1884), by Helen Hunt Jackson. The impact of the Spanish Colonial buildings created by Bertram Goodhue and Carleton M. Winslow for the 1915 San Diego Exposition made the Mediterranean style seem inseparable from California; and clients and architects became more familiar with terms such as *Plateresque* and *Churrigueresque* than the next generation would be with the names Schindler and Neutra.

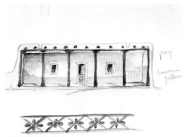

Morgan evinced interest in the Mediterranean style early in her career, with her additions to Phoebe Apperson Hearst's Hacienda, begun a year after Morgan returned from Paris, and with her Mills College bell

Blanding house (The Casino), Belvedere, 1913–14

tower. Always an engineer as well as an architect, she was particularly interested in using reinforced concrete for both domestic and public architecture, and she found it easily adaptable to styles originally created in adobe bricks and plaster. Morgan's grasp of the Mediterranean style, developed as she enlarged and remodeled the Hearst Hacienda at Pleasanton from 1903 to 1910, carried over into her later work. Her last two Spanish-oriented commissions, the Babicora Hacienda and the San Francisco Medieval Museum, kept her busy in the 1940s.[2] (During World War II she went to neutral Mexico to find craftsmen who could train farm workers to make adobe bricks and Mediterranean ornamentation for Babicora.)

Diverse styles may have inspired Morgan, but her primary attention was directed to the client's wishes and to the site; everything else followed from those two considerations. Before designing a house for someone, Morgan would visit the family, often sitting on the floor with the children, and make every attempt to understand what the client wanted, however quirky (including designing a house without any rectangular spaces[3]). After this information was gathered, the plan itself became her most significant concern, for in Beaux-Arts fashion she designed each building from the inside out, with the exterior being of secondary importance. Her plans varied. Sometimes she favored the popular rectangular organization with a central hall as axis; sometimes she preferred the Mediterranean plan of rooms located around a patio; sometimes she used butterfly or open plans. The kitchen was placed at the front of the house if the chief view was at the rear of the lot. Side entrances gave the whole front of the house to the living room. Morgan delighted in the purposeful variation of scale. She used vaulted ceilings or left trusses open to extend the height of even small rooms and favored open plans that created a feeling of expansiveness, while sometimes juxtaposing that openness with an enclosed recess to give a sense of shelter and privacy.

Details were all-important to Morgan. Her entrances were often subtle exercises in opposition, expressing welcome while gracefully excluding the world. At a time when many modernist architects were trying to dissolve the wall, Morgan enhanced it, glorifying the wall's importance by the ways she used windows to punctuate it. Never merely openings, her windows were often major design features, shaped and ornamented, with various forms and sizes unified into pleasingly rhythmic patterns. She used reflective light to call attention to the richness of surfaces, arranging for illumination to come from more than one direction to avoid glare. Her stairways were central features, using the light as part of the design. Fireplaces were many and varied, with the hearth often becoming the heart of the home. Paneling and built-in furniture were scrupulously thought-out parts of the aesthetic and practical scheme, satisfying in their use of fine wood and cabinetry. Meticulous care for such elements was a major, ongoing consideration, and she presented full-scale drawings for all-important details to

Left: Donaldson house, San Francisco, 1921–22

Center, top: Newell house, San Anselmo, 1908

Center, bottom: Yates house, San Francisco, 1911

Right: Chapel of the Chimes, Oakland, 1926–30

Stenciled ceiling panels, Berkeley Women's City Club, 1929–30

the artisans who would carry them out. A Morgan building could come equipped with custom-designed buffets and bureaus, tables, chairs, lighting fixtures, even dishes and linens.

Morgan's preoccupation with light and color characterizes her buildings of all styles and sizes. She used courtyards, colonnades, and sleeping porches to link inside with outside; skylights were another favored device for funneling light into a building or a swimming pool. Highly polished wood floors and plain white walls intensified the light within some of her structures. She calculated curved ironwork balconies to cast decorative shadows on bright white exteriors, providing unexpected ornamentation. Color appeared throughout her buildings in many different guises: polychrome terracotta tiles, wreaths, and garlands, stenciled borders, even elaborate murals. Her lavish pools at San Simeon and elsewhere are dazzling in their use of vibrant peacock hues. But color could be more subtly employed, as in Morgan's use of unpainted local wood and stone to blend into the surroundings and in her advice to one client to match the leaves and bark of the eucalyptus tree in decorating the interior of a house Morgan had just designed.

Morgan's great skill in accommodating the tastes of her middle-class clients kept her far from the cutting edge of architecture. Reluctant to push beyond what her clients wanted, she had a tendency to put the practical ahead of the spatial. Efficient, pleasing solutions to design problems took precedence over innovation or drama. Bold flights of uninhibited imagination would hardly have been welcomed by her typical clientele, and her nature seemed content with this restriction. Morgan made no revolutionary city plans, though she was an effective urban designer, and she created no new style. She could, however, be innovative when given a free hand on an expansive building project, as at Asilomar and the Hearst estates, and she often worked out original solutions that derived from her knowledge of the past but were uniquely her own.

Julia Morgan chose to be anonymous. She steadfastly refused to enter competitions, write articles, submit photographs to architectural magazines, or serve on committees, dismissing such activities as fit only for "talking architects." In her day the national architectural magazines were all headquartered in the East and paid little attention to what was happening on the West Coast. Polk, Maybeck, and the Greene brothers were other California architects who, like Morgan, did not receive their just due from the architectural establishment. Her refusal to exploit the usual methods of making one's name known guaranteed her almost complete anonymity outside the circle of her clients and peers.

When Morgan closed her office in 1951 at the age of seventy-nine, she had her files, blueprints, and drawings destroyed because she thought they would be of interest only to her clients, who already had their own copies of relevant material. By this time architectural fashion had moved far from the styles Morgan favored, and she seemed out of step in a world dominated by the International Style. Cycles of architectural fashion made her eclipse almost complete, but a few more turns of the wheel of fashion have made a reappraisal of her achievements inevitable. The new respect for and understanding of Beaux-Arts architecture is equaled by a surge of interest in California regional work. Bay Area domestic architecture, long the object of local interest and admiration, now appeals to architects from all parts of the country. Morgan's interest in crafts and ornamentation seems progressive today, and her sympathetic response to her clients' desires an admirable and much-needed lesson. The buildings that Morgan designed in numerous cities for the YWCA helped to solve problems still plaguing cities, and with magazines now showing new, innovative YWCA designs, attention is again being paid to those earlier structures. Morgan's role as a woman in a field still largely dominated by men has been another factor in the growing appreciation of her achievements.

But it is the particular quality of Morgan's buildings that most evokes interest today. Her preoccupation with light, with the relationship of a structure to its site, with flexibility of plan, with indoor-outdoor living, and with the use of color and decoration make her work relevant to contemporary designers. Her devotion to quality, to craftsmanship, and to the most exacting standards is appealing even though it is unlikely ever to be duplicated. Her generosity of spirit, as evidenced by the profit sharing in the office and her support of her staff and their children, is unfortunately not a practical working model for most contemporary firms, but the evidence of it helps make her come alive as a person dedicated to her associates and to the practice of architecture.

THE EARLY YEARS

Looking back on a long and satisfying career, Julia Morgan reflected, "My own experience is that it is a decided advantage to grow up in the general environment one is to work in."[1] She had been born in a still raw and rowdy San Francisco on January 20, 1872, and her life's work revolved around that rapidly maturing city. Morgan's father, Charles Bill Morgan, had abandoned a secure upper-class life in New England to sail around the tip of South America to California in 1867.[2] After becoming convinced that he could make a fortune in minerals, the twenty-three-year-old mining engineer returned to his home in New York City and married Eliza Woodland Parmelee. Both sides of Eliza's family, the Woodlands and the Parmelees, came of old Virginian stock and were proud of it. Eliza's father, Albert Osias Parmelee, had made a fortune before the Civil War by dealing in cotton futures on the New York Commodity Exchange, and he was eager to use his money to provide the young couple with a house, furniture, and frequent cross-country visits.

In 1870 the Morgans settled in a family hotel in San Francisco. When their first child was born, a son they named Parmelee, the Parmelee family paid for a trip to New York via the new transcontinental railroad so that the child could be christened at Grace Church in Brooklyn Heights. Julia was born two years later, and the family crossed the continent again when she was ten months old. The Eastern relatives were assembled for Thanksgiving, and the baby was christened in the family church and named for Eliza's sister Julia. The same journey was repeated, at the Parmelees' expense, for the other three children: Emma, born in 1874; Avery, born in 1876; and Gardner Bulkley, born in 1887.

The security offered by the Parmelee money had an important influence on Julia's younger years. When she was a preschooler, her family moved to the milder climate of Oakland; they would stay there for fifty years in the same commodious Victorian house at 754 Fourteenth Street —bought and furnished by Julia's grandfather. The family maintained an

Opposite: Julia Morgan, Brooklyn Heights, c. 1878

Left to right: Parmelee, Emma, and Julia Morgan, Brooklyn Heights, New York, 1875–76, on the occasion of Emma's christening

Julia Morgan, Brooklyn
Heights, c. 1878

Charles Bill Morgan,
1901

upper-middle-class standard of living, with servants, formal calls, summers by the seashore, participation in civic affairs, and a firm belief in the importance of education for daughters as well as for sons. Julia's father worked in the world of mining stocks, commuting by ferry from Oakland to San Francisco. A solid citizen who voted the straight Republican ticket, he would occasionally imperil the family finances by taking a flier— sometimes in gold mines, and once, during the late 1890s, in voting machines. A wistful letter to Julia in 1902 mentions that his planned sale of a mine promised such wealth that "I do not know what extravagances may be indulged in," even as he acknowledged that the source of his hopes was his "gold-brick man."[3] A calling card reveals that Charles Morgan ran for city treasurer in 1901, an unsuccessful venture he seems never to have repeated. He was proud of Julia, but hardly serious when he wrote in a letter of congratulation upon her 1898 acceptance into the Ecole des Beaux-Arts, "It seems as if I might go down in history as the father of the distinguished architect, Julia Morgan."

Eliza Morgan's parents made several trips to California to spend time with their grandchildren; and at least once, when Julia was six, Eliza took the four children to live with her parents, first in their summer house in Morristown, New Jersey, and then in Brooklyn Heights. This Eastern stay, from July 1878 to June 1879, was admittedly undertaken because of Charles's straitened finances—his mining investments had not realized the hoped-for profits. His wife's letters to him from this period (always addressed "Dear Boy" and signed "Your Girl, Eliza") record a series of disasters: scarlet fever, diphtheria (which took the life of a young cousin), various illnesses of the Morgan children (no doubt worsened by the custom of dos-

C. B. MORGAN

REGULAR REPUBLICAN NOMINEE FOR

✿ ✿ ✿ ✿ CITY ✿ ✿ ✿ ✿

TREASURER

Election March 11, 1901.

TRIBUNE UNION LABEL PRINT

ing with paregoric and opium), and a fire that severely burned Eliza's hands, incapacitating her for weeks. Despite the assistance of several servants (a nurse was in constant attendance on Eliza's invalid mother), Eliza was exhausted by the rigors of fumigating and washing everything in carbolic acid to stem the diseases. After California's milder climate the ice and snow of the New York winter seemed an added hardship. Julia suffered a severe ear infection that winter, a condition that later became chronic. She was kept indoors most of the time because of her ear, but possibly also to save the expense of a private school. Nonetheless, the Parmelee family could still afford to make the end-of-summer move from Morristown to Hoboken by private railway car, then from Hoboken to Brooklyn by ferry and carriage. They shopped at the best New York stores, visited Henry Ward Beecher's fashionable church, and sent Parmelee to a nearby private school.

Eliza's letters to her husband include frequent references to "Dudu" (the family nickname for Julia, derived from Parmelee's childish attempt to pronounce *Julia*). By December 1, 1878, Julia had recuperated sufficiently from a "very bad" case of scarlet fever for her mother to write: "Dudu has never made any fuss. She accepts the inevitable and is composed and serene. She is a real darling. She sits up in her bed as pleasant as an angel and it will be a week or two before she can leave it." On January 7 Eliza wrote that the six-year-old Julia "denies herself stories, fearing there'll be no more left for Papa to read." Two weeks later she wrote, "Dudu is thin but bright and pretty. She had a splendid birthday party [on January 20] with grandmother, cake, books, doll, clothes (over $10) and kid gloves." A day later the ear infection had her in tears from pain. Eliza's letters also indicate that Julia was dissolved with longing for her absent father and raged against taking the required medicine. She was the most determined and the most emotionally intense of the children, and remained so in later years.

The family returned to Oakland in the summer of 1879, resuming their comfortable home life and the children's schooling. Like all her siblings, Julia took dancing and music lessons, and along with Avery she continued to study violin and piano beyond youthful competence. A studious child, Julia attended Riverside Grammar School, then went on to Oakland High School, which had a strong classical curriculum with advanced mathematics, physics, Latin, and German.[4] The Morgan girls were more studious than their brothers, none of whom ever evidenced any conventional drive to succeed. Julia considered both medicine and music as careers before settling on architecture, and Emma contemplated art and the law before choosing the latter. Their commitment to professional careers is especially remarkable given the absence of any immediate role model: Mrs. Morgan wanted her daughters to fulfill their potential, but she also expressed all the traditional

Julia Morgan, Oakland, c. 1879

The Morgan family
house, Oakland

hopes that they would marry and repeatedly urged them to enjoy life rather than studying so hard.

Julia and her older brother, Parmelee, were apparently not very close, but she, Emma, and Avery went around together; the youngest brother, Gardner Bulkley (called "Sam" by family and friends), was fifteen years her junior and almost seemed to belong to another generation. In 1900 Parmelee took a trip around the world, then worked in his grandfather's brokerage firm back East before marrying and moving to southern California, where he maintained little contact with his relatives in the Bay Area. Julia's younger sister, Emma, nicknamed "Baby" by the family, was a lively and pretty young woman, much taken up with clothes, parties, and boys, as well as with more serious pursuits. After earning her bachelor's degree from the University of California, Berkeley, she graduated from law school in San Francisco, complaining in a letter to Julia that she would "rather be working at art but am bent over Blackstone." Emma married Hart North, a fellow lawyer who had been a high-school and university classmate of Julia's. Although Emma maintained a lifetime membership in the Queen's Bench (the association for women lawyers) and shared her husband's office, she practiced little. The sisters remained close until Julia's death; Emma died at age ninety-six in 1970.

The fourth child, Avery, was gifted in music and art but graduated from Berkeley with a degree in engineering. He had never been particularly close to his father, but when Charles Morgan suffered a stroke in 1923, Avery stayed by his bedside for the remaining year of his father's life. His devoted round-the-clock nursing reportedly broke his own health and caused a nervous collapse, although there is evidence of previous instability. Avery had followed Julia to Paris, where he studied architecture in an atelier for a year, but he designed little. He later did some drafting in his sister's office, but his favorite role was as chauffeur of her Hudson automobile. Julia served as his companion and protector until his death in 1940.

The youngest son, Sam, seems to have been the family favorite. After high school he started a moving and storage company, for which his sister designed a warehouse. He worked for a time in the San Francisco office of Aetna Insurance and then joined the Oakland Fire Department when professional fire fighters replaced volunteers. He was only twenty-six years old and engaged to be married when the fire truck on which he was riding brushed against a cement wall, killing him instantly. Julia designed a classical tomb to erect over his grave in Oakland's Mountain View Cemetery, but her mother decided instead to donate in his memory the entrance gates for the Kings Daughters Home, an Oakland hospital designed by Julia (see chapter 5).

In 1890, at the age of eighteen, Julia enrolled at the University of California, Berkeley, which had been chartered in 1868, admitting its first female students two years later. During her first year Avery had to escort her on the horsecar to and from Oakland, then she settled into the Kappa Alpha Theta sorority residence at the edge of campus. The Thetas were a group of twenty-seven young women who organized in 1890, rented their own house, and hired a cook-housekeeper. Berkeley had so few women students at the time that the support provided by a sorority was very important, and many of the women developed close bonds that remained significant throughout their lives.

Individual records for Berkeley students in the 1890s are sparse, but Julia's do indicate her interest in mathematics and science. According to family sources, she favored architecture as a profession early in her undergraduate studies; since there was no architectural school in the West, she enrolled in the engineering program at Berkeley. She was the only woman there at the time, although at least two others had preceded her. For an undergraduate engineering class she wrote "A Structural Analysis of the Steel Frame of the Mills Building [a commercial structure in San Francisco]." It caused a fair amount of professional comment. When Julia was in France, Mr. Morgan proudly wrote to her that Arthur Brown, Sr.—architect and father of Julia's classmate Arthur Brown, Jr.—had told him on the commuter's ferry that "not more than two or three men in San Francisco" would have been capable of writing that paper.[5]

Eliza Woodland Parmelee Morgan, in mourning for her son Sam, 1913

Professor George Washington Percy of the College of Engineering was reportedly one of Julia's mentors and even offered to help pay her expenses to study architecture back East or in Europe, as he did for other students. By far the most significant person in her engineering studies, however, arrived at Berkeley in 1894, when she was a senior. This was Bernard Maybeck, a thirty-two-year-old architect hired to teach descriptive geometry, the subject in which he had recently won a major prize at the Ecole des Beaux-Arts in Paris. In addition, he energetically gathered the most able students around him for a series of informal seminars. Maybeck was starting a small architectural practice, and these students, eager to continue their education outside the classroom, worked with him on additions to his house and studio on Berryman Street, in Berkeley. Julia Morgan was one of the group, which included John Bakewell, Edward Bennett, Arthur Brown, Jr., Lewis Hobart, and G. Albert Lansburgh. All studied in Paris and became prominent architects in the West during the early twentieth century, but none ever rivaled Maybeck's charismatic personality or his innovative approach to work and to life.

Julia graduated from the College of Engineering in the spring of 1894 and worked for Maybeck the following year, while she also studied drawing at the Hopkins School of Art Instruction (now the San Francisco Art Institute). The Berkeley campus newspaper recorded one of her earliest architectural efforts, announcing on October 20, 1894, that she was in charge of building a house for Andrew C. Lawson, a professor of geology at Berkeley. This was one of Maybeck's first commissions, a "Gothic" house destroyed in the 1906 earthquake.

Maybeck had kept in touch with his Paris colleagues and passed on to Julia the rumor that the Ecole des Beaux-Arts might be ready to accept women into its heretofore all-male ranks. His encouragement strengthened Julia's resolve to continue her architectural studies. Eliza Morgan (who always controlled the family's purse strings) agreed to finance a trip for her daughter to investigate the possibilities of enrolling at Polytechnic Institute (now Massachusetts Institute of Technology) in Cambridge, to visit various family members, and to undertake a study tour in France, after which she was to decide if she wanted to return to Cambridge. Arthur Brown, Jr., was going abroad with his mother, who planned to make a home for her son in a Paris apartment for a year or so. Mrs. Brown invited Julia to accompany them, and Julia's mother consented. This plan fell through when Mrs. Brown became ill, but Julia found another former Berkeley student to accompany her. Jessica Peixotto, one of a distinguished family of Oakland artists, was going abroad for graduate studies in economics. The Morgans gave their consent to the trip and made arrangements for both women to stay at a club for American women at 4 rue de Chevreuse. Avery would graduate in engineering in two years; if he wanted to go to Paris and if Julia had not yet returned to study in Cambridge, they might share quarters.

Kappa Alpha Theta sorority, U.C. Berkeley, 1894. Emma Morgan is at far left, Julia Morgan, at bottom right.

Opposite: Julia Morgan, 1896, just before leaving Oakland for Paris

The elasticity of the plans suited Julia. She and Jessica set out together in March 1896 by cross-country train, visiting Morgan relatives in New England, evaluating the Polytechnic Institute, and stopping over at the LeBruns, who lived near the Parmelees in Brooklyn Heights. A New York City cousin, Lucy Thornton, had married Pierre LeBrun, a member of the distinguished Napoleon LeBrun and Sons architectural firm in New York. It is obvious from their years of correspondence that Morgan came to value Pierre LeBrun not only as a kinsman but also as a practicing architect to whom she conscientiously reported her architectural progress and ideas. LeBrun in turn admired her character and, later, her ability to manage her office. When he closed his office in 1910, he sent her his architectural library, a formidable collection that unfortunately was later dispersed by her nephew, along with her own.

Filled with high purpose and a lively sense of adventure, Morgan and Peixotto sailed for France. The Morgans, like Julia's teachers, had recognized her talent and her determination, and they provided financial and emotional support for her unconventional plans. Her confidence, her diligence, and her ambition made the Ecole des Beaux-Arts the inevitable next challenge.

2

ECOLE DES BEAUX-ARTS

The renowned school that attracted Morgan to Paris had existed almost unchanged since the seventeenth century. Originally called the Académies Royales, the Ecole des Beaux-Arts provided state-supported training for aspirants in the fine arts. The architecture division, founded in 1671, was the last to be formed; it retained its powerful status until it was closed in 1968 in response to the New Left revolution. French citizens who emerged from the Ecole des Beaux-Arts were prime candidates for positions as state architects. Foreigners were actively discouraged from applying and permitted to enter only in never-explicit quotas; once accepted, they were required to write *étranger* on their submissions to the all-important competitions. Foreign students were never allowed to compete for the Grand Prix de Rome, the annual prize that underwrote study and travel in Italy and nearly always resulted in a state appointment.

Students could present themselves for the entrance examination annually or sometimes semiannually if there were a great number of applicants. Preparation for the entrance examinations took place in ateliers run by trained architects who were usually in private practice and were often former Grand Prix winners; some even served as instructors at the Ecole. The atelier was an independent organization composed of students invited to pay for the privilege of criticism by the patron and of apprentices who worked for him on independent commissions. In addition to criticizing the efforts of aspirants seeking entrance into the Ecole and helping students hone their skills by working on group atelier projects, the patron was responsible for encouraging each student to develop independent ideas based on a wide knowledge of precedents. On the one hand, a successful student had to be familiar with historical solutions to architectural problems, and on the other, the student was required to work out a personal solution, not simply a copy of the past. Personal choices were made at each step, but those choices were guided by awareness of

Opposite: Ecole des Beaux-Arts, Paris

Julia Morgan in front of Notre Dame, Paris, 1897–98

earlier examples and a rational ordering of possibilities.

The aspirants who passed the Ecole's entrance examination began the prescribed scientific, architectural, and arts courses of the Second Class. This process emphasized school-administered monthly competitions, which were considered to be training for the final Grand Prix de Rome competition; students also attended lectures. Both the competitions and the lectures inculcated classical principles of symmetry, proportion, and harmony, with geometric clarity in design a primary aim.

Once a student acquired a total of sixteen points, which could be accumulated only in competitions, he was permitted to enter the First Class. Scientific subjects such as mathematics, descriptive geometry, stereotomy (the elements and materials of construction, including stonecutting), perspective, and construction theory were weighted more heavily than arts such as drawing, sculpture, and the history of architecture. A medal in stereotomy counted twice as much as a medal in design; a "mention" in construction weighed twice as heavily as one in drawing. The basic Beaux-Arts training focused on design and theory. No one made models for the competitions and no one constructed a building. Experience after certification was expected to provide whatever practical skills were necessary.

The subject to be designed for the monthly competition was usually a monumental public building, or certain elements of one, which was never meant to be built. Competitions alternated between *esquisses* ("sketches") and *projets rendus* ("complete projects," which included plans, sections, and elevations—often several large drawings). At the beginning of a competition each student was confined for twelve hours to an individual closed studio at the Ecole to ensure that the work was independent. From this session each student would emerge with a fairly elaborate sketch solution, or *esquisse*. The student took a tracing with him but left the sketch to be judged (it was identified by a number drawn at entry—numbers were used in all the competitions to preserve the anonymity of the contestants, who were judged by a jury of Beaux-Arts architects not associated with any atelier). In the *esquisse* competitions the juries voted on each sketch and awarded points; in the alternate months *projets rendus* were delivered to judgment after the plans, sections, and elevations had been prepared in the atelier, where they were often completed by the group and criticized by the patron.

Delivering the final rendition of projects usually became a frantically rushed affair, with students pushing a cart ("charette") holding the precious drawings through the Paris streets to meet the midnight or noon deadlines. (Hence the phrase "en charette," still used to describe last-minute delivery of drawings for a competition.) The jury would then examine the meticulously detailed studies of building parts that the student had synthesized into a final design. If the work diverged in any essential way from the sketch, it could be thrown out of the competition.

Once students achieved the First Class, they concentrated exclusively on the art of design, applying theory and method to their own original ideas. They would still enter competitions, some of which, called *grands concours*, were more advanced and difficult, with formal names and even cash awards; all were designed to lead to certification and, for a French student, a chance to compete for the Prix de Rome. When a First Class student accrued a total of ten points or more, he had completed the course and achieved certification—*if* the student was still under the age of thirty.

At the age of forty-five, Julia Morgan looked back on her own experience in Paris:

> Almost without exception the American students were preparing for the competitive examinations for entrance to l'Ecole des Beaux Arts, but to my regret, these examinations were not open to women, and the best I could do was to enter the private atelier of M. de Monclos, drawing at Colarossi's and modeling with [Jean-Antoine] Injalbert,—an experience not entirely regretted as it rubbed one up against students of many nationalities and ideas, but giving more time to the allied arts than to architecture. I was about to come home when, unexpectedly, the French Government decided to admit women painters and sculptors to the competitive examinations for admittance to the Beaux Arts. They did not say anything about the Department of Architecture, either way, it not entering their heads that there might be women applicants. There was no preparation for such a case and no word against it; so I was given the benefit of the doubt and allowed a chance with the other competitors, and was received as a student by M. Chaussemiche, Government Architect and Grand Prix de Rome, with whom I spent the next years, working at l'Ecole des Beaux Arts and outside and winning a fair share of medals and mentions.[1]

Morgan had arrived in Paris about the first of June 1896. She entered an atelier recommended by Bernard Maybeck, began learning French, and immediately started to study for her entrance examinations. On June 8 she wrote to Lucy and Pierre LeBrun: "I'm so glad I came. It wakes one up so

Architecture Atelier Pascal, Ecole des Beaux-Arts, Paris, 1890s

Julia Morgan, identification card, Ecole des Beaux-Arts, 1899

wonderfully more than Boston [where she had also considered studying]." Women would be allowed to enter the Beaux-Arts that fall, "but without separate ateliers—and I don't think from the few days I have been here that it is a very possible arrangement." The ateliers were rough-and-tumble fraternities for the most part, enlivened by hazing and pranks. Nonetheless, Morgan decided "to try for it [the Beaux-Arts], working half a day all summer on drawing at least, to sort out the possibilities."

Her first atelier, on the third floor of a building overlooking a courtyard in the rue de l'Ancien Comédie, was a small studio headed by Marcel Pérouse de Monclos, a friend from Maybeck's Parisian days. He was a young architect who had "little work to show"—that is, he had not designed or built very much—and he spoke no English, despite having an American wife. Morgan worked on atelier projects for over a year and assisted on one of the prize competitions (the one each year that was open to aspirants as well as matriculates), an experience she described for Pierre LeBrun with enthusiasm, even though their entry won no prize.

Morgan took the entrance examinations in October 1897 and placed forty-second of 376 aspirants—a most respectable score, especially considering that she had become confused in some of her mathematics because she was unaccustomed to working in meters. Unfortunately, only the top thirty applicants were accepted. She tried again in April 1898 and failed again, although Monclos said angrily that her only mistakes were the marks—lowered by the jury because "they did not want to encourage young girls."[2] Her third try, in October 1898, was an unqualified success.[3] She was ranked thirteenth, with only ten French students and two other foreigners ahead of her. The *San Francisco Examiner* headlined that fact:

CALIFORNIA GIRL WINS HIGH HONOR
Miss Julia Morgan In the Ecole des Beaux Arts
First Woman Who Has Entered the Architecture Department
Is a Graduate of Berkeley
Stood very near the Head of the Long List of Applicants

Another California girl is added to the long list of those who have won honor for themselves and for their State abroad. The latest on the list is Miss Julia Morgan, who has just successfully passed the entrance examinations for the Ecole des Beaux Arts, department of Architecture. The honor is all the more marked that Miss Morgan is the first woman in the world to be admitted to this special department.

Morgan wrote to Lucy and Pierre LeBrun on November 14, 1898:

The judgement [result of examinations] was given today only, and am the 13th—ten French and two foreigners—they take forty [thirty] in all. It's not much but has taken quite a little effort. If it had been simply for the advantages of the *Ecole,* I would not have kept on after M. Chaussemiche was arranged with, but a mixture of dislike of giving up something attempted and the sense of its being a sort of test in a small way, of work itself overcoming its natural disadvantages—made it seem a thing that really had to be won.

In the same letter Morgan reported her experience of the oral exam:

None of those received had tried less than twice. Everyone takes this defeat in the most cheerful way, for you are always with the majority. . . . The oral examination broke down about a hundred at least. It's the most trying ordeal for its simpleness. . . . There were thirteen examined before me the day I came up and everyone failed entirely—those big strong fellows would get up, tremble, turn white, clutch their hands and seem to have no thinking power left. . . . When I was called there was a room full. I tried to pretend I was not afraid, and perfectly steady, and actually believed it until at the end of the first problem I discovered that my hand was rattling in the air, and the discovery so surprised me, I could not do any more mathematics—it was enough for a pretty good mark, but you see so many did nothing.

In the spring of 1898 Honoré Daumet (Grand Prix, 1855) and Jean-Louis Pascal (Grand Prix, 1866) had both expressed interest in Morgan's work as a result of her high placement in her first, unsuccessful attempts. Now, however, she chose the atelier of Benjamin Chaussemiche (Grand Prix, 1893), a favorite student of Victor-Alexandre-Frédéric Laloux (Grand Prix, 1878). Laloux, patron of the most prominent atelier in the 1890s, had told Maybeck that Chaussemiche wanted to discuss with Morgan the possibility of forming a women's atelier (a plan that was never realized). She went to see him and, brought together in this rather circuitous way, Morgan and Chaussemiche both recognized a good combination. Of Chaussemiche, Morgan wrote to LeBrun on May 30, 1898: "He is considered the finest of the younger school of architects—especially as to draughtmanship. He criticizes from an entirely different point of view from M. de Monclos, and it feels like a sort of weight has been lifted—and one could work in a bigger, freer, happier way." He became a lifelong friend and regular correspondent.

Once she entered the Ecole, Morgan made rapid progress, accumulating the sixteen points she needed to complete the Second Class in under two years. Of course, she was also racing against time. In January 1902 she would reach her thirtieth birthday and, by the rules of the Ecole, would no longer

Julia Morgan, photographed by her brother Avery, Paris, 1899

be eligible to accumulate points toward a certificate. Morgan's mother meanwhile wrote supportive letters, which were reinforced by encouragement from Maybeck and Le-Brun. Morgan had written as she crossed Nevada on the transcontinental train that she was "never going to write anything about homesickness," and for six years she kept that vow, with the exception of confessing to LeBrun that she was "hungry for home" and occasionally expressing hope that her brother Avery would join her in Paris.

By 1898 Morgan must have felt that she had finally hit her stride. After two years she felt at home in Paris and

with French, especially once Avery arrived in the fall of 1898 and she found the apartment they would share until he went home in 1900. Paris in 1899 was preparing for the Exposition Universelle of 1900. A decade before, the city had made its mark with the extraordinary Eiffel Tower, and now it was attempting to duplicate that feat with the Grand and Petit Palais and with a new bridge to the Champ-de-Mars. Julia and Avery took long walks in the soaking winter rains to observe the construction but "decided we'd put off further sightseeing for the real weather, for physical comfort has a good deal to do with one's appreciation of artistic things, has it not?"[4]

Although she worked hard and steadily, submerging herself in her designs for long stretches, Morgan was no recluse. She enjoyed the company of John Van Pelt, an American from upstate New York who was working at the Ecole in architecture. After winning the 1902 prize in composition, he returned to teach at Cornell University; Lucy LeBrun later made sure that Julia knew he had asked a mutual acquaintance "particularly about you." His mother had accompanied him to Paris, and Julia also enjoyed her company. Her own mother urged Julia more than once to buy new clothes and opera tickets, to take more trips, and to enter into society in general. She did spend time with Bernard and Annie Maybeck when they arrived in connection with an international competition sponsored by Phoebe Apperson Hearst for a new plan for the Berkeley campus. In her early art classes, before her acceptance into the architecture section, Morgan met a number of Russian women whom she characterized as "fine strong workers, and very intelligent and good—but they smoke and drink tea—the first almost I've seen of bohemianism, and I immediately thought of the exhibition I promised Cousin Pierre of all I learned in that way—that I practiced."[5]

Morgan explored Paris, enlarging her architectural vocabulary; took vacations around Europe that always involved visiting sites and sketching; and laid the foundation for her splendid library, the delight and challenge of her future colleagues. She wrote to LeBrun on May 30, 1898, that she had about $250 to spend on books but felt "fairly lost at the choice." Among the volumes that she purchased were a series on ornamental design by H. O. d'Espouy, selections from the Ecole des Beaux-Arts series published at the end of the century, photographs, and "a few odd atelier works like Otto Priths." She continued: "If that meant six books as full as the d'Espouy's it would be enough to take a long while for this worm to digest thoroughly."

It is ironic that Morgan's student work should have survived, forgotten among the letters and papers returned to her at Pierre LeBrun's death, whereas she destroyed the major records of her mature career when she retired. Morgan's Beaux-Arts drawings not only document her development as an artist but also reveal the excellence of her design work. Each is of interest in its own way, but her submissions to special competitions are worth examining in detail because of the rarity of such examples documenting the evolution of finished Beaux-Arts drawings.[6]

Julia Morgan, photographed by her brother Avery in the kitchen of their Paris apartment, 1899

33

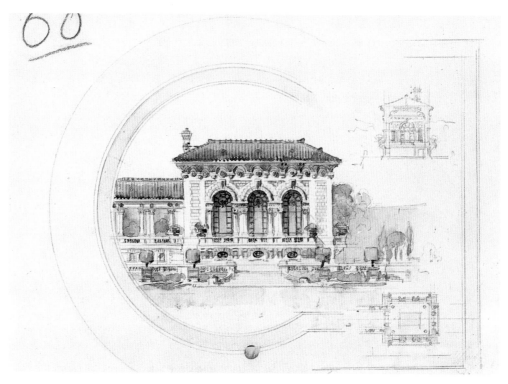

Morgan's initial first mention in the First Class came in December 1900, when she had been a student in that group for four months. The Concours Godeboeuf—an important annual competition of the *"grand concours"* variety—was for an architectural work of a special nature. This one required the contestants to design a bell tower to top the roof of a city hall. Morgan's friend Arthur Brown, Jr., who had arrived for study in 1898, won a medal in that competition and gave Morgan the winning drawing for a Christmas present, inscribed "pour Mlle. Morgan, en bon souvenir" (for Miss Morgan, with good wishes).[7]

About five months later, in April 1901, Morgan received a first mention for her *projet rendu* of a museum designed for the principal square of an urban neighborhood. Her sketch on coarse gray paper shows elevation, plan, and skillfully rendered section framed by a broken circular border; Morgan and other students used this curve as a decorative device to present a drawing in competition. By July 1901 she had won a first mention for the lecture hall of an institute (presumably scientific but possibly humanities), including an outdoor court of honor for public ceremonies that would accommodate about two hundred people and an interior court for members only. In October 1901 Morgan received a second mention for her sketch of a scaffold attached to a church, and in December she won another for a vestibule running the length of a building. Her vaulted vestibule, comparable to that of the Louvre, opposite the Palais Royale, had a central passage for cars or carriages and two side passages for pedestrians. It measured 25 meters across, 10 meters high, and 70 meters long. Her drawing, delicately washed in watercolor, shows a colonnade comprising a series of arched windows with decoration between them and an entrance that gives a sense of ceremonial introduction into the space.

December again brought the Concours Godeboeuf. It opened on December 6, 1901, and closed on December 21, with judging three days later. The subject was an iron and bronze balustrade for the principal staircase of a palace. Typical of Beaux-Arts subjects in its institutional grandeur, it was unlikely to have practical applications in twentieth-century architecture. The instructions, or program, for the competition specified the following:

> Destined for the stairway of honor of a monumental building, the projected balustrade should bear the luxury of materials and of decoration that one encounters in beautiful examples of French architecture.
>
> The balustrade should rest on a curved base of marble holding the ends of the steps and should link in the most supple way with a metal newel, which should be arranged in an interesting and ingenious manner. Toward this end, contestants are given the most complete freedom about the base and starting point and in the number and degree of projection of the steps curving around the newel, preceding those that gradually merge into the base.
>
> The balustrade itself, meeting the newel by whatever curve, ought in any case to present, in the straight part, some ornamentation, sculptured motifs, or panels where possible repetition would facilitate the carrying out of the work and would give to the whole the indispensable unity of conception.
>
> The stairway in the flight from the starting point should consist of thirteen steps between the level of the floor and the level of the first landing. It is the study of the balustrade in the part between the floor and the landing that is the object of the present program.[8]

Morgan's first sketch of the staircase shows a flowing ornamental scroll of ironwork between paired columns as balusters, with a rather abstract suggestion of acanthus leaves for the newel. In her second sketch she trans-

Drawing for a vestibule running the length of a building, which won a second mention, December 3, 1901

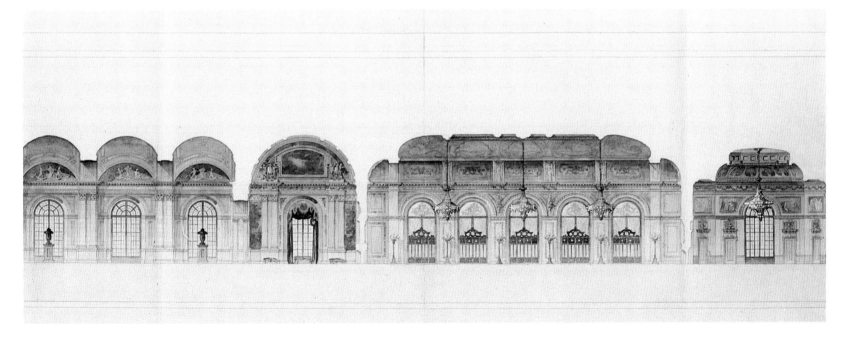

1

2

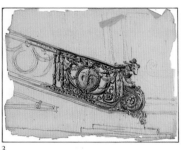

3

4

5

6

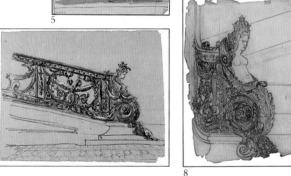

7

8

9

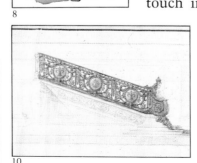

10

formed the newel into a ramlike head and ornamented the sides with round shields bearing fleur-de-lis. The third effort shows the ram's or sheep's head clearly, this time with a round knob or finial suggesting a crown. Next Morgan made two attempts to work out a vertical presentation. The first version, quite rough, shows a ram's head wearing what is definitely a crown; the second is more polished and more open, abandoning strict verticality. The royal beast, designated as bronze, may be an allusion to the possible origin of the Ionic column in the shape of a ram's horn. At any rate, Morgan abandoned that motif after she had worked it through in the four sketches.

Beginning afresh, she changed back to the horizontal and used floral scrolls on the sides with oval insets for the newel post. This new design featured, at the newel, a nude female trunk and head, with a horizontal crown on the figure's bent head. In the next version the woman's head is erect, but the hair under the crown is distracting, and we see the artist's correction of the chin line. Morgan's interest was evidently engaged, for she followed this sketch with a close study of the nude, hair restrained (it would end braided at the sides with a suggestion of wings) and crowned. Another attempt at a vertical solution placed the figure in front of the post with the suggestion of round shields on the sides. After nine versions sketched and set aside, Morgan's final drawing, of the stairway seen from the side, incorporates the torso as the newel—a crowning touch in an elaborate staircase with the round shields between the banister and base alternately ornamented by fleur-de-lis and by a sun figure (an Apollo head); slender paired columns between each shield are linked by festoons of garlands. The marble base was to be carved in stylized waves and foliage, a design echoed in miniature under the banister. The torso,

Ten drawings for the principal stairway of a palace. The final version won a second medal, December 24, 1901.

Opposite: Morgan's drawing for a stairway, reproduced in *Les Médailles des concours d'architecture à l'Ecole des Beaux-Arts,* 1901–2

HÉLIOTYPIE E. LE DELEY, PARIS

ARMAND GUÉRINET, ÉDITEUR, 140, FAUBOURG SAINT-MARTIN, PARIS

Concours Godeboeuf: Une Rampe en fer et bronze pour l'Escalier d'un Palais - Mme MORGAN, Elève de M. CHAUSSEMICHE

Sketch for a theater in a palace, December 3, 1901

Drawing for a theater in a palace, which won a first mention, February 4, 1902

perhaps meant to represent the goddess Flora or the French character-symbol of Marianne, merges naturally into acanthus leaves at the base, where a cornucopia of fruits and flowers spills out. Morgan specified that the carpet, in blue and gold, was to be held in place by brass rods with weighted ornaments at the ends.

That this is the final drawing is shown by the gold tape, which served as a frame for drawings exhibited after a judging. The rating, "1ère mention," is inscribed in the corner beneath the large number 188, which Morgan had been given when she handed in the work for the competition. In addition to the first mention, this work was awarded a second medal, worth two points. The finished drawing, reproduced in Armand Guérinet's *Médailles des concours d'architecture à l'Ecole des Beaux-Arts, 4e année scholaire 1901–1902*, appears to be the only prizewinner for those years to use the female form in any way. As far as we know, Morgan used the form of a woman in only one other project at the Ecole—the theater in a palace described below—and in one built design: the caryatid busts along the crimson damask walls of the movie theater she built at San Simeon.

In January 1902 Morgan entered her last Ecole competition. Her thirtieth birthday was approaching at the end of the month, and with it the end of her allotted time to earn the Ecole des Beaux-Arts certificate. The competition's program called for a theater in a palace, with loges for the president and ten guests and access through the palace rather than a public lobby. Morgan used eight caryatids linked by swags of garlands to uphold the roof of the lower-level loges. Medallions, portrait busts, and classical figures in niches adorned the walls, while the ceiling was ringed with garlands and shields crowned by Apollonian sunburst figures. For examples of theaters within palaces, the contestants had been referred to palaces such as Trianon, Compiègne, Versailles, and Fontainebleau. Ironically, the Old World would see few theaters within palaces in the years to come, but Julia Morgan, the American from San Francisco, would actually design two: the one at San Simeon and another at Wyntoon, both for William Randolph Hearst.

The judges' decision arrived on February 4, 1902: a first mention carrying one point, which meant that her certificate was assured. As Morgan reported laconically fifteen years later, she had earned her "fair share of medals and mentions."[9] She had also refined her talents and absorbed a classical idiom that would shape her architectural repertoire without constraining it. Barely breaking stride, she was ready to begin her life's work.

THE MORGAN ATELIER

Morgan was determined to have an office of her own. After getting her certificate, she spent some months working in Chaussemiche's atelier in Paris, but she was eager to return home. She did not leave Paris, however, until she had completed her first real commission. The client was Harriet Fearing, an American expatriate from Newport, Rhode Island, and New York who had purchased a fine seventeenth-century house in Fontainebleau and required more space for her protégés' concerts and exhibitions. Morgan designed a *grand salon* 34 feet long, which featured four tall arched French windows, one of which led into the house. Murals of pink Chinese hydrangeas by a painter named Dresant ornamented the room. The salon was demolished in 1954, but the specifications remain (in the Documents Collection at the College of Environmental Design, University of California, Berkeley), detailing the names and contracts of locksmiths, ironworkers, masons, chimney men, glaziers, and other artisans.

After Morgan's six-year stint in Paris, she returned to the United States late in 1902, stopping off to visit the LeBruns in New York. They urged her to establish a practice either there or in Newport, and she did work briefly in the LeBrun office but soon took the train home to Oakland. There was work available at the University of California, where John Galen Howard was in charge of a building program, and she could have spent her entire professional life on the staff of the university's new School of Architecture, where her Beaux-Arts background would have been highly prized. But Morgan wanted to head her own office. For about a year and a half she designed for clients from an office in the family home in Oakland. She also assisted Howard in drafting for the Hearst Mining Building and as project director for the Greek Theater on campus.

Morgan took the state examination for certification in February 1904 at Sacramento and was certified the next month. She was ready for practice in San Francisco. Less than two years after

Opposite: Unidentified draftsmen working in Morgan's office at the family home in Oakland (probably the carriage house), 1902–4

Morgan's seal, used on early blueprints

she opened her first office, at 456 Montgomery Street in San Francisco, it was completely demolished in the earthquake of April 18, 1906. Books, drawings, records, typewriters, every pencil—all were destroyed. Fortunately that office was so small that Morgan had kept the library she had collected in France at home in Oakland, where it survived unscathed. The earthquake and the ensuing fire created a desperate need for architects, and Morgan was among those who received numerous commissions. Pierre LeBrun wrote from New York on May 9, 1906, to thank his cousin for her account of the destruction in the city, commenting on her graphic picture of "vacant sites, displaced foundations, shifted paving lanes and stones, not sufficient water to make mortar for bedding for new footing"; he offered to send her materials to replace what she had lost. LeBrun added that "the worst thing to be feared is that the city would be rebuilt too quickly."

By the summer of 1907 Morgan had moved into a suite on the thirteenth floor of the Merchants Exchange Building at 465 California Street in San Francisco.[1] This building, a pioneer high-rise of 1903 designed by Daniel H. Burnham of Chicago (with some drawings signed by Willis Polk), had stood firm during the earthquake and still stands today. Here Morgan established a vigorous practice that ranged all over the state of California and from Utah to Hawaii, always with the Merchants Exchange Building at its center. For six years she had as junior partner Ira Wilson Hoover, who had come west from Philadelphia with John Galen Howard and served as his chief draftsman until starting with Morgan late in 1904. For the brief period before he returned to the East Coast, Hoover did his share, especially in domestic work, and he signed the building permit for Saint John's Presbyterian Sunday School and other projects. After his departure in 1910 the Morgan office was always "Julia Morgan, Architect," with no other name on the door during her forty years of practice.[2]

The heart of the Morgan office was the library. Bookcases lined the walls of the 12-by-14-foot room, at the center of which was a table where Charles Adams Platt's *Italian Gardens* (1894) or huge leather-bound French volumes on art might be open. At least five hundred books related to architecture were available for study, and everyone in the office was expected to consult them. The larger area of the main drafting room, with long, broad tables around which the designers worked (nine or ten of them in good times), had a massive drawing file topped by a bust of Dante. Here for reference were the drawings for earlier Morgan buildings. A prominent bulletin board featured different architectural photographs from Morgan's collection each week, and every member of her staff had to be familiar with these. Morgan had a high-backed desk in the drafting room, where she made many sketches and conferred at each step with those who drafted the working drawings. There were also at least one separate office for a secretary-bookkeeper and one small room, its door frequently closed, where Morgan met with clients and made her own original sketches.

Merchants Exchange
Building Trading Room,
San Francisco

Morgan's training in Paris had well prepared her to manage an atelier. Her methods were derived in large part from her years with Chaussemiche, although they were certainly determined by her own nature as well. Those methods brought satisfactory results, for her office was a valuable training ground and a center for work of very high quality. But for both the men and the women working under her, the strict supervision of the *patron d'atelier* was not always easy to take. Everyone in the office was on a first-name basis except Miss Morgan, who set a standard of diligence and skill that none of her associates could match. Dorothy Wormser Coblentz stated in no uncertain terms that "wherever she was, she was boss." Morgan's policy of being the only one to see clients caused occasional problems, such as Coblentz's designing a breakfast nook that was far too tight for a portly doctor she had never met. Nevertheless, as Coblentz recalled:

> Her office was a real apprenticeship. To work with her was to work from the ground up, and it had certain drawbacks because you learned to be so thorough that you couldn't put your pencil down unless it meant something. So, I think anybody that had been trained at Julia Morgan's office was welcome at any other office because probably nobody else would have taken the time to give such a thorough training. She would say, "Think it out at the start and finish everything as you go along." She'd give you a little 8-inch sketch of something and then you had to work from that . . . and you did not depart from what she had assigned you, until she came back and gave you permission.
>
> You worked when you were in Julia Morgan's office. You worked from 8 to 5 and you didn't stop and you didn't take time off . . . . She didn't build in a style. She built functionally; the plan came first.

No one was allowed to use shortcuts or any but the finest materials. Full-size drawings were done of all details, and these full-size details were what the painter, wood-carver, or ornamental plasterer was given. Coblentz remembered: "If you worked in Julia Morgan's office, you used the details she used and liked, and your reference library was all the drawings of everything that had ever been done in the office, and if you were in doubt about something, you could look up such and such a job. . . . You learned to apply her thinking. She was a perfectionist and each job was a maximum effort. Nothing was left incomplete and . . . nothing was left to chance."

Model making was also important in the Morgan office, especially for the Hearst commissions, which were located far from both the office and the client. C. Julian Mesic, a talented sculptor, did most of this work in the earlier years. For Morgan's last important commission, the Medieval Museum for San Francisco in the 1940s, she hired Cecilia Bancroft Graham, a sculptor who had won medals at the 1939 Treasure Island Fair. Graham built the model (now in the M. H. de Young Memorial Museum in San Francisco) under Morgan's supervision, with landscape details by Coblentz; art historian Margaret Burke has recently made additional models and catalogued material important to the project.

One of Morgan's closest associates, Walter Steilberg, moved to San Francisco in 1910, just out of Berkeley's College of Engineering. He had already had some experience at home in southern California, working as a draftsman for Myron Hunt and Irving Gill while still in school. He headed straight for the office of Morgan's friend and colleague Arthur Brown, Jr., who had no work for him but suggested that he contact Morgan, as she had several jobs and was looking for help. When Brown noticed Steilberg's expression of doubt at the idea of working for a woman, he assured the young applicant that she was one of the best architects in the city: "I know because I had to compete with her." Convinced, Steilberg applied at the Merchants Exchange office and was hired immediately.

Steilberg recalled: "She ran as efficient an office as I've ever been in." No time was wasted, no nonsense was tolerated, and an enormous amount of work was accomplished. At the same time, an ongoing process of education was encouraged. For example, during the Panama-Pacific International Exposition of 1915 Morgan bought tickets for her six draftsmen to spend half a day there once a week to make sketches of whatever interested them. She wanted her staff to learn, and she herself was always a student, sketching and taking notes on buildings during her trips to the East Coast, to Europe, and to South America.[3]

In a 1969 draft for a never-finished article on Morgan, Steilberg wrote: "Not only was she one of the most talented of West Coast architects; she was also far more accomplished in the area of building technology than any of the men I have known." He continued with emphasis on the significance of her frequent site inspections during construction and her close observation and deep understanding of crafts workers, and then noted:

> Miss Morgan was tops as a construction craftsman in her cautious but unhesitant courage in making inspections, or just observing whatever interested her. When I first worked for her as a junior draftsman in 1910 repairs were being made to the terra-cotta cornice of the Merchants Exchange Building,—in the top story, of which J. M. had her office. I came in early one morning; no one in the drafting room or outer office, but I noticed that there was a ladder in the library leaning out of the window to a suspended scaffold on which two masons were working,—and Miss Morgan was coming down the ladder. When she reached the floor (her neat gray suit all dusty and spattered with mortar and her wide-brimmed hat over one ear) she was quite a-glow with enthusiasm with learning what the masons had discovered: that the cracking of the terra cotta was not so much due to the effects of the 1906 earthquake as it was to faulty engineering in that the steel beams, although of ample strength, had excessive deflection. She urged me to go up on the scaffold and see for myself. It was a fearful experience; but I went, conquered my trembling, and did see for myself.[4]

Among those drafting in Morgan's office over the years were Eleanor Jory (wife of architect Stafford Jory), Alice Joy (sister of architect Thaddeus Joy, whom Morgan had encouraged to set up his own practice in New York); two of Thaddeus Joy's daughters and his son; Marjorie Tyng (said to be a relative of Morgan); Avesia Atkins; Harriet Young; and a Miss Delius. Not always in the office but closely connected to it were engineers, contractors,

Dorothy Wormser unpacking part of the collection at San Simeon, 1921

and craftsmen who followed Morgan from job to job. Her own education in engineering had taught her to hire expert engineers. (Walter Steilberg, James LeFeaver, and Walter Huber were her chief engineers throughout her practice.) She let them do the work on their own, making sure they knew that she demanded the highest skills and would settle for nothing less. This division of labor is common in large firms today, but it was rare in the early part of the century.

Morgan paid good salaries and when she had a good year shared the profits with her employees, which was very unusual among architectural firms. During hard times she kept many going, one way or another. For example, when the war was on in 1918 she paid Steilberg to photograph some of her work. She was not at all pleased, however, when he published an article about her in the *Architect and Engineer* of November 1918, the chief source on her early work. Her admiration for the anonymity of the medieval artisan may have been at the root of this unwillingness to appear in print, or perhaps it was just her personal reticence. At any rate, Steilberg's article was the first and last about her work that she countenanced, except for C. Julian Mesic's article on the Berkeley Women's City Club in the *Architect and Engineer* of April 1931. Adela Rogers St. John told of her own frustration as a journalist when she tried to interview Morgan in 1928 for a *Good Housekeeping* series on important American women. Confronted with Morgan's adamant refusal, St. John said, "But Mr. Hearst gave me permission," to which Morgan replied, "Then you may interview Mr. Hearst."[5]

Morgan also rebuked any of her staff who violated the privacy of clients, especially during the decades when some of her personnel were always at San Simeon and tempted to regale the others with gossip. "She sure gave me hell for it, because that was private," said Coblentz, who had spent time at San Simeon in 1921, photographing and cataloguing Hearst's treasures.

Despite her high standards and her formality, Morgan seemed to think of her staff as family. She was godmother for her secretary's daughter, she found work in the office for the children of Thaddeus Joy (probably her best designer), and the children of her artisans still delight in recounting her generosity and understanding. Morgan gave roller skates to the daughter of a conservative old-world craftsman

Left to right: Louis Schalk, Walter Steilberg, Dorothy Wormser, Thaddeus Joy, and Camille Solon in Morgan's office, c. 1922

in order to get the child in motion out-of-doors. When George Loorz, her engineer at San Simeon after 1932, mentioned that his son's teacher had called him a "daydreamer," Morgan fumed: "No one worth his salt was *not* a daydreamer; tell her to help him express those dreams." Another child, a daughter of Alfredo Gomes and his wife, who repaired the tapestries and had charge of the greenhouse at San Simeon, had to have an operation in San Francisco. Since the family lived in Alameda, Morgan insisted that the girl come to her house to recuperate, to shorten the trips back and forth to the doctor. When one little boy had the measles, she visited him every day, always taking a toy from Woolworth's. To many children she sent books; Constance Spencer's bookshop at 470 Post Street had a standing order from her for children's books in small sizes, "to fit their little hands." Silver cups or porridge dishes were sent to new babies and are still treasured by the now-elderly recipients. In many cases Morgan provided more substantial gifts in the form of boarding-school and college scholarships.

An engineer in the Morgan office, Bjarne Dahl, had much to thank her for. He worked on several of her projects over the years, including the Honolulu YWCA. Having discovered Hawaii, Dahl refused to return to California: he found a government job there and received architectural certification. Morgan remained a good friend and mentor, writing to cheer him on during the Depression: "What is needed is young courage, and a realization that money in itself is but a small part of living, a means, not an end. I think the simpler living and a return to simpler pleasures is a healthful and worthwhile result, if the high level of wage and income is never reached again."[6]

Years later, after the bombing of Pearl Harbor, Morgan took Bjarne Dahl, Jr., into her home for a school year.[7] His father was in the Army Corps of Engineers by then, and his mother was a nurse needed in the hospital, so they sent the twelve-year-old boy by Red Cross convoy and taxi directly to Morgan's office. The next day she interviewed teachers and enrolled him in the local public school, after taking him to a shoe store (he had run barefoot in Hawaii) and outfitting him "as a young gentleman." After school each day he would go to her office, look through her books, and do little tracing jobs. She took him to the newsreel movies every other day, to the zoo, to museums, to Coit Tower, to an amusement park (and on the roller coaster). She told him they must watch Charlie Chaplin movies twice, once to laugh and again to appreciate the art.

The architect most closely associated with Morgan was Bernard Maybeck, and their collaboration was a matter of friendship and long-term mutual respect. Room was always made available in her office for Maybeck, who never maintained a spacious office; for an occasional large project he would hire some of her staff or come in to work there himself, doing his expansive and colorful drawings. In 1894–95, just out of engineering school, Morgan had worked for Maybeck, drafting and supervising construction on

Bernard Maybeck in
characteristic costume,
c. 1945

a house for Professor Andrew C. Lawson, which was demolished in the 1906 earthquake. (His second house, also by Maybeck, is a celebrated Berkeley landmark.) In Paris in 1898 she had lived in an apartment below the Maybecks, sharing everything from their piano to the responsibility of caring for the Maybeck's critically ill visitor, Professor Lawson's first wife. At that time Morgan assisted Maybeck on the drawings for Hearst Hall (the earliest University of California gymnasium for women) and possibly also on the drawings for Mrs. Hearst's castle at Wyntoon. In 1925–26 Morgan and Maybeck collaborated on plans for the Phoebe Apperson Hearst Memorial Gymnasium for Women for the Berkeley campus (see chapter 4). When Maybeck's castle at Wyntoon, near the Oregon border, burned to the ground in the winter of 1929–30, he and Morgan were asked by William Randolph Hearst to plan a replacement. Maybeck's extravagant drawings for the project were clearly beyond the budget, and Hearst placed Morgan alone in charge. On January 8, 1930, she sent a letter to Hearst, with copies of Maybeck's bills for the unbuilt Phoebe Hearst memorial projects and the Wyntoon drawings, saying that she was willing for the full fee for her sketches to go to Maybeck because

> It is difficult to arrive at a basis for division of commissions with Mr. Maybeck on account of the different way in which we do our work.
>
> In recent years he has devoted himself to one project at a time, making his beautiful studies and sketches personally, carrying very little overhead, and leaving to others the development and carrying out of his ideas. We carry many projects at a time from sketch to completed building, requiring the most competent available people, entailing a very considerable capital investment as well as the personal work.
>
> But with us, if we lose on one project, we make up on the next, actually the years bringing a remarkably even, if modest average of return—while with Mr. Maybeck, each project, he feels, must bring its own return for his investment of personal time, experience and gift. So, all considered, he is welcome to whatever our contributions to these projects up to now have been. It will be necessary, however, to think out a working basis for future mutual work.

It is significant that Morgan, originally trained by Maybeck, did not make him her mentor. She loved and respected him but went her own way.

Other architects throughout the Bay Area knew and appreciated the work coming out of Julia Morgan's office. One good friend and admirer of her skills was Warren Perry, who had followed her in graduating in architecture from Berkeley and attending the Ecole des Beaux-Arts, then returned to work under John Galen Howard. Perry, who became dean of the Berkeley architecture school, recalled that when he was at the Ecole people were still talking about the remarkable Mademoiselle Morgan who had broken the barriers and won so many awards. Her old fellow student Arthur Brown, Jr., also continued to be her advocate, and she respected his skills, although she expressed only reserved approval of his 1934 Coit Tower. Albert Evers, longtime president of the northern California branch of the American Institute of Architects, talked of his respect for Morgan and her work, although he also complained rather bitterly of her insistent refusal to serve on committees or to enter competitions sponsored by the AIA.[8]

The warmth evident in Morgan's relationship with fellow architects also characterized her relations with some of her clients. Many gave her multiple commissions and many became friends. Agnes and George Wilson in Vallejo, for example, directed commissions to her for a YWCA building and alterations on the bank in that community as well as for a downtown store and their own handsome house at the crest of a hill. One client frequently mentioned by Steilberg as a particular friend of Morgan's was Dunning Rideout, of Marysville, California. Not only did he commission her to design his house (which still stands), but he also steered several commercial commissions in his hometown her way, including an elementary school, the first Marysville Golf Clubhouse, the bank, and the American Legion building, all since demolished. Rideout admired Morgan's work and often visited her office when on business in San Francisco. His wife sent Morgan a miniature watercolor showing the house she designed for them, which the architect saved among her valued papers.

Julia Morgan, June 1929, the day she received her honorary degree at U.C. Berkeley

The Morgan atelier, remembered with fond respect by her employees, colleagues, and clients, was responsible for between seven and eight hundred projects during its forty-seven years of operation. Working for private and institutional clients, Morgan designed buildings that balanced her lifelong commitment to Beaux-Arts values and her profound understanding of the California landscape. In 1929, when she was still in midcareer, the University of California granted Morgan an honorary LL.D. President William Wallace Campbell aptly cited her as "distinguished alumna of the University of California; artist and engineer; designer of simple dwellings and of stately homes, of great buildings nobly planned to further the centralized activities of her fellow citizens; architect in whose works harmony and admirable proportions bring pleasure to the eye and peace to the mind."

4

ON CAMPUS, IN CHURCH, AND
AT THE MARKETPLACE

When Julia Morgan returned to California in the fall of 1902, she readily found work in the office of John Galen Howard, architect in charge of the University of California campus.[1] The original Berkeley campus had been planned by Frederick Law Olmsted in 1867, in a rambling parklike style that was picturesque rather than formal. The first two buildings, by David Farquharson (a Scottish architect working in San Francisco) and Henry Kenitzer (a German architect working there), were built in the fashionable Second Empire style, without relation to Olmsted's plan, except for respecting the axis he had established with the Golden Gate harbor. The next few buildings on campus followed no single plan.

When Phoebe Apperson Hearst approached the university in 1896 with a proposal to fund a building for mining studies to honor her late husband, Senator George Hearst, the president called on Bernard Maybeck, the only architect on the faculty, to present an appropriate design. Maybeck had a decidedly theatrical flair; he also had a friend, Jacob Reinstein, a brilliant attorney on the Board of Regents, who joined him in proposing an international competition to design not just one building but a master plan (to be supported by multiple donors) that would rival the much-acclaimed architecture at the 1893 World's Columbian Exposition in Chicago. When Maybeck improvised a model for the Mining Building and suggested that it be the keystone of a new plan, Mrs. Hearst promptly agreed to sponsor the international competition with $200,000 and to serve as its chairwoman.

Annie and Bernard Maybeck spent the next two years traveling with Reinstein to promote the competition; they distributed the program, published in three languages, to architects all over the world. The Maybecks and Mrs. Hearst also spent a good deal of time in Paris, where Maybeck gave out thousands of copies of the program. When the international jury met in Berkeley in 1899, the first place among the 104 entries went to Emile Henri

Opposite: El Campanil, Mills College, Oakland, 1903–4

Hearst Mining Building, U.C. Berkeley, 1901–7, designed by John Galen Howard

Bénard of France for a traditional Beaux-Arts design, with John Galen Howard of New York and his engineer partner, Samuel M. Cauldwell, in fourth place with a rather similar design. Bénard gladly accepted the $10,000 award in exchange for his drawings, but he refused to stay and work on any actual building. The jury then decided to employ Howard to implement the Bénard plan. This put Howard in command as supervising architect for the next quarter of a century, giving him the opportunity to found and direct the architectural school (1903) and enabling him to design the new buildings. For Maybeck, who had clearly been ineligible to compete in the competition he had organized, the results were a certain international acclaim but the loss of the opportunity to shape the Berkeley campus.

Howard began his transformation of the campus as early as 1901, with a new study for the Hearst Mining Building, completed in 1907. This was the building that Phoebe Hearst had originally proposed, and its prominence was reiterated in the prizewinning plan for the campus. Howard's plan for the building was based on classical tradition, but the design also incorporated elements from the California missions, notably red-tile roofs, broad roof overhangs, and missionlike walls composed of stark white granite over a steel framework. The result expressed the force of the mining industry and the new spirit of this "edge of the world." Morgan drafted for this building during her first months with Howard, then she was made assistant supervising architect for the Greek Theater, which he had proposed in 1901.

The Greek Theater, adapted from the semicircular one at Epidaurus, was the first such classical open-air theater to be built in the New World. The cost of constructing the theater in reinforced concrete came to $447,000, financed by William Randolph Hearst at his mother's urging. Morgan's role in the project may have included participation in the design; her primary responsibility was to deal with the quantity and quality of the concrete necessary to provide seating for more than six thousand spectators. She had studied ferroconcrete in the Ecole's construction course and had observed its use at the Paris Exposition Universelle of 1900. When President Theodore Roosevelt came to Berkeley in May 1903 to give the commencement address at the new Greek Theater, the structure was not completely finished. Morgan had worked day and night to meet the deadline, but in the end she had to design canvas banners to cover the still damp concrete of the skene (the wall behind the stage, measuring 42 feet high by 113 feet wide by 23 feet deep). The theater was dedicated that September with a university production of *The Birds* by Aristophanes, and it is still in active use, its acoustics excellent, although it can no longer seat the entire student body.

Her experience on the Mining Building and the Greek Theater gave Morgan confidence to go out on her own to practice. The imperious, authoritarian Howard apparently never forgave her for opening her own office and for taking with her as junior partner a young man from his staff, Ira Wilson Hoover. Thus, Morgan was effectively barred from making any important contributions to the campus architecture until Howard's influence had waned; in 1925–26 Maybeck and Morgan planned the Phoebe Apperson Hearst Memorial Gymnasium for Women, which was commissioned by William Randolph Hearst as a memorial to his mother. The original plan had been for a great Beaux-Arts complex that would include a gymnasium, a theater, a music building, and a museum. Morgan visited college art museums on the East Coast and at the University of Michigan, Ann Arbor, to check on prototypes, while Maybeck was drawing up a grand plan. By September 15, 1926, however, after the gymnasium had been built, Hearst wrote to Morgan: "I find that I am not in a position to begin work on the University Museum at present. I have just bought some papers in Pittsburgh and it has left me pretty well exhausted for ready money."[2] And that was the end of the grand plan.

The most conspicuous feature of the north side of the gymnasium is a large marble-lined pool, which was to serve as part of the promenade for the vast complex and features a view of the campus and the distant hills. The

Greek Theater, U.C. Berkeley, 1903, designed by John Galen Howard, with Julia Morgan as assistant supervising architect

templelike structure, complete with urns and sar-
cophagi, establishes a classical atmosphere for
physical and mental relaxation. On the south side
is a sunny smaller pool, protected from view by
shrubbery. A third pool, the length of the space
between the two wings, reflects the gymnasium's
Beaux-Arts fenestration on its surface and provides a quiet haven in the midst of all the physical
activity. The pools and the ornamental rein-

Three views, c. 1927, of
the Phoebe Apperson
Hearst Memorial
Gymnasium for Women,
U.C. Berkeley

forced-concrete urns seem to have been Morgan's contribution to the design.
She also supervised construction of the complex, dealt with all the workmen, and was unquestionably the on-site architect, although the design for
the whole was worked out by the two architects in partnership. In newspaper reports and in accounts by workmen, it was called the "Morgan-
Maybeck gym."

Just as Morgan was completing her work for Howard, another campus,
the only secular women's college on the Pacific Coast, was ready to embark
on a development program. Mills College, in nearby Oakland, had received
a chime of ten bronze bells (weighing ten thousand pounds) from a friend of
the college, and President Susan Mills had secured funds for a tower in
which to hang them. Wanting to build a bell tower such as her alma mater,
Mount Holyoke College in Massachusetts, boasted in its Mary Lyon Hall,
Mills turned to Julia Morgan. Morgan's background in engineering and her
recent experience in working with reinforced concrete made her the logical
person to design the bell tower, while her training at the Ecole enabled her
to determine how an overall plan at Mills might be developed. The campus
at this time consisted of wooded acreage plus the Main Building—a three-
story Victorian house designed by S. C. Bugbee in 1871 with a mansard roof
and a cupola (now called Mills Hall). That was where the students lived and
took most of their classes; other small buildings included a one-room library
and a music and science classroom.

Morgan sited the bell tower, called El Campanil, on a grassy oval surrounded by live oaks and eucalyptus. Her use of an oval rather than a grid
or quadrangle as an organizing principle was in decided contrast to contemporary campus planning, and the placement of the tower on a diagonal line
from the Main Building rather than directly facing it was a daring departure
from the symmetry of Howard's design for Berkeley. The tower itself,
though dominant, respects the scale of the three-story Main Building. The
design departed from that of European and East Coast bell towers, which
were usually square and solid, tapering at the top (as is true of Howard's
later 307-foot Sather Tower at Berkeley, which recalls the Venetian campanile of San Marco). Morgan's drawing shows a 72-foot tower that is twice as
wide at front and back as it is on the sides. It follows the building tradition
of the California missions, with a low-pitched red-tile roof and redwood
brackets. The reinforced-concrete mass is broken up visually by two de-
vices: first, graduated arched openings at four levels, in which the bells hang
mission fashion; and second, suggestions of red-tile roofs over the buttresses
and the entrance. A low terrace at the base has a parapet ornamented by
twenty-eight urns designed by Morgan in the style of the Spanish Alhambra.

Elevations for the Mills
College Campanil, 1903

Opposite: Postcard of the
Margaret Carnegie
Library, Mills College,
1905–6

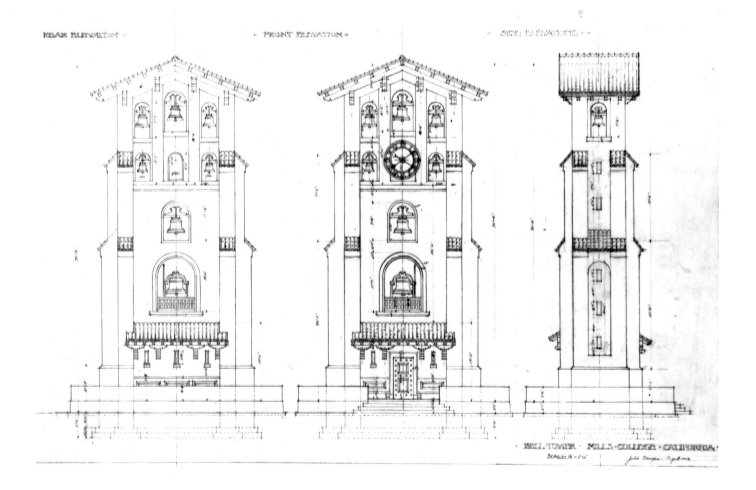

Two contemporary accounts give some idea of how the tower was received. The Mills magazine of January 1904 says:

It is a pleasure in this first number of the *White and Gold,* for the new year, to announce that work has already begun on the tower, in which the chime of ten bells . . . will be hung. The plans for this building, which is soon to add new beauty to our campus, have been prepared by Miss Julia Morgan, of Oakland. Those who have been privileged to see them are much impressed by the architectural and artistic skill displayed by this lady, and feel assured that when completed this first campanile to be erected on the Pacific Slope will be a model of strength and refined sentiment. It is interesting also to note that a work of so much promise has been designed by a carefully trained woman architect for a woman's college.

A report in the October 1911 *Cement Age* notes:

The dimensions of the tower are 12 feet by 24 feet (exclusive of the buttresses and platform), with a height of 72 feet. It is of the natural grey color of the concrete, but a roof of red tile resting upon heavy timbers gives a contrasting touch of color. The tiles are used to good purpose over the portal and buttresses as well.

The surroundings of "El Campanil" are designed to bring out its beautiful lines and quiet yet effective color scheme, as it is flanked by huge oaks and eucalyptus trees and rises from a broad expanse of lawn.

1202 — MARGARET CARNEGIE LIBRARY, MILLS COLLEGE, _____ A.

The Campanil was not erected without conflict. The builder, Bernard Ransome, was proud of being a third-generation concrete worker, and he did not believe that Morgan understood the material, in spite of her engineering degree, her Paris study, and her experience on the Berkeley campus. Ransome recommended directly to the donor, Frank "Borax" Smith, that 6-to-8-inch walls be used between the buttresses rather than the 12-inch walls planned by Morgan, pointing out the economy of this change, to which Morgan acquiesced. He also advocated "picking" done with a single blade, rather than brushing off with brick as in her specifications. Smith backed up Ransome and urged Mrs. Mills to credit his name ahead of the architect's, which she did at the dedication ceremony. Morgan's skill in working with reinforced concrete was proved when the 1906 earthquake left the Campanil and her new library untouched.

The library was the next building added to the campus, in 1905–6. Morgan designed it to continue the mission effect, using the same materials as the Campanil, with the addition of wrought-iron balconies in front and at each end. The result is as balanced and symmetrical as a Beaux-Arts jury could demand, with five full-length arched windows on the front and one at each end, over groups of three windows on the first floor. Morgan continued the relationship with the main oval here, placing the library at an angle

alongside it. The interior—clearly influenced by the Arts and Crafts tradition—provided administration and reading rooms on the first floor, with the second floor as the library proper.[3] Natural light pours in through the high mullioned windows of this latter space, illuminating the lofty open construction, the exposed hardwood supports, and the handcrafted details, including furniture that Morgan designed herself.

Mills commissioned Morgan to design a gymnasium for the college in 1909. This expansive redwood structure has pergolas and both open-air and indoor sports facilities. An annex with a pool was planned for placement along the axis behind the Main Building, but it was not built until 1916, after the death of Susan Mills. Both interiors were of highly polished wood, with fireplaces large enough to heat the buildings. The annex is now used as a social hall, having served earlier as bowling alley and then as an alumnae building. The sturdy wooden columns on its porch have been painted white, producing a severe classical effect never intended by Morgan.

Another Mills building by Morgan is located on a road adjacent to the oval. Originally built in 1909–10 as the Kapiolani infirmary (commissioned by Mills alumnae from Hawaii), it now serves as faculty housing. A modest frame structure with upstairs sleeping porches, it must have seemed a homelike haven for indisposed students. This—along with the Ming Quong Chinese Girls School built by Morgan in 1924–25 and later absorbed by the campus (see pages 64–65)—completed the architect's work for Mills. Susan Mills's presidency ended in 1912, and her successor, Aurelia Reinhardt, favored Maybeck, Walter H. Ratcliff, and a variety of other architects in the next phase of campus development.

A sorority was an important feature in the life of a woman student during the early days at Berkeley, as no dormitories existed. Julia Morgan and her sister, Emma, were both loyal members of Kappa Alpha Theta, known as Theta. When the sorority was ready to build its own headquarters, it naturally turned to Morgan. Her redwood-shingle building was heralded in the *Berkeley Independent* of May 28, 1908:

HANDSOME NEW HOME FOR KAPPA ALPHA THETA
A large force of workmen are at work building the first University of California Greek letter sorority clubhouse ever erected by a local chapter in Berkeley. The Kappa Alpha Theta sorority, one of the oldest and most prominent of the co-ed organizations at Berkeley, has the distinction of planning, purchasing clubhouse property and building the first home in the college town.

The house was built the long way of the lot, with wide bays on each side and sleeping porches in the rear. A plan for the street side shows a band of five windows on the first floor and a bay with five casement windows above; leaded panes were used in the upper part of the casement windows on all three floors. A belt course marks the third floor, where the front windows are set back under a kind of bargeboard that parallels the verge above. The balcony thus formed added visual interest and kept the building from seem-

ing too tall for its two-story residential neighbors. The building served its users well; but after the Berkeley fire of 1923, despite the fact that it survived unscathed, Morgan completely remodeled the building, as wood had become a decidedly unpopular material. After reorienting the building to the side on a new brick foundation, she sheathed it in stucco and created English bays, with an open loggia above the new entrance.

Phoebe Hearst, who helped underwrite the Town and Gown Club designed by Maybeck in Berkeley in 1899, had commissioned him in 1897–98 to build Hearst Hall as a social and athletic center for women students. At first it adjoined Mrs. Hearst's own house, but in 1902 it was moved to the newly reorganized campus, where it remained until destroyed by fire in

Kappa Alpha Theta sorority house, Berkeley, seen in 1916

Kappa Alpha Theta sorority house, as remodeled c. 1930

Opposite: Elevations and plan, Girton Hall, U.C. Berkeley, 1911

1922. Mrs. Hearst reportedly offered to pay for a women's dormitory at Berkeley as well, but the plan was rejected by the president on the grounds that "women in groups tend to become hysterical."

In 1911 the Berkeley women students asked Morgan to build them a simple meeting place similar to the Men's Hall designed by John Galen Howard. Essentially one rough-finished room with a central fireplace plus facilities for light cooking at one end and a porch at the other, it was named Girton Hall in a burst of enthusiasm for the Cambridge University col-

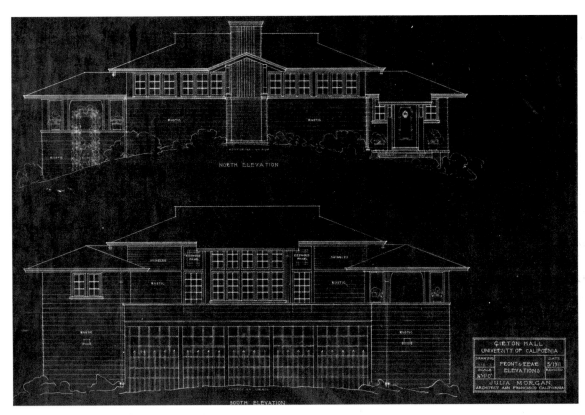

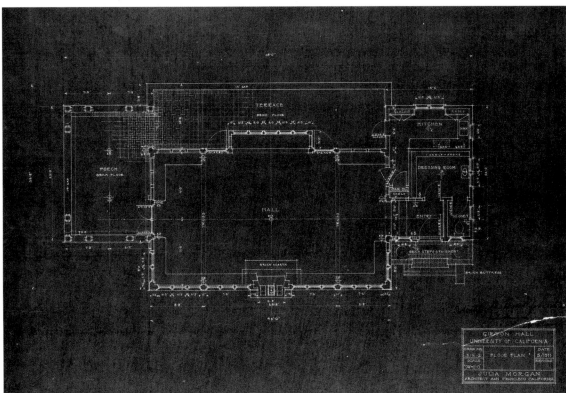

61

lege for women. Its low roof and redwood shingles make it merge into the
landscape, even on its new site near the east entrance of the campus, where
it was moved in the early 1940s.

Designed for students and still serving them is a Berkeley residence
originally built for the Delta Zeta sorority in 1923; it was next used by a
fraternity and then leased to a group of students who now run it as a coop-
erative. The blocky concrete structure is sited on an unusual "gore corner"
lot between two streets that run diagonally down the hill to meet at Hearst
Avenue, north of the campus; the sloping lawn and shrubbery at the apex of
the triangle reinforce the English look of the architecture. The plan has a
bent-U shape, accommodating the residence to a lot much wider at the rear
than it is at front. The third floor of the building has three or four dormers
punctuating each side of the low-pitched, all-encompassing roof. Its second
floor is outlined by a long balcony at front, with casement windows opening
inward and French doors at either side of the central windows. The principal
doorway, set between pairs of pilasters, repeats the form of the arches linking the porch columns. The door has six panels; in the center of each is
carved a different variation of the Tudor rose, while stylized roses form the
capitals of the pilasters. Details such as a waterspout and iron brackets
under the balcony repeat the rose motif.

The interior uses concrete frankly and appropriately: thin-shell construction is used in the entrance hall for the curve behind the wide arch.
Windows below and above the stairs are cut on the curve, modeling the
curve sensually and flooding the stairway with light. The large main dining

room to the right and the balancing living room at the left feature structural elements faced in wood and ample fireplaces with cast-stone mantels decorated with heraldic designs. The open feeling created by having all the main rooms flow into the patio (formerly a rose garden, now a basketball court) recalls Arts and Crafts ideals, but the effect of this structure, originally painted a dark rose, is decidedly English.

Morgan's largest early commission in the English style was built for the Berkeley Baptist Divinity School in 1918–19. This structure is on the south side of campus, opposite Maybeck's First Church of Christ, Scientist. Claiborne Hill, a Baptist official, has indicated that a competition was held for this building and that "three well-known architects competed."[4] The building committee asked that the Oxford Hall Tower be considered in the design, "not a copy of the Oxford Hall Tower but . . . that [type of] Tudor gothic." The committee had almost certainly seen the work of Thomas Graham Jackson (1835–1924), whose work on the New Quad Buildings at Oxford played a significant part in the efforts to develop an English style for institutional buildings. At any rate, Julia Morgan's design was unanimously chosen. The result is a four-story building framed in reinforced concrete with brick facing and cast-concrete ornamentation. The slate roof, though typically English and also common on the East Coast, is unusual for Berkeley. The plan for the school was U-shaped, with a cloister and pergola at the rear creating a rural effect. The urbane street-side entrance, surmounted by a bay and a turret with finial, opens into a wide hall that leads to the chapel on the left and to the library on the right. Lecture rooms and dormitory facilities occupy the rest of the wings. The interiors on both floors are paneled in oak, the extra cost for which was contributed by the architect.

Another campus building by Morgan in the English tradition is a women's dormitory at Principia, a Christian Science college for women in Elsah, Illinois, just across the Mississippi from Saint Louis. This commission came as part of a new campus design that Maybeck was asked to do in 1930. He brought the whole project to Morgan's office because his own facilities were not large enough for this scale of drafting. The Jacobean revival, which had also been in favor at Oxford early in this century, was at the heart of the plans: both Maybeck and Morgan worked out free versions of that style. Morgan visited the site just once; but Edward Hussey, from her office, and the Maybecks lived there during design and even during some of the construction. Funds were never sufficient to complete the project as lavishly as Maybeck had envisioned, but the campus nevertheless reflects the stamp of the two California architects who worked on it.

Drawing for the Berkeley Baptist Divinity School, 1918–19

Some of Morgan's San Francisco school buildings were for clients involved in missionary work. The Methodist Chinese Mission School (1907–10) and the Chinese Presbyterian Mission School (1908)—both built in Chinatown just after the earthquake—are examples. Both still flourish as Chinese centers. For the Methodist Chinese Mission School (called Gum Moon), which is recorded in Walter Steilberg's photographs and description from 1918, Morgan used clinker bricks. The arched entrance of the three-story building on Washington Street has Chinese motifs, tiles, and lanterns. The vaulted doorway uses a cast-stone peony design as key block, while its soffit (or exposed undersurface) shows stone latticework with the same flower. Iron balconies across the upper story serve as decorative fire escapes, a favorite device of the architect. The building has been recently restored, and the original bright colors recalled by the Chinese orphans who studied there have been carefully recreated.

Overview and detail of arched doorway, Methodist Chinese Mission School, San Francisco, 1907–10

The Chinese Presbyterian Mission School was started in 1894, but its building was destroyed in the 1906 earthquake. Morgan's new center was known as Donaldina Cameron House in honor of a Scottish missionary who rescued young Chinese girls from the brothels and sweatshops of the flourishing child-slave trade. Cameron later moved the school to a farm in Oakland, which seemed a safer environment for her young charges. In 1924–25 Morgan designed the Ming Quong Chinese Girls School on Cameron's two-acre site, adjacent to Mills College. It features a Beaux-Arts–style square courtyard and cast-stone balconies within the symmetrical spreading wings of the school building. Stone Fu dogs and many other Chinese symbols of hospitality greet the visitor. A frieze of polychrome tiles imported by Morgan from China is reminiscent of Chinese country houses, as are the cast-iron and stencil designs over each entrance and throughout the interior. Red-tile roofs cover the whole, as is the case for all of Morgan's buildings on the Mills campus. Ming Quong became part of the college in 1936, where it now serves as the Alderwood Center for conferences.

Many of Morgan's school buildings, private and public, reflect Mediterranean antecedents. One of the earliest, built in 1908–16, was Ransom and Bridges, a private college-preparatory school for girls in Piedmont (a suburb in the hills east of Oakland). The design emphasized a courtyard formed from wings and a central section, with some additional buildings (notably an open-air gymnasium) at the sides. At the entrance bulky concrete columns supported a high arch, which was flanked by side openings the height of the capitals; oval designs decorated the space above the openings. Curving iron brackets held up a balcony in front of four tall windows or French doors, while third-floor gables featured broad windows. Having served as a Piedmont showplace for two generations, the

Ransom and Bridges School, Piedmont, 1908–16

Ming Quong Chinese Girls School, Oakland, 1924–25

school and campus were demolished after World War II.

Marion Ransom, head of the school, was not only an appreciative client of Morgan's but also an enthusiastic promoter, as witness a letter in the Mills College library (undated, presumably 1915) addressed to Aurelia Reinhardt, the president of the college. In the letter Ransom gives a list of reasons to choose Morgan as architect "for the memorial building" (which seems to be the proposed Ethel Moore Memorial Alumnae Building). Since the school prepared students for Mills and other colleges, Ransom's endorsement would have carried weight, but Morgan did not get the job.

The Katherine Delmar Burke School, another college-preparatory school originally for girls, occupies a generous site in the Pacific Heights area of San Francisco, its Mediterranean style blending well with the streetscape. Designed in 1916, it has a plan that follows decidedly Beaux-Arts rules. The glazed interior courtyard (which would have been left open in a more Mediterranean climate) is well suited to the moderate Bay Area weather, and there is a pleasingly rhythmic relationship of inside to outside that is characteristic of Morgan at her best. The courtyard, with fountain and flower bed at the center, is visible from the formal entrance. Wide corridors with vaulted ceilings (squared off, alas, in a recent remodeling) and expansive windows form the sides of the building. Circulation through the library on one side and a hall on the other leads to classrooms at the sides. The second floor has similar halls with loggia classrooms that were originally open but have now been glazed. The axis and cross axis function easily, and it is an impressive structure to walk through. The building now serves as an independent coeducational high school with a program very similar to what has worked well for seventy years.

Morgan created other schools that emphasized a link between the outdoors and the interior. In 1910, for example, she designed a dormitory and classroom for the Montezuma School for Boys in the Santa Cruz Mountains near Los Gatos. The buildings are now used as a retreat by the Catholic Church. The Lakeview schools in Oakland (1905–17) and the Marysville Grammar School (1916) have all been demolished. Morgan's earliest Lakeview schools were two-story structures, but both of her 1916–17 buildings there were one-story public elementary schools with access to the outdoors from each room, designed at a time when most architects were still constructing two-story schools with staircases and halls.

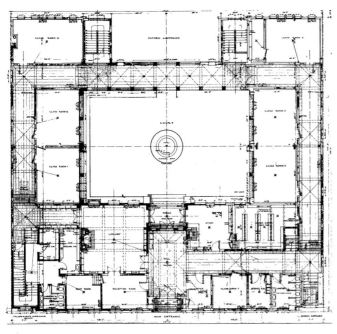

Main-floor plan and
courtyard, Katherine
Delmar Burke School,
San Francisco, 1916

Increased construction of churches as well as of schools resulted from the mood of expansion that pervaded the early years of the twentieth century. As more and more people settled in growing communities, splinter groups would break off to form new congregations, as was true of Saint John's Presbyterian Church in Berkeley and the First Swedish Baptist Church in Oakland. Population shifts to the outer edges of cities also created a demand for new small churches, such as the Ocean Avenue Presbyterian in San Francisco, the High Street Presbyterian and the United Presbyterian in Oakland, and the Thousand Oaks Baptist in Berkeley. Morgan designed several Baptist and Presbyterian churches, as well as related buildings such as columbaria (vaults to hold cinerary urns) and theological schools.

Morgan's first church commission, in 1906–7, was to redesign the interior of the First Baptist Church in Oakland, which had been severely damaged in the earthquake. She worked with local Swedish carpenters, for whom she later designed the First Swedish Baptist Church. For the First Baptist auditorium these craftsmen used local wood to carry out her design, which featured a dynamic curve around the centerpiece of a great organ. Brackets and supports for the open ceiling, which were centered in an octagonal ring with all the construction elements revealed, were products both of the designer's skills and those of her talented craftsmen. Morgan used the sweep of the pews and the wood overhead to create a space that may evoke for some worshipers the wilderness experience of John the Baptist; others may focus on the geometric perfection of the simple curves, trefoils, and triangles within triangles used as design elements. This interior, built three years before Maybeck's famous First Church of Christ, Scientist in Berkeley, has some of the excitement and tension of his more colorful and complex interior, although it is much less elaborate.

In 1908 a commission came to the Morgan office from a newly organized Presbyterian group in Berkeley. One of its leaders was Professor Clifton Price, a classicist for whom Morgan built a Crafts-style apartment building and for whom she would design another larger and more urbane apartment building four years later. The Presbyterian group had a large double lot on College Avenue, not far south of the campus. They first wanted a simple and economical building for a Sunday school, with a main church to follow in the next year or so, to be called Saint John's Presbyterian Church. Ira Wilson Hoover's name appears on the 1908 building permit for the Sunday school, but by the time the church was under way in 1910 he had left Morgan's office, and Walter Steilberg joined her on the project.

The Sunday school is a small, single-wall frame structure with a side entrance recessed on the north side of a bay; the modified Tudor arch lines of the large five-part window parallel the rooflines of both the bay and the basic structure. A parlor with fireplace was originally at the rear, and the bay area was labeled "Infant Class." When it

Interior and carved-wood bracket, First Baptist Church, Oakland, 1906–7

came time to design the church, the congregation was without adequate funds. Morgan, mindful of Maybeck's conviction that drawbacks could be transformed into opportunities, focused her skills on designing a minimal structure as sanctuary. Her early training at the Ecole had led her to examine and to love Romanesque architecture, which was also minimal. Saint John's may appear to derive from the California barn tradition, but in fact it relates more closely to the Romanesque and to the Tudor English style, to which the British Arts and Crafts movement looked back so fondly.

Saint John's is an extraordinary small building of large significance. It was designed to be a modest addition to a residential block, low to the ground and with its gable linked by a glazed corridor to the Sunday school. Like the music of Bach, the building reveals a play of repetition and variation. The angles of the roof and bargeboards, the timbers beneath the clerestory windows, and the gable over the main entrance parallel the modified Tudor form of the main church doorway and of the Sunday school roofs and window. The horizontality of the upper cross members of the window frames is carried across the face of church and Sunday school. Verticals also play a role in this harmony: narrow sections of wall punctuate the clerestory windows, which have a modified Gothic form that reinforces the subdued verticality. This verticality is continued by the bands of long, narrow windows below. The rich complexity evolving from such simple forms is powerful testimony to the architect's geometric imagination.

Saint John's Presbyterian Church and Sunday School, Berkeley, 1908–10

Opposite: Elevations and section for Saint John's Presbyterian Church

-REAR ELEVATION-

-FRONT ELEVATION-

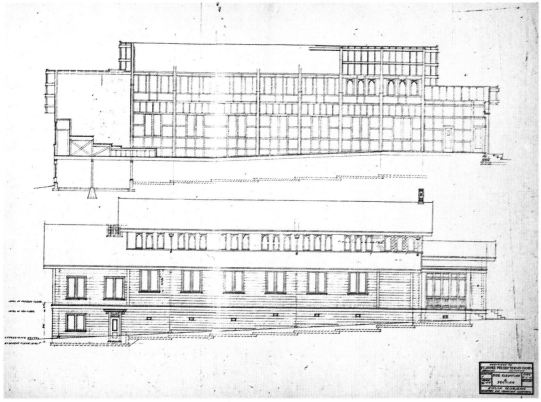

Detail of Celtic cross, clerestory window, Saint John's Presbyterian Church

Bottom and opposite: Early views of interior, Saint John's Presbyterian Church

The interior of Saint John's was originally lighted from all four sides by a diffused glow through clerestory windows of smoked glass common to industrial buildings; one end has since been blocked in. The sloping floor and simple wood pews give visual access from everywhere in the building, but the visitor's eyes are inevitably drawn to the overhead beams and supports. All hardware is exposed. The warm, rich color of the wood reflects the changing light and takes away any sense of cool austerity that such economy of material and design might have created. Although the natural lighting is perfectly suited to the space, artificial light was also provided by the Morgan office in the form of wood and iron "electroliers," with bare bulbs pointed down. The acoustics are remarkable, which has helped to make the church an admirable performing-arts center since the expanded congregation built a large modern church down the street in 1970.

A variety of spatial treatments leads a visitor from the main interior of the church through a narrow redwood-paneled and glazed passage to the open-timbered hall of the former Sunday school building and the lower-ceilinged offices at either end of it. The hall is lit by wood fixtures holding bare bulbs set into cross-shaped electroliers. Early light bulbs gave a softer light than their glaring contemporary counterparts, but it is not difficult even now to imagine the effectiveness of the original light.

Saint John's interior can be compared with Morgan's earlier First Baptist of Oakland, as both derive from the Crafts style. Both use native redwood, both are geometric, both are original in composition and in execution. But the effect of the two is quite different. The Oakland church is impressive and moving in the sweeping curves of its pews and supports, while Saint John's has a kind of harmony that looks simpler but is in fact more sophisticated. The ingenious play between the inside and outside and the relation of details to the whole at Saint John's have rarely been equaled in American urban architecture.

Most of Morgan's ecclesiastical designs were small-scale neighborhood buildings. Usually she had a connection with someone on the building committee, either a previous client or an artisan. In 1923–24 Morgan built three modest churches in the Mediterranean style, all still in use today. The Federated Community Church in Saratoga, the Thousand Oaks Baptist Church in Berkeley, and the First Swedish Baptist Church (now called Lake-

side Baptist) in Oakland all feature a square tower, white walls, red-tile roof, and Mission-style windows; good acoustics were assured by Morgan's continued use of wood for interiors. The straightforward style was appropriate in that it was popular with clients during the period and relatively cheap. As all three were Protestant churches, it is unlikely that the religious associations of the mission-derived elements were a factor in Morgan's choice of that style.

Top: First Swedish Baptist Church, Oakland, 1923–24

Bottom: Morgan designed this Catholic church, San Carlos Borromeo, with a bell tower, tile roofs, and twin towers flanking an entrance that was to have been decorated with pilgrim figures. She made this watercolor elevation for the archbishop's consideration in 1928 and drew up a set of plans, but before funds could be allocated for construction the Depression put a halt to church building.

Oakland's Chapel of the Chimes, a crematorium and columbarium with Romanesque and Gothic features designed by Morgan starting in 1926, has an irresistibly exuberant vitality. The massing of the spaces creates a strong rhythm, and the decoration is sumptuous, where it had been spare in her earlier churches. The white concrete walls are broken by Gothic tracery and accented by arches, medallions, and arched stone trim. The chapel glows with light filtered through stained glass made by Marian Simpson of Berkeley, who said she was working for "an orchestration of color" and exploring the "medium of glass to its utmost intensity as light."[5] Paintings by another local artist, Doris Day, and decorations by practitioners of the art form called *parget* (ornamental plaster decoration), enrich the appeal of this building, which in other hands might have seemed gloomy or rigid. Morgan placed gardens and cloisters and chapels of varying scales on two levels in a spatial progress distinctively her own, alternating vaulted ceilings with clerestory light so that the whole effect is dazzling. Each detail was important to the architect, and each was calculated for maximum effect. The theatricality evident at San Simeon is very much a part of the Oakland columbarium.

Morgan considered all visual aspects of her buildings. She used decorative arts skillfully, working closely with craftsmen and choosing furnishings with care. In a January 10, 1935, letter to Lawrence Moore, the client for the Chapel of the Chimes, Morgan described purchases she was making for him:

Pictures are out of the question, as a good original is way beyond our fund even as a whole. Here in Florence I have accumulated for you things which are lovely but which you may not necessarily feel are suitable. You do not need to keep such items as they can easily be placed.

The finest item is a beautiful Della Robbia—a great wreath enclosing an angel in the circle—young, graceful and of comforting suggestion. I have never seen a finer wreath, or one beginning to equal it.

Then, there are two large vases with bouquets of lilies all of Majolica, in colors. (No need of daily watering).

. . . A fount (baptismal or otherwise) of marble and stone—Byzantine in character, the base of an antique animal bearing on his back a carved shaft supporting a bowl (this carved alone), and enriched with an inset band of old mosaic. It will be interesting in the entrance hall.

Next, pair of Majolica water things, which will not try to describe. I thought could be used in the flower rooms, or possibly as drinking fountains. Am sure these will be admired, and provide talking points.

. . . Tomorrow, when the final prices are checked up, if the allowance for packing, etc., is not eaten up—will order, *lastly*, a really lovely marble top table of inlay work on an iron stand—which would go well in one of the entrance ways, or another Della Robbia figure in relief, good sized.

. . . The things selected are at extremely good figures and are all excellent of their kind. If there is any small sum left over, will try to pick up some bits of embroidery or damask for runners for the altar and reading desk.

She closed the letter "with greetings to you, and kindest regards to all the 'C.C' [California Crematorium] family."

In 1930, when a group of Congregational churchmen in Hilo, Hawaii, was ready to build a columbarium on church property at their cemetery, their leader wrote to the national church organization in New York for advice. The response noted that the most beautiful columbarium in the United States was in Oakland and that a visit there would provide all the advice needed. Levi Lyman took the next ship to the mainland, saw the building, visited Morgan in her office, and commissioned her at once to design the Homelani Columbarium in Hilo. It is modest compared to the splendor of the Chapel of the Chimes, but it still stands and has been awarded landmark status.

Chapel of the Chimes, Oakland, 1926–30

Three views of Chapel of
the Chimes

W hen San Francisco suffered the disastrous earthquake followed by a devastating fire in April 1906, architects enjoyed an immediate bonanza. Morgan was no exception. The earthquake had so seriously damaged the luxurious six-hundred-room Fairmont Hotel that some experts thought it should be demolished. Designed three years earlier in Italian Renaissance style by James and Merritt Reid, it had recently been purchased by Herbert and Hartland Law and was being readied for a grand opening in the fall. After the earthquake struck, Herbert Law was determined to reopen the hotel within a year, so he commissioned Stanford White to come out from New York to renovate it. When White was shot and killed a few weeks later, Law turned to Julia Morgan, in private practice only two years and herself without an office as a result of the earthquake. Her experience with reinforced concrete while working on the Berkeley and Mills campuses, plus her training in engineering, may have brought her to Law's attention.

Morgan supervised the Fairmont project from a primitive construction shack on the slope behind the hotel, where the "flowing terrace stairs" (as described on an early postcard) and Italian garden were to be. There she worked on engineering problems, with rats jumping over her feet late at night, until the hotel was in shape to provide an office for the rest of the year. Photographs published by the insurance company clearly show what a demanding reconstruction job confronted the young architect. An accompanying report noted: "Columns covered with wire lath and

Postcard of the Fairmont Hotel after reconstruction

The Fairmont Hotel after the 1906 earthquake

plaster were generally defective. Thirty-seven such buckled and a portion of the floors settled down about seven feet from normal position."[6] What a triumph it must have been for Morgan and for Law to have the building ready to receive guests in time for the first anniversary of the earthquake.

While solving the engineering and landscaping problems for Herbert Law at the Fairmont, Morgan was also designing and constructing the international headquarters of a patent medicine company founded by Herbert's brother, Dr. Hartland Law, whose earlier building had exploded in the fire set to block the spreading flames started by the earthquake. The Viavi Building, located on the steep slope of Nob Hill, was also pledged to open for business one year after the disaster. The massive rectangular block that Morgan designed as Viavi headquarters followed the Italian Renaissance urban tradition. It had three stories at the main entrance on the north side of Pine Street, and four stories at the other end, where a distillery and press occupied the lowest floor. The elevation shows large arched windows under an almost flat tiled roof, with an overhang supported by ornamented brackets and cartouches between the windows. A strong horizontal line, or string course, below these arched windows separated the floors, and the second one (or piano nobile) had five tall rectangular windows with balconies, with five smaller ones along Pine Street.

The entrance, marked by an inset arch with a small-paned semicircular transom above the oak and glass doors, was surmounted by an ornamental arch incised in a design of herbal leaves and plants, with Roman letters spelling out the name *Viavi* ("way of life").[7] The procession through the plan began in the marble lobby, which was lit by a skylight in the center of the building. Manufacturing took place on the main floor: salve preparation, emulsion mixing, capsule stamping, labeling, and other preparation of the materials. Above that level were Dr. Law's offices, laboratories, and classrooms for the "practitioners," as the saleswomen were called. An early photograph shows them grouped around a diagram of the female body, learning about the way of life before starting out two-by-two to promote these herbal universal homeopathic cures to women on ranches and farms. The Viavi building was demolished when the life-insurance companies adjacent to it expanded in the 1920s.

A curious little commercial building designed by Morgan in 1910 still stands in Port Costa, a suburb east of San Francisco on the Carquinez Straits. Commissioned by William Clark Barnard of San Francisco, the Port Costa Water Company, a private waterworks, is basically one rectangular brick building with a wide overhang and Morgan's characteristic brackets. A frieze of vertical bricks runs around the entire building, just beneath the overhang.

Viavi Building, San Francisco, 1906–7

Women practitioners in the Viavi training rooms, 1907

The strictly functional interior has a small office space and places for machinery, although it is no longer in use.

Morgan later designed another unusual commercial building on a far vaster scale—the Sacramento Public Market (1923). The commission came through the Glide family, whose interest in revitalizing the downtown district was part of the pervasive civic enthusiasm of the 1920s. That the state capital, the center of the most productive agricultural valley in the nation, should have a noteworthy public market to replace the makeshift facilities that had grown up since the turn of the century was the idea of Elizabeth Glide, already a client and friend of Julia Morgan. The architect designed a brick building in Beaux-Arts style; her plan shows the corner siting to be significant, with a wider sidewalk at that point marking the main portal. This entrance is classical, framed by brick pilasters with ornamental capitals below a clearly marked string course; clerestory windows bring in light at the top. Along the sides additional two-story brick pilasters with capitals punctuate wide sixteen-panel windows both upstairs and down; further classical reference was provided by metopes (carved blocks) placed above the columns between sections of the clerestory windows. Awnings over the lower-floor windows provided protection from Sacramento's summers.

The interior has the large, central open space of a traditional Beaux-Arts plan, which offered easy circulation to the stalls and shops. Structural steel pillars and brackets were unsheathed, and the encircling balcony had wooden balusters with cutout urn designs and boxes for ferns and flowers provided from the start. After marketing patterns changed, the building was used as a sports arena as well as for shops, then was converted in 1979 to

Left: Sacramento Public Market under construction, 1923, and an early view of the interior

Above: Two contemporary views of the Sacramento Public Market, now used as offices for the California secretary of state

offices for the secretary of state as part of a program of adaptive use of historic buildings.

In 1916 Morgan built an early shopping center in Oakland for Fred C. Turner, an entrepreneur for whom she had already built a house in Oakland and for whom she would later design other speculative buildings. The brick building, which contains a block of shops plus apartments on the second floor, is at Piedmont Avenue and Fortieth Street, where the trolley cars used to turn around, making it a favorable place for trade. The circular windows are wreathed in della Robbia–style polychrome terra-cottas designed by Gardner Dailey of Morgan's office. Turner was publicly criticized for offering his parents one of the apartments above the stores, but they always professed delight to be in the center of activity on Piedmont Avenue with an unsurpassed view of the lively streetscape. The building still stands, unchanged in any major way.

In 1938 Turner called on Morgan to design another, more extensive shopping center just opposite the Berkeley campus, near the Hearst Memorial Gymnasium for Women. The expansion of the campus to Bancroft Way at Telegraph Avenue had necessitated the demolition of a block of small buildings. The favorite of these structures had been the Black Sheep Restaurant, which was to be relocated to Turner's new complex. Morgan's plan utilized a cobblestone courtyard in front of the restaurant, with shops along the side and flanking the entrance on the street. The one-story buildings were composed of reinforced-concrete blocks, but copper-roofed bays and copper suggestions of capitals above concrete columns give the complex an air of distinction, while diagonal entrances unite the composition.

Fred C. Turner stores, Oakland, 1916, with detail of terra-cotta wreath

THE · DURANT · WAY · ELEVATION.

SKETCH · FOR · THE · BERKELEY · WOMENS · CITY · CLUB · BUILDING.

THE WOMEN'S NETWORK

The social and economic ferment in turn-of-the century America made it a profitable place for architects. To the economic advances of the late nineteenth century was added the spirit of optimism common to new centuries. Pervasive interest in city planning had emerged from the 1893 Chicago world's fair, and the City Beautiful movement gave people confidence in the future of urban development.[1] Accumulation of wealth in those pre–income-tax days meant that clients had plenty of money on hand, and inevitably some of them spent it on showcase offices and dwellings, churches and clubs.

For the woman architect practicing in the early part of the century, these favorable factors were reinforced by others related to the improved status and new professionalism of women. Financial resources came with professional status, and high-school teachers, college professors, physicians, even journalists, did not hesitate to commission an architect for a house or a club building. The networks that women had developed while campaigning for abolition, temperance, and women's suffrage had made them aware of, and eager to hire, other women with diverse skills, including architects.

Morgan was not the only woman architect to benefit as women in various parts of the country established an astonishing number of clubs to provide centers for recreational, educational, and civic activities. In southern California, Hazel Wood Waterman (1865–1948) designed buildings for service organizations such as the Wednesday Club of San Diego. She trained another woman architect, Lilian Rice (1888–1938), who designed and supervised the Rancho Santa Fe community near San Diego in the early 1920s and a Rowing Club house (1932) in San Diego. In other parts of the country Minerva Park Nichols (1861–1948) was the architect of the New Century Club in Wil-

Opposite: Sketch for the Berkeley Women's City Club, 1929–30 (now the Berkeley City Club)

The YWCA Committee for Asilomar Leadership Conference, 1912. Phoebe Apperson Hearst is toward the right, wearing a silk-brocade Chinese robe.

mington, Delaware; Louise Blanchard Bethune (1856–1913) of Buffalo, New York, designed commercial and institutional buildings in partnership with her husband, Robert Bethune. In Chicago the work of Marion Mahoney Griffin (1871–1961) was submerged in that of her three collaborators: Walter Burley Griffin, Hermann von Holst, and Frank Lloyd Wright. Only now are her designs being studied by Chicago architectural historians as an independent contribution.

Morgan's preeminence among women architects is indisputable. Particularly relevant here is the fact that she designed and built an extraordinary variety of institutions planned for women's use. Some attention to her attitude toward women in architecture and to her relationships with them, both as clients and as staff members, may help to explain her success in promoting the interests of women through her buildings. Morgan was nearly apolitical, although she listed herself as a Republican in her biography for *Who's Who in California*. A friend, Dr. Mariana Bertola, formerly the Mills College physician, tried in vain to interest her in Hiram Johnson's progressive campaign for U.S. senator. Morgan's mother had attended a women's suffrage talk while Julia was in Paris and had written enthusiastically about the cause, but there is no record of any answer nor of any later recognition of women's rights as a political issue. Socially, however, Morgan was certainly aware of a women's network, beginning with her affiliation with the Kappa Alpha Theta sorority at Berkeley. Several of the women she met there became clients for important institutional as well as domestic commissions, and many were lifelong friends.

As early as 1905 one friend, Louise Goddard, commissioned the first of at least five speculative houses in Berkeley. Theta member Lucretia Watson, later Mrs. B. Grant Taylor, commissioned a house in Saratoga with a special music room that had its own separate entrance, where she pursued her career as a piano teacher. Grace Fisher Richards, also a Theta, brought Morgan a commission for the Saratoga Federated Community Church as well as for two major YWCA buildings and a house. Thetas Mary McLean Olney and Mary Olney Bartlett between them accounted for at least four Berkeley houses designed by their sorority sister. Elizabeth Glide of Sacramento had Morgan design three very different houses for her daughters, and another member of that Sacramento family commissioned a concrete house with cast-stone pillars and a carved-wood door; Morgan also designed the family hay barns in nearby Lisbon. Mrs. Glide, a powerful lumber heiress who took a vigorous part in the development of her city, also arranged Morgan's most important commission in the state capital: the Sacramento Public Market (see chapter 4). Morgan and Glide disagreed over the architect's proposal for a Glide Memorial Methodist Church to be built in San Francisco and the commission went to an architect willing to build it more cheaply, but the women remained friends.

During the 1920s Morgan employed several women artists whose work later became familiar in other contexts. For example, Maxine Albro, whose frescoes ornament the entrance and courtyard of Morgan's 1928 house for Seldon and Elizabeth Glide Williams in Berkeley (now a part of the University of California), went on to assist Diego Rivera on his San Francisco murals.[2] In 1934 Albro was commissioned to paint *California Agriculture*, a fresco in Coit Tower, and she later did a mosaic mural of flower and animal motifs for the entrance to the Hall of Natural Sciences at San Francisco State University. Marian Simpson, whose stained glass for Morgan's Chapel of the Chimes (1926–30) in Oakland contributes to the rich late medieval atmosphere of that building, had a long and successful career in the Bay Area. She also worked with Rivera, but her own style and interest in historic craft techniques prevailed, as is evident in her colored-marble

mural *Exploration and Settlement of California* (1937) in the lobby of the Alameda County Courthouse in Oakland.

Margaret Herrick of Stanford painted the frescoes (now painted over) and stencils at Morgan's Oakland YWCA and at her 1928 building for the Native Daughters of the Golden West in San Francisco. Doris Day escaped a lonely existence as a ranch wife in the 1920s by running away to San Francisco to find work as an artist. Her ambition was happily fulfilled as she received various commissions, first from Morgan, for paintings, stencils, and wall decorations at the Chapel of the

Stained glass by Marian Simpson, Chapel of the Chimes, Oakland, 1926–30

Chimes and at the Monday Club in San Luis Obispo, and later with federal New Deal projects and assorted private decorating projects. In the 1930s she painted fairy-tale motifs on the exterior of the Wyntoon houses that Morgan designed for William Randolph Hearst and painted folk-art designs in the large rusticated living room of Morgan's house for Else Schilling on the shore of Lake Tahoe.

Morgan also employed a series of women for drafting, but no one ever stayed very long or showed the dedication that would have been necessary to carry on the firm after Morgan retired. Some, such as Charlotte Knapp (called Kid Knapp by everyone but Morgan), worked for Morgan while attending architecture school and then went on to practice in other cities. Morgan sent money and encouraging letters when Knapp was in New York with a new degree in architecture and a job selling upholstery in Macy's;

she later worked as architect for the state government. Dorothy Wormser worked for four years before her marriage but not much afterward, and Elizabeth Boyter went off to practice on her own until a brain tumor terminated a promising career. C. Julian Mesic (originally named Charlotte) had changed her name when working in an office that was reluctant to have drawings signed by women. Morgan encouraged Mesic to take her licensing examinations, and she later built at least one house in Berkeley. In about 1920 Rose Luis, who had graduated from the architecture school at Berkeley, was refused a job in the Morgan office because several women architects were already there and Morgan said she did not want to have a majority of women. This must have seemed harsh to a qualified beginner, but it shows hardheaded business sense on Morgan's part. She did not want to risk putting off men clients with a single-sex firm.

Louis Schalk, a draftsman who had worked in the Morgan office since his high school days, expressed dissatisfaction with office policy as he grew older and more independent. He wrote a letter around 1921–22 upbraiding Morgan for her choice of personnel and especially her policy of taking on associates less talented than herself. In a letter that Morgan carried with her on a trip to San Simeon, as witness sketches for the latter on the envelope, he wrote:

> I believe that if you had selected prospects for their ability . . . instead of personality or sentiment, that we would be prepared after ten years of *grind* to carry on *nice* work, *big* work, *picked* work and *lots* of work. Consequently and incidentally we would now have a force of all around men, like myself or better.
>
> No doubt you have often wished for at least one girl who would amount to something but I am convinced that there will not be any in another 10 years. There are no reasons why girls should follow up Architecture in preference to marriage, but there are many good reasons why they should do just the reverse. . . . You cannot quote yourself as an example because I firmly believe that you are one in centuries, as a woman architect. Further it is my honest opinion that you have not been excelled by any architect of my reading acquaintance & most of the good architects are only reading acquaintances. Now then, I want to work in a group of capable hustlers, or for a capable hustler alone, or by myself, but I don't want to work with or train, hopeless prospects. . . . Of course it is good for the novice and as long as I stay I shall make friends with them and teach them a great deal. My aim is to do *quality* of work and not *quantity*. In your desire to satisfy all these so-called "connections" you are apt to sacrifice quality to quantity.

This letter continues for three more pages, in a rather repetitive but sincere effort to reform Morgan's office practices. She must have taken Schalk's criticism seriously, since she kept the letter (one of the few papers she preserved) for more than half a century, but she never changed her way of working.

Morgan rarely answered interviewers' questions about her views on architecture as a profession for women. In the *California Alumni* paper of October 23, 1915, she said: "Few women persevere as architects though many take up the study. Many are impatient to reach the top of the ladder too soon, matrimony takes others, but the greatest lures are the teaching positions in the high schools. There is a large field for women there, and as the salaries are good one cannot blame them for accepting unless they are determined to become architects." Sixteen years later Morgan was interviewed by Marcia Mead, herself a successful architect. In the *Christian Science Monitor* of November 27, 1931, Mead wrote:

> Miss Julia Morgan of San Francisco, one of our first successful women architects, says: "I think it is too early to say what contribution women are making in the field of architecture. They have as clients contributed very largely except, perhaps, in monumental buildings. The few professional women architects have contributed little or nothing to the profession—no great artist, no revolutionary ideas, no outstanding design. They have, however, done sincere good work along with the tide, and as the years go on, undoubtedly some greater than other architects will be developed, and in fair proportion to the number of outstanding men to the number in the rank and file.

Morgan understood women's organizations, their goals and their limitations, not just because of her gender but also because she shared their determination to improve the lives of individuals and groups who could not take social action on their own. Because of her own compassionate and pragmatic character, the idea of building new solutions to new problems always appealed to her. At the time Morgan was actively developing her career, women's clubs were establishing headquarters, community houses were being built, orphanages and specialized hospitals for children, for tubercular patients, and for the terminally ill were all being constructed. The Young Women's Christian Association (YWCA) and the Emanu-el Sisterhood for Jewish women were playing an especially active role in providing havens for young women flocking to the city to take relatively low-paying factory and office jobs. Morgan's practice included a large proportion of such projects over the years.[3]

The YWCA represented the kind of institutional client that an ambitious architect might well enjoy, for the National Board was supported by affluent and forward-looking citizens eager to ameliorate the widespread problems caused by the rapid growth of the cities. There had been a scattering of homes for "working girls" set up in houses donated or purchased for that purpose, but now the board was ready to build new centers, working in partnership with the regional offices and with local leaders. The stimulus to their construction efforts was the serious shortage of housing and recreation facilities for the newly urban young female workers, who rarely earned more than the minimum wage. Boardinghouses were few and often unsavory, if not actually unsafe, while healthy recreational activities were almost nonexistent. Providing these services along with educational and vocational opportunities required complex structures that had to house and entertain and instruct, providing, beyond beds and a few amenities, spaces for swimming, "amateur theatricals," English language and typing courses as well as classes in nutrition, cooking, money managing, sewing, and folk dancing—all that and more in an atmosphere that attempted to be "home-like." During the period of major building by the YWCA in the West (1913–32), Morgan designed YWCA structures at Asilomar (1913–28), Oakland (1913–15), San Jose (1915), Vallejo (1919), Salt Lake City (1919–20), Pasadena (1921), Fresno (1922 and 1924), Long Beach (1923), Hollywood (1925–26), Honolulu (1926–27), and San Francisco (1929–30), as well as special buildings for the 1915 Panama-Pacific International Exposition in San Francisco and World War I "hostess houses" in Camp Fremont, San Pedro, San Diego, and perhaps elsewhere.

Entrance gates to
Asilomar, Pacific Grove,
1913

Tent houses, Asilomar,
1913. The last tent house
was not torn down until
1971.

In order to staff their mushrooming centers the YWCA in the West developed a series of summer leadership conferences in small seaside towns. When the Santa Cruz hotel where they were to meet in 1912 burned down, Phoebe Apperson Hearst, already a patron of the YWCA, invited all three hundred participants to meet at the Hacienda, her ranch in Pleasanton, thirty-five miles inland from San Francisco. She arranged for tents, hotel beds, and supplies (even umbrellas, although it was unlikely to rain in the California summer). Not only did she provide

hospitality, but she also encouraged the group to think of starting a conference center·of their own. She went so far as to secure thirty acres of land at Pacific Grove, near Monterey, with the proviso that improvements worth at least $30,000 be made within ten years. She also recommended the architect who had been adding to her Hacienda for the past ten years—Julia Morgan.

By the next summer, 1913, the conference center at Pacific Grove opened, with large stone gateposts marking the entrance, one general assembly building (underwritten by Phoebe Hearst), and the ten elegant tent houses and beds that had been used at the Hacienda. A splendid plan was to be realized there during the next sixteen years. Using local wood and stone, Morgan designed buildings clustered around a campus circle in the redwoods and Monterey pines. A competition was held among YWCA members to name the conference center, with *Asilomar* (meaning "refuge by the sea") the winning entry. Morgan kept the buildings unobtrusive and sensitively coordinated with nature, in part by her use of local materials, in part by a determined horizontality. The first structure built, now the Phoebe Apperson Hearst Administration Building, is basically one large rectangular room, glazed on the two long sides, with offices, clubrooms, and rest rooms at either end, its stone base and redwood walls linking it to the landscape. The interior has exposed timbers and a massive fieldstone fireplace, with unpainted wood walls revealing every element of structure. With its high, open ceilings and sweeping views down to the sea, this generously proportioned room is as effective an introduction to the conference center today as it was seventy-five years ago.

The successful food sales in the YWCA building at the Panama-Pacific International Exposition of 1915 and additional contributions by California women funded construction of Morgan's next two important buildings at Asilomar: the chapel, dedicated in 1915 to the memory of Grace H. Dodge;

Asilomar, with a view of the Phoebe Apperson Hearst Administration Building (1913) in the distance.

Interior of the Administration Building. Ella Schooley of the YWCA wrote to Phoebe Apperson Hearst regarding this building on May 19, 1913: "Miss Morgan is A-1, and she is sparing no pains to give us the greatest possible result for the least expenditure. The builder, in looking over her plan for the administration building, said, 'There is nothing like it in these parts.' I said, 'Do you think it compares favorably with Pebble Beach Lodge?' His reply was, 'It has it skinned a mile.'"

and the dining hall and kitchen, a gift from Mary Crocker in 1918. The chapel, which also served as auditorium and music hall until Merrill Hall was erected in 1928, was sited so that its wall-size altar window frames a natural picture of pines, sand, and sea. This modest cottage-like building, again in unpainted wood inside and out, is distinguished not only by that window wall but also by a carved frieze of gold-incised letters punctuated by shell motifs:

> Sing, O Heavens and be joyful O Earth:
> And break forth into singing O Mountains! (Isaiah 49:13)
> For ye shall go out with joy, and be led forth with peace:
> The mountains and the hills shall break forth before you into singing (Isaiah 55:12)

The chapel is warmed by another huge stone fireplace and chimney, similar to that in the Administration Building. Crocker Dining Hall recalls the large tent under which meals were originally enjoyed, bring-

Rear view and interior of the chapel, Asilomar, 1915

rrerrrerrrerrrerrrerrrerrrerrre
Dear Mrs. Hearst:

Yesterday I returned from Asilomar. . . . It reminded me, as things constantly do, of your own kindness to me in connection with Asilomar. It has been a real happiness to see the little "general plan" you went over and approved gradually take form, and now even begin to grow beyond.

Then this work brought acquaintance with Miss Gerry and others of the National Board which in turn has brought other interests, the pleasantest being the work last fall and winter, and even now finishing, in their New York center on war work problems. They have asked me to come to them permanently and over look their Building plans nationally—but on acct. of my family here it would not be possible to accept, attractive as it could be in the way of service in the very dreary middle west towns I had glimmers of the life of this winter.

And so through it all is the thread of your kindness since those Paris days when you were so beautifully kind to a most painfully shy and home sick girl. My mothers and yours are the greatest "faiths" put in me, and I hope you both know how I love and thank you for it.

I hope you are feeling very much better and that the Spring will bring complete restoration. [Mrs. Hearst died the following month.]

> *Sincerely and affectionately,*
> *JULIA MORGAN*
> *March 26th, 1919*

ing the outdoors in and making a minimal separation between site and structure. The exposed trusses are like tree branches overhead; the window walls, bentwood chairs, and rustic stone fireplaces establish a joyful link with the landscape.

Land was added to Asilomar in 1915, doubling the original acreage, and the next year Morgan completed a visitors' lodge, also in Arts and Crafts style, with sleeping porches held up by stone pillars. Building at Asilomar ceased briefly during World War I. In the meantime Morgan was engaged by the YWCA to design "hostess houses" at western military camps, where soldiers and their families could meet. Morgan's two surviving hostess houses, both in Crafts style, follow lines similar to the Administration Building at Asilomar. Both are also quite like the later Berkeley YWCA, featuring open trusses, fireplaces, and a balcony over the service and club-room areas at either end of the long main room. Asilomar meanwhile had been utilized as a training ground for "soldierettes." Dorothy Wormser Coblentz, later an architect in Morgan's office, reported that she marched, drilled, and camped out there in 1918, shortly after earning her degree in architecture from Berkeley.

In a surge of postwar building at Asilomar, Morgan produced several new housing units, notably the shingled Scripps Lodge (named after another

California family in honor of its support); the director's cottage; Hilltop (a cottage for women employees, with "The House of Happiness" incised over the mantel), Viewpoint Cottage, and Tide Inn (for men employees). Facilities for basketball, volleyball, softball, and tennis plus the earlier saltwater swimming pool for those not ready to risk the Pacific were built on the periphery of the central area. Warehouses and garages were also constructed following Morgan's design, hidden behind the trees and under a hill so that they disappeared almost as effectively as later underground garages.

The most important addition to Asilomar in this period was the auditorium, Merrill Hall (1928), designed to seat a thousand. Again made of local wood and stone, this large rectangular hall has natural lighting from French doors and clerestory windows framed in laminated wood arches. Open trusses with brass braces, nuts, and lighting fixtures make this elegant building a rusticated rather than a rustic version of Crafts architecture. Morgan alleviated the long stretches of unpainted wood by adding colorful stenciled friezes of seashells, sea horses, and the like, which celebrate the site and remind conference-goers of where they sit. Merrill Hall exhibits all the characteristics that make Morgan's Crafts residences so appealing, although its very size was a distinct departure from the scale of most Crafts structures. Surrounded by Monterey pines and cedars and sited on a slight

Opposite: Crocker Dining Hall, Asilomar, 1918

Living room, hostess house, Camp Fremont, 1916–18

rise above the original center of the complex, the building emerges from stone and sand like one of the natural elements. Reflecting the client's and the architect's feeling for preserving the landscape, it clearly was built from the inside out, with an economy of means emphasized by leaving the structural elements visible.

Designed so successfully that it seems to have grown naturally on the site, Asilomar is perhaps the largest institutional complex ever built in the Arts and Crafts style. A California State monument since 1958, it is still being used as a conference center and is one of the two most profitable units in the state park system, San Simeon being the other.

The use of Asilomar as a conference and training center meant that YWCA personnel and board members from all over the West and even nationally were familiar with its architecture and its architect. It is not surprising, therefore, that commissions for other buildings came from the same source. Two major Morgan buildings still in use by the YWCA are those in Oakland and in Honolulu. Although both have plans recalling Beaux-Arts principles, they differ in basic ways. The Oakland building was designed to serve as a women's hotel as well as a center for recreation, education, and job training. In Honolulu, Morgan had already built a YWCA women's hotel, called the Residence, so the need there was for a recreational center.

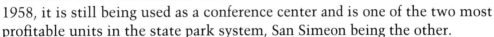

Plans for the Oakland building were begun in 1910, when Grace Fisher, a sorority sister of Morgan's, was president of the local board. The need was felt for one multipurpose building in rapidly growing Oakland and another in San Jose. *Architect and Engineer* announced in January 1913 that Julia Morgan had "recently returned from a tour of Eastern cities where she made a study of YWCA clubhouses for the purpose of getting ideas that might be utilized to advantage in the erection of the Oakland YWCA home. A home for young women will be a distinct and separate feature of the building."

In April of that year plans were approved and a budget of $125,000 was established. It is difficult to know whether any particular East Coast YWCA had influenced the architect, as Morgan left no notes about the trip, except a brief fragment regarding her response to the Minneapolis YWCA, and the archives of the national association have not revealed any records of what buildings she visited. *Architect and Engineer* noted in March 1913, however, that the plans showed "all the newest features to be found in the finest buildings of this type in the East." Morgan followed the tradition of the

Opposite: Merrill Hall, Asilomar, 1928

Interior of Merrill Hall and detail of stenciled frieze

95

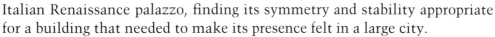

Italian Renaissance palazzo, finding its symmetry and stability appropriate for a building that needed to make its presence felt in a large city.

Morgan's changes from the elevation of 1913 to the final building yielded a bolder handling of the entrance and a more rhythmic placement of the two-story arched windows. Rather than classical columns or pilasters to frame the windows, she used rich designs of California fruits and flowers in polychrome terra-cotta, manufactured and glazed in nearby Alameda from Morgan's drawings. Such use of regional motifs in ornamentation has a long history, notably exemplified by Benjamin Latrobe's choice of tobacco leaves and corn to grace the Capitol in Washington, D.C. Morgan's use of brilliant natural colors here provides a purely Californian element. The top floor of the building, set back to provide a balcony on all sides, has oversize square windows framed with more mat-glazed polychrome terra-cotta. The iron-railed balcony serves as the required fire escape, as an amenity for the classrooms on that floor, and as a decorative band on the exterior.

The interior follows an axis and cross axis plan with a central court modeled on the outdoor courtyard of Donato Bramante's church of Santa Maria della Pace in Rome. The columns have a combination of orders similar to the one used there, and in both structures a frieze of biblical verses is used for design as well as for content. Morgan's wood-frame brackets are in the East Bay vernacular, and the skylight suits Oakland's climate, giving the courtyard a feeling of the outdoors' having been brought indoors. A fountain originally played in the courtyard, and wicker furniture chosen by Morgan further enhanced the patio atmosphere. The building as a whole functioned exactly as programmed, offering shelter and recreation to the minimum-wage woman in a period of transition. It still serves as a YWCA, although the hotel has been replaced by offices and classrooms.

Pools were planned as prominent features of both the large urban YWCAs completed by Morgan in 1915, at Oakland and at San Jose. The San Jose pool was pictured in the *Architect and Engineer* of November 1918,

Opposite: Assembly room, Oakland YWCA, 1913–15

Drawing for the Oakland YWCA, 1913

Terra-cotta exterior decoration, Oakland YWCA

Three views of the
Oakland YWCA

Pool, Long Beach YWCA,
1923

showing the flood of daylight provided by a broad Palladian window at one
end and the effect of open sky through the skylight roof supported by two
heavy trusses. Five years later Morgan built a pool with a skylight and five
tall double windows at each side for the Long Beach YWCA. Here the reinforced-concrete arched forms were in a decorative open design, and a spectators' balcony with wire mesh and stone posts ranged around the whole.
This balcony was cantilevered over concrete columns, with supports carrying out the line of the arches. The San Jose and the Long Beach YWCAs
have both been demolished.

At the same time that Morgan was building the YWCAs in Oakland and
San Jose, she was engaged on perhaps her most notable community service
building—notable partly because it came and vanished so fast, almost without a trace, and partly because it was the only structure allocated to women
at the Panama-Pacific International Exposition in San Francisco in 1915.
Architects as well as exposition fanciers have long been aware of the Wom-
en's Building at the 1893 World's Columbian Exposition in Chicago, a building designed by Sophia Hayden and ranked among the twelve major
buildings at that fair. Despite that successful example, when plans were
made for an exposition in San Francisco to celebrate the completion of the
Panama Canal and the linking of East and West, the committee of architects

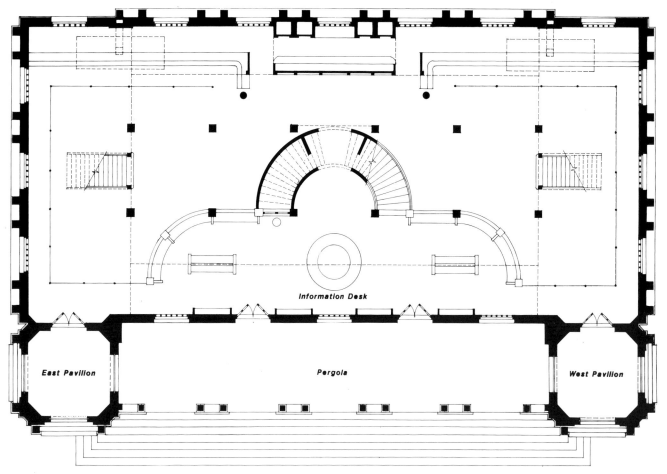

Information Desk

East Pavilion   **Pergola**   **West Pavilion**

headed by John Galen Howard made no provision for a women's building. Nor did they include Julia Morgan among the architects, although Howard and the other members of the committee were certainly aware of her impressive Beaux-Arts background and her established practice in the Bay Area. (By 1913 Morgan was engaged in planning and building Asilomar and the two large YWCAs for Oakland and San Jose.) Yet it was only through the insistence of Phoebe Hearst and a few of the other committee members that she was commissioned to design the interior of one of the exposition buildings.

Because there was to be no women's building as such at the fair, the national YWCA was finally invited to collaborate on a structure to serve the needs of women visitors and to provide a quick-service lunchroom for all. The exterior design was furnished by the Panama-Pacific International Exposition Company, to match the appearance of the Press Building at the other side of the Scott Street entrance; both exteriors were designed by Edward F. Champney of San Francisco. It was the interior of the YWCA Building that Morgan was chosen to design.

A November 1913 report from Helen A. David, executive secretary of the national YWCA's fieldwork committee, illuminates some of the difficulties in planning the project: "My week in San Francisco was a most

Main-floor plan for the YWCA Building, Panama-Pacific International Exposition, San Francisco, 1914–15

exciting one. I have never in Association work faced as many complications as this San Francisco situation offers. . . . I have been to the Exposition grounds twice, have talked with the men there in charge of the concessions and they are relying on us. . . . The Women's Board of the Exposition have said in public that there was no hope of the YWCA doing the work. Last night I had a most interesting interview with Mrs. Hearst who felt that if the National Board could assume some responsibility it could break this apparent deadlock."[4] As a result of David's report, the national board lent money for construction, with additional funds contributed by other women's organizations, and the idea of a women's building on the exposition grounds became a reality, with at least the interior designed by a woman.

Champney's ornamental plaster-and-stucco exterior conformed to the overall design of the exposition. It was a two-story rectangular box, with a low-pitched roof supported by ornamental brackets. A porch across the front featured six pairs of caryatids, with another four pairs on each side; these were probably designed by Morgan, although this is not documented. Domed, glazed pavilions at the front corners extended the interior beyond the walls of the box.

Three views of the portico, YWCA Building, Panama-Pacific International Exposition

Morgan dealt with the interior in a purely functional way. An article by Frances A. Groff in the May 1915 *Sunset*, "Lovely Woman at the Exposition," describes the YWCA Building:

> Its interior is the only architectural work of any importance in the Exposition entrusted to a woman architect; and the remarkable airy, cheery, welcoming arrangement reflects much credit upon Miss Julia Morgan. Every foot of space has been made available. Even the ends of the porch have been glassed in and utilized as reading and writing rooms. Just inside of the entrance is the information bureau. The rest of the main floor and all of the mezzanine are occupied by the lunch room, where "real food" is served at moderate prices. On the second floor are kitchens, offices, club rooms, a rest room with trained nurse in attendance, and an assembly hall seating 250 people, which is available free of charge to suitable organizations. Prominent men and women speak here on home economics, hygiene, physical training and recreation, thrift and economy and kindred subjects. Jane Addams will be among the lecturers this summer. There are classes and social gatherings for the girl employees on the grounds; and the association is endeavoring through what is called "The Big Sister" work, to see that girls discharged from the various concessions shall not drift out into the city friendless, discouraged and open to temptation.

Although Morgan generally followed the Beaux-Arts principle of first conceiving a plan that in turn dictated the exterior, it was evident here that she could devise an imaginative and functional interior with a predetermined exterior. The resulting space—with its circular information desk and its broad, curving staircase—expressed a welcoming hospitality. The well-lighted mezzanine, also used to serve food, gave a sense of openness to the cafeteria below and added flexibility to the cafeteria's seating arrangements, allowing the adjacent kitchen to serve small groups or large in one or both

First floor and
mezzanine, YWCA
Building

areas. Bentwood·chairs and square tables harmonized with the total design. The lunchroom, one of the most successful in the exposition, turned a profit of $15,000, which the YWCA invested in other building projects, notably the chapel and dining hall at Asilomar.

In addition to the interior of the YWCA Building, Morgan built two separate facilities for the women employed in the international food stands and entertainment booths of the concession area, known as the Zone. Essentially one-room structures in Crafts style, these small board-and-batten structures had banks of windows grouped for a light and airy effect, enhanced by open-trussed ceilings. Writing materials, a kitchenette for snacks, a sewing machine, and some books and games made these centers a pleasant refuge during time off from the Zone. As works of architecture, they were simple and functional, but not skimpy or cheap. They were demolished, as planned, along with most of the exposition buildings when the year was over.

Both the highly visible YWCA Building and the inconspicuous shelters for the Zone personnel have been omitted from most accounts of the Panama-Pacific Exposition. The fair itself has attracted attention in the current revival of interest in exposition architecture; but because exposition historians Louis Christian Mullgardt, Ben Macomber, and others have overlooked Morgan's work, her contributions were almost lost to history. Thanks to the archives of the national YWCA, these unusual examples of design for specific, if ephemeral, community service have been rediscovered.

Top: Resting room, YWCA Building

Center: Main lobby, YWCA Building

Bottom: Clubhouse for Zone workers, Panama-Pacific International Exposition

More indirectly related to the exposition was the Oakland Juvenile Court Probation Building, which was commissioned by a group of women in 1913 but never built. The women had begun lobbying for the building in September 1913 because they were concerned that numbers of young people would run away from home to see the exposition. They predicted that the youths would arrive in Oakland, the chief railway terminal, with no means of support and without funds to return home. The city was urged to construct a juvenile facility that would be quite distinct from a jail, where young people in difficulty could be sheltered and probation could be supervised. Morgan was to design the building, and she presented drawings and cost estimates as her contribution to the women's campaign, but funds were not raised in time to build the facility. San Francisco had Mullgardt design and construct a large probation building in an attempt to solve the same potential problem.

Pasadena YWCA, 1921

Concern for the powerless members of society continued to be characteristic of the YWCA and of Julia Morgan's commissions for them. In southern California the city of Pasadena, in the throes of expansion, planned a
City Beautiful center. Here was to stand a YWCA building that would emphasize the city's care for minimum-wage women who needed shelter and
amenities. Mary (Mrs. David E.) Gamble, of 4 Westmoreland Place (the most
celebrated of Greene and Greene houses), was chairman of the YWCA building committee, which commissioned a structure that would fit well with
plans for a civic center. Instigated by Dr. George E. Hale, director of the
Mount Wilson Observatory, and carried out by the Pasadena Planning Commission, the decidedly Beaux-Arts civic center included city hall, the main
library, the civic auditorium, and both the YMCA and the YWCA.

Preliminary drawings for the YWCA were published in *California
Southland* in December 1920, titled "Proposed Group for the YWCA of
Pasadena, California, Julia Morgan, Architect." As originally planned, the
Pasadena YWCA was composed of three sections. The central three-story
portion had a columned loggia at the top, flanked by open corner porches; a
two-story building at either side provided office and residential space.
Marked by a Palladian doorway, the central part projected somewhat and
was altogether readable as a recreational and educational center. As actually
built in 1921, the central section has a band of five windows (three square
panes above rectangular ones in each) instead of the loggia, while the second
floor has tall windows with iron balconies, and the entrance has a plain
archway with iron lanterns. Pool and gymnasium are at the rear. The building still reads as clearly as a Beaux-Arts elevation, while the plan (as carried
out by associate architects Marston and van Pelt in collaboration with Morgan) shows her concern for circulation, for the hierarchy of spaces, and for
the function of the program.

In between commissions from the YWCA, Morgan designed another landmark building to aid young working women. Similar to the YWCA buildings in program was the Emanu-el Sisterhood Residence at Page and Laguna streets in San Francisco. The Jewish women's group asked Morgan in 1921 to design a residential facility with assembly rooms, gymnasium, and other recreational features. The three-story brick building (plus basement) is on a difficult corner site, with hills at different angles on the two street sides. The facade is formal, with broad steps used to give a level base to the slope. The windows are spaced and framed in classical Beaux-Arts symmetry. The entrance leads to a formal hall that provides the central axis, with a large assembly room to the right and offices to the left. Tables and chairs built by Morgan's craftsmen to her designs are still in use after sixty-five years. Across the large courtyard, in the center of which a fountain was originally located, a parallel wing serves as classrooms and living space. The cross axis marked by a broad staircase leads up to the living spaces and down to the gymnasium, with natural lighting on the landings both above

Exterior and courtyard, Emanu-el Sisterhood Residence, San Francisco, 1921–22

and below the main level. After wartime duty as headquarters for female military personnel, the building was bought in the 1950s to serve as the San Francisco Zen Center.

One of Morgan's major YWCA centers still serving its original purpose is the YWCA Metropolitan Headquarters in Honolulu (1926–27). Morgan had first worked for the YWCA in Hawaii around 1917, when she remodeled a Waikiki beach house belonging to the Atherton family. The Athertons then gave the property to the YWCA to be used as an international center for young women. This was a simple Crafts building, much beloved during the period between the two world wars. It was demolished in the 1950s so that the YWCA could lease the beachfront property to developers, an arrangement that has provided income for the organization ever since.

When the Athertons' daughter Kate died in about 1919 they gave their homestead ("Fernhurst"), plus some land and money, to the YWCA as a memorial to her, and they called

Above: Metropolitan Headquarters, Honolulu YWCA, under construction, c. 1926

Below: Honolulu YWCA, 1926–27

Opposite: Floor plan, Honolulu YWCA

on Morgan to remodel the mansion into a women's hotel. The Honolulu newspaper reported Morgan's arrival on October 15, 1921, to design the alterations for Fernhurst and announced that she might also help with plans for a new YWCA administration building. While Morgan was busy creating the Residence, as Fernhurst was called, she was also thinking about the need for a nonresidential headquarters on the island. By September 1925 she produced blueprints (revised in 1926) for an imposing three-story structure opposite Honolulu's historical park surrounding Iolani Palace.

After a visit in December 1925 Morgan put one of her office engineers, Bjarne Dahl, in charge of the Honolulu headquarters. He recalled in 1980 that she had shown him the plans and "laid them out ready for us to start the working drawings. She said this building is in the center of the city. I

said the drawings look like it would be out in the country someplace. This remark delighted her, and she said that was the impression she wanted to convey."[5] Because of the complex demands of her wide-ranging practice, including weekends allotted to San Simeon, Morgan had to work out a long-distance plan as complicated as that of a Paris architect designing a colonial structure in Madagascar. She made Edward Hussey her architectural representative, with Dahl his assistant. Her ablest draftsman, Thaddeus Joy, took a ship out periodically to consult, as did her engineers Walter Steilberg and James LeFeaver. She remained in control of the operation by requiring that Hussey write, in duplicate, full daily numbered reports to be mailed by the weekly boat (which took ten days to two weeks to reach San Francisco), along with a roll of eight exposures of film and annotated and dated floor plans. For emergencies, radiograms went to "Julmorgan SF." These notes, on file in the Morgan Collection at Cal Poly, show exactly how the building was designed and erected from two thousand miles away. Some of Morgan's

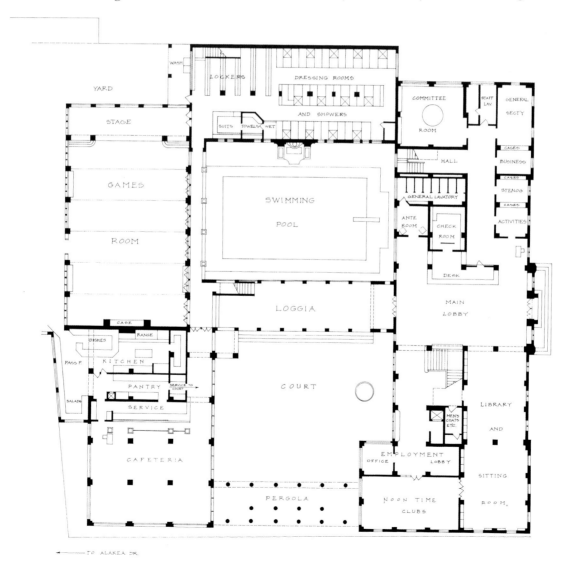

HONOLULU YWCA RECREATION CENTER
1926

0 1   5   10
FEET

responses reveal a personal point of view, as when the women of the YWCA wanted opaque glass in the doors to the Committee Room and she wrote: "Wish they could use sash curtains. The obscure glass is not friendly looking and has the effect of being dirty when clean."

Morgan used only clean, well-graded beach sand, crushed blue lava, or Palola rock for her reinforced concrete, with all new steel, no bars from scrap permitted—examples of her scrupulous care as an engineer. The *Honolulu Star Bulletin* of June 18, 1927, reported that "an allowance of 2,000 pounds of steel more than required for reinforcements was made in the contract to provide bondings and earthquake ties where it might seem advisable. Even the roof trusses are concrete. Practically all the floors with the exception of the gymnasium and the games room will be of concrete." The same paper elaborated on the beauty of the building revealed when the wooden forms were torn off by the crew of seventy workmen:

> A spacious lobby, sitting rooms and library, a gymnasium, outdoor swimming pool, games room, club rooms, classrooms, rest rooms, community room, cafeteria, picturesque loggias and balconies took definite shape as the wooden frames were cast off. Interesting arches, distinctly "Morgan" in design, are a feature of the entire building, which is designed by Miss Julia Morgan, Architect. . . .
>
> Already there is a feeling of rest and beauty, a distinctly tropical atmosphere, as one enters the front of the building opposite the Iolani Palace on Richards Street. One needs but to pass through this arch to know that here will be hung beautiful carved teakwood doors, flanked on each side by plate glass openings to keep all of nature's rare beauty within as without. Especial care has been taken to guard all the trees in the yard during the course of construction.
>
> To the right of the spacious lobby, which faces Richards Street, will be the desk, checking room and offices. To the left is a beautiful sitting room and library where comfortable seats and books will be at the disposal of all visitors. Back of the library is a clubroom and kitchen. Connecting the two main portions of the building, and directly through the center, is a two-floor loggia. As one crosses this loggia from the lobby, the swimming pool, about 30 by 60 feet, is to the right and connects directly with the dressing rooms, showers and the offices of the health education secretary.
>
> The back wing of the building, or the wing which runs parallel with Alakea Street, includes on the first floor a large games room and cafeteria. A feature of the cafeteria, as well as the girls' club rooms, directly above it, is the series of diagonal arched girders which give the ceilings an interesting effect.
>
> On the second floor is a community room, designed especially for the club women of Honolulu. Here it is expected that many women will take advantage of the spacious quarters which have been set aside for their convenience.
>
> On the third floor are educational department quarters. Another feature of the second and third stories will be open galleries looking down upon the swimming pool.

In one of her rare letters describing a completed work, Morgan wrote to the national headquarters of the YWCA in New York: "The Honolulu building is unusually frank and sincere architecturally. There is practically no false work or furring in the building—the girders, beams, great arches, openings of all types, being the structural concrete, sometimes plastered upon, sometimes not, always the form used expressing (or trying to) a given more or less decorative quality."[6] Here Morgan reveals her feeling for materials,

Main entrance and
carved-teak doors,
Honolulu YWCA

Two views of the pool
and courtyard, Honolulu
YWCA

her understanding of the plasticity of concrete. Her graceful use of this material established a rhythm with the three sections of the building, each marked by quoining to make a readable facade. The portico, with broken pediment above an ordered doorway framed by pilasters, has the distinctly local feature of double teakwood doors. Each door has ten squares carved in low relief, representing local flowers: the ubiquitous plumeria, the hibiscus, the orchid. The ironwork of the balconies and fences was calculated to cast decorative shadows as well as to be pleasing against the plaster and concrete.

The Honolulu plan offers an unexpected open courtyard in the middle, a special delight in a fast-growing city. An unusual aspect of the courtyard is the two-story central arcade that bisects it, with a large outdoor swimming pool on one side and um-brella-topped tables in the dining area on the other. This arcade leads to the wing holding the cafeteria, gymnasium, game room, and theater, with a canti-levered balcony overlooking the pool. Again, orna-mental ironwork catches the light in varying patterns throughout the day.

It was in Honolulu that Morgan's skill with pools and her sensitivity to climate and atmosphere created what is probably the most effective of all her YWCA pools. Impressive as part of an exceptionally clear and functional plan, it also reflects her remarkably sensuous approach to pools, which was to culminate in those at San Simeon. The architect's provision for spectators from the gymnasium balcony and from the two levels of the arcade underlines the pool's importance and speaks for the physical and aesthetic values of swimming. This Spanish-style building refers back to Islam in its presentation of precious water within an enclosure, while celebrating the modern freedom of young women to learn to swim, rather than merely "bathe," for recreation and health. It is in marked contrast to many institutional pools that are hidden away. Adapting Mediterranean traditions to this Pacific outpost, Morgan created a structure that still functions admirably well as a place for physical, mental, and spiritual recreation.

While the Honolulu YWCA was being constructed, the Los Angeles YWCA commissioned the Hollywood Studio Club, with Mrs. Cecil B. deMille as chairman of the building committee. Morgan's task was to design a building to house and provide recreational facilities for the endless stream of young women who came to Hollywood in the hope of establishing movie careers. The local YWCA had sponsored efforts since 1916 to provide low-cost, high-quality housing for such women and had worked with industry leaders, notably Will Hays (who headed the self-censoring film board), to secure funds for a building. The lot they purchased at the corner of Lodi Place and Lexington Avenue cost $36,640. Morgan first submitted plans for the structure in 1920. The earliest surviving drawing (undated) shows a Mediterranean building of three stories with two towers in the rear, separated from the lower part of the building fronting the street by a courtyard with pergola. A center section was set back be-

First drawing for Hollywood Studio Club, c. 1920

Second drawing for Hollywood Studio Club, c. 1925

tween two gabled wings. Three blocky concrete pillars at the entrance under another tiled gable formed four arched openings, flanked by Mission-style windows. Each gable section had a wide-arched full-length window with balcony, again with Mission-style windows at each side. An unglazed loggia at second-floor level united the facade and gave a feeling of openness, which was repeated in the enclosed courtyard.

After some changes made in a subsequent drawing, the Studio Club was completed for $229,604, including furnishings, and was officially opened in May 1926. It provided a secure shelter over the years for some ten thousand young women in the entertainment industry, some of whom, like Ayn Rand and Marilyn Monroe, later achieved fame. In 1968 it was merged with the Los Angeles YWCA and is currently rented to the city for use as social-service offices. According to recent seismic regulations the structure is unsafe for use as housing, and it is in constant danger of demolition.

The Hollywood building shows Morgan at the height of her powers, freely responding to the client's program and to the urban setting with a creative use of the Mediterranean style. Its development from the original drawing to the actual structure reveals her liberation from the strict Mission style as she balanced Moorish complexity with her own rational symmetry. During this period, when she also designed the Honolulu YWCA, the Riverside YWCA, and the Berkeley Women's City Club, the contrapuntal work at San Simeon stimulated her imagination, resulting in a sense of disciplined excitement that communicates directly to the viewer.

The Riverside YWCA (1929), set on a generous corner lot in southern California, is another of Morgan's urban Mediterranean designs in concrete with tile roof. It differs from her other YWCA buildings in being a complex of blocks of varying scales rather than a single mass. There is an orderly progression of height toward the corner, where one massive Italianate component features a gable that shelters a frieze and a loggia. Set-in arched Palladian windows at street level continue the Italian effect. Quoining demarcates each section of the major part of the building and emphasizes its separate function: it contains a theater, a gymnasium, and two rather Mannerist loggias (one is around the corner, next to the outdoor gymnasium). An ornamental seal of the YWCA with scrolls unites the low-pitched roof with the protruding gable. The building's central portion, indented in Palladian fashion, has the four columns of an unglazed loggia over an entrance

Opposite: Hollywood Studio Club, seen c. 1927

Riverside YWCA, 1929

The Residence, YWCA, San Francisco, 1929–30

Living room and a
bedroom, the Residence

Opposite: View from the
Residence of Morgan's
Chinese YWCA, 1930

framed by pilasters and originally topped by broken pediment and urn (removed as a seismic risk, now leaving a bare semicircle). At its side is a section with iron balcony and central arched openings, then a wing that continues the parade of tall Palladian windows on a residential scale.

The unusual combination of monumental and residential scales, the progression left to right in size and significance, and the richness and unexpected juxtaposition of Mannerist details give this building a Postmodern aspect. Compared with the adjacent Glenwood Mission Inn (1902–31), probably the greatest and certainly the most lavish example of the Mission Revival style—built through the successive efforts of Arthur Benton, Myron Hunt, Elmer Grey, and G. Staley Wilson—the Morgan building might seem merely a "tasteful, somewhat neutral Mediterranean design."[7] Yet, looked at for its own rhythm, for the clarity and wit of its historical allusions, it reveals itself as a lively and vigorous example of southern California architecture. It is now used as an art museum and has even begun to be called the Julia Morgan Museum.

A women's hotel called the Residence (1929–30) on Nob Hill in San Francisco was Morgan's last major building for the YWCA. Its formal exterior of brick with tile decoration is well suited to the Powell Street site; the building turns the corner to adjoin the Chinese YWCA, also designed by Morgan. Tall arched windows along the front illuminate formal public rooms, a paneled library with a fireplace imported from France, and a large assembly room. Originally located along the axis to the large formal living room (40 by 60 feet) were a central dining room and kitchen on one side and smaller dining and sitting rooms on the other. The living room's tall windows look out on Chinatown, and its long interior wall, which Morgan had decorated with a silk wall covering, now has a Chinese mural.

Morgan wanted this building to signify the importance of working women, and she sought to provide them with amenities that at times seemed excessive to the YWCA board. Her determination to provide private dining rooms and kitchenettes for the young women, so they could occasionally entertain friends for meals, met with opposition. "But these are minimum-wage girls," was the protest, "why spoil them?"

To which the architect replied: "That's just the reason."[8] The building, remodeled by Worley Wong, now serves low-income older people in studio apartments with many of the same amenities provided by Morgan.

While the Residence was under construction, Morgan designed the adjoining Chinese YWCA down the hill behind it. That recreation center, designed for a complex program of sports and education, presents a discreet Chinese face to the street. Within are sequestered a quiet private garden, a

bustling gymnasium, and many other facilities. The building varies from one to three stories on the steep slope, with its most conspicuous section the large gymnasium. This in itself is evidence of the acceptance by Chinese women of certain American traditions, as physical exercise for girls had not been acceptable to most earlier generations. Crenellation (with special tiles imported from China) and three towers with wooden spires give interest to the roofline. A cast-stone arch over the double doors has leaded glazing, and above it is a circular cast-stone window with steel sash. Presently called the Chinese Community Center (although the YWCA sign remains to speak of its history) and sensitively remodeled on the interior by architect Philip Choy, the building continues to function as it was designed, though now serving both men and women.

Morgan designed the Japanese YWCA (1930) on Sutter Street in San Francisco to recall elements of Japanese culture. The rooflines, the stone wall and gates surmounted by iron lanterns, and the interior details, especially the cutout screen over the auditorium stage, all suggest Japan. After the demographic and economic upheavals of World War II led to a change in the composition of the neighborhood, the building was renamed the Western Addition YWCA, which it remains today.

Top: Entrance, Chinese YWCA

Center: Stairwell, the Residence

Opposite: Courtyard, Chinese YWCA

Settlement houses and orphanages, retirement centers, and various specialized hospitals were other forms of community service for which Morgan created buildings. Potrero Hill House Community Center has been in continuous service since its establishment in a Crafts-style building by Morgan in 1921. She designed about eight California hospitals for tubercular patients, each underwritten by adjoining counties and planned to provide the fresh-air therapy that was the treatment of choice during the first half of the century. She also built pediatric facilities in Santa Barbara and in Los Angeles, the latter commissioned by Marion Davies.

Kings Daughters Home, Oakland, 1908–12, with detail of the gate designed by Julia Morgan as a memorial to her brother Sam

By far Morgan's most significant hospital structure was the Kings Daughters Home (1908–12) in Oakland, which covers a whole city block on Broadway. It was built of brick masonry with tile roofs and comprised five major three-story structures around a landscaped courtyard. Ornamental polychrome-tile accents and iron lanterns add Mediterranean touches, while a tile-roof pergola at street level and an ornamental iron gate give dignity to pedestrian and vehicle entry, respectively. The gate had special meaning for Morgan. When her youngest brother, Sam, was killed in 1913, her mother (who was on the board of the Kings Daughters Home) donated the gate as a memorial to him. For some seventy years the hospital served cases not accepted in other hospitals, but it was eventually purchased by the Kaiser Health Plan and partially demolished for parking space.

In 1924–25 Morgan designed another important service institution, this time in the English style, on land that had once been part of the Panama-Pacific Exposition. The Ladies Protection and Relief Society (established in 1853) had acquired the land at Laguna and Bay streets as a gift in 1922. The society had originally helped homeless women and cared for orphans, but by the 1920s foster homes had replaced orphanages, and the group was ready to assume new responsibilities. They soon realized that the kind of protection and relief most needed by ladies in modern San Francisco was attractive housing and permanent care for the elderly. Morgan was commissioned to design a residential facility for older women; the plans for a building to cost $50,000 were approved in 1924, and the board met in the new building in March 1925.

The Heritage, as it is now called, is made of reinforced concrete with red-brick facing and salmon terra-cotta trim.[9] The elevation reveals the interior plan by two large bays of seven windows, which mark the principal public rooms. The original plan, which covered a large city block, was for a long rectangle under one roof. A richly planted formal garden around a fountain was a major part of the project, with a gardener's cottage to one side. Much of the garden was absorbed by an insensitive addition to the original building made by Warren Perry in 1958. The gardener's cottage was upgraded to superintendent's home and finally became an apartment connected with the institution.

The concrete of the interior is unfurred and cast in forms suggesting a Tudor arch, with squared pillars. Oriental carpets on tile floors and screens, paintings, and antique furniture fit the manorial atmosphere, as does the cast stonework of the main fireplace, with its wide arch and quatrefoils in four square panels. A small chapel, a library, a health-care wing, and a beauty shop (all in the original plan) add to the quality of life in this retirement community, now home to more than a hundred residents, both men and women. The enthusiasm of the residents and the long waiting list testify to a carefully conceived and executed environment for the aged that has rarely been equaled.

Women had gathered in private homes and in church or grange buildings during the nineteenth century for purposes as varied as organizing the abolitionist and temperance movements, reviewing books, and discussing capital punishment, child labor, and women's rights. These meetings continued over the years almost entirely without permanent headquarters, although men's clubs, both social and political, were plentiful and elaborate. The general spirit of expectancy that characterized the coming of a new century kindled what has been called the Progressive Era, and educated women eager to be a part of it began commissioning buildings for their own use. Morgan designed the Friday Morning Club in Los Angeles in 1908 for women in that

Exterior and interior views of the Heritage, San Francisco, 1924–25

city, and in 1914 she altered and enlarged the headquarters of the Century Club in San Francisco, an association for sophisticated urban women. She designed several independent women's clubs along Arts and Crafts lines. The Saratoga Foothill Women's Club, for example, had been chartered in 1907. When Morgan was called in to design a building for them in 1915, she offered four possible plans for their site (according to club records and local newspapers), and built the one unanimously chosen for under $5,000. The gabled redwood structure with pergolas leading to the gardens is simple and timeless, evoking a kind of sophisticated country style. Wooden benches at the sides of the doorway express a welcoming hospitality.

That the Foothill Women's Club was up-to-date for its period is shown by Morgan's inclusion in the original blueprints of a motion-picture projection booth, opposite an alcove where a screen could be pulled down. The main assembly room, equipped with a stage, has served as auditorium for many local presentations, from dancing-school classes to serious drama. Windows make up two sides of the room, and more light pours in through a large round window above. Another glazed wall faces the broad hallway, which leads to rest rooms and kitchen. In its parklike setting the club discreetly brings the outdoors in.

On a crest in Sausalito, the Women's Club (1916–18) takes full advantage of the spectacular views of San Francisco across the bay. The windows in this redwood-shingle clubhouse stretch from floor to ceiling on two sides, with simple balconies and terraces on side and front. A second story at the far end adds interest to the roofline and provides four-way views from the board room. The design as a whole is provocative, almost playful; and details such as the door carving, almost but not quite minimal, exemplify the enrichment that results when details are in harmony with the overall form.

Various stories are told about the design and construction of the Sausalito club. One such comes from Mrs. Edwin G. Klinck of Sausalito: "A Mr. Robbins gave the land and a goodly amount of money for the construction of the Clubhouse. Because the architect chosen by the members was a woman and/or because he thought a redwood building would fall down in a few years, Mr. Robbins left a trust to the Club which can only be used for major reconstruction. Needless to say, the building has endured beautifully and we've never had to touch the trust."[10] The club, dedicated to Grace McGregor Robbins in September 1918, became the first historic landmark designated in Sausalito, in 1976. Other of Morgan's small Crafts-style clubhouses include structures for the Monday Club in San Luis Obispo and for Santa Maria's Minerva Club, both still flourishing. For the latter, Morgan suggested that the club sponsor a competition to find designs for furniture that would relate to the room and that they appoint a committee of one extra-tall, one short, and one overweight member to test the chairs by a trial sit-down. Samples were offered by ten decorating firms; those designed by Gaylord Jones were selected as most comfortable and suitable. Fifty-five

Elevations and main-floor plan, Saratoga Women's Foothill Club, 1915

SOUTH EAST ELEVATION

NORTH WEST ELEVATION

SARATOGA FOOTHILL CLUB
20399 PARK PLACE, SARATOGA, SANTA CLARA COUNTY, CALIFORNIA

HISTORIC AMERICAN BUILDINGS SURVEY
SHEET 3 OF 10 SHEETS

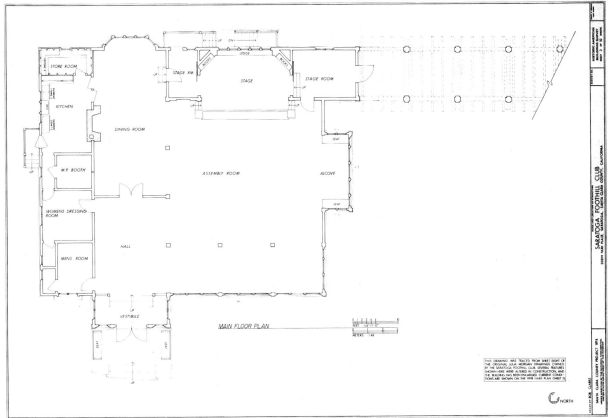

STORE ROOM

KITCHEN

DINING ROOM

M.P. BOOTH

WOMENS DRESSING ROOM

MENS ROOM

HALL

VESTIBULE

STAGE RM

LEDGE

STAGE

STAGE ROOM

ASSEMBLY ROOM

ALCOVE

SEAT

SEAT

SEAT

MAIN FLOOR PLAN

NORTH

SARATOGA FOOTHILL CLUB
20399 PARK PLACE, SARATOGA, SANTA CLARA COUNTY, CALIFORNIA

HISTORIC AMERICAN BUILDINGS SURVEY
SHEET 3 OF 10 SHEETS

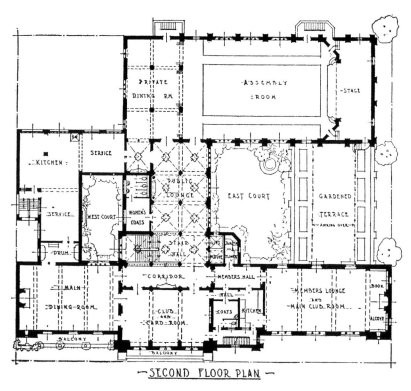

— SECOND FLOOR PLAN —

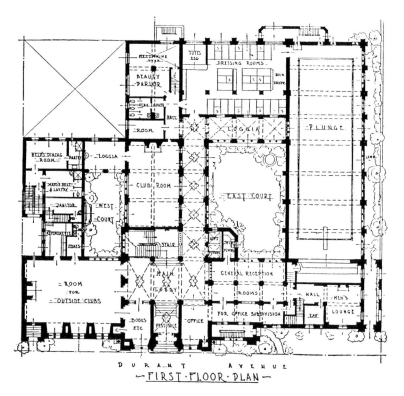

— FIRST · FLOOR · PLAN —

years later they are still in use.

In 1929 the Women's City Club in Berkeley called on Morgan to design a building on their property near campus. They wanted reception and assembly rooms for educational and recreational use; a large ballroom-auditorium for dances, theatrical performances, and lectures; and a public dining room and smaller private dining spaces for special parties. They also asked for a library, a swimming pool, a beauty parlor, a tearoom, and several floors of residential accommodations. Morgan designed a castle-like six-story building, attending to every detail, including the lights, furnishings, dishes, and linen. She chose the late medieval style because she loved it but also because she had available many skilled craftsmen trained at San Simeon who could carry out ornamental details. Her favorite material, reinforced concrete, was just right for the great arched doorway, for the vaulted or beamed ceilings, and for the grand staircase tying together the two public levels. The plan is designed around two interior courts, "the camellia" and "the rhododendron," which are wells of light and filled with colorful flowers or greenery all year round. Huge windows in the rooms and hallways and glass doors open to the courts bring in ample natural light.

The Women's City Club took special pride in "waterproofing" its members, and indeed it pioneered in having a special swimming membership at a time when no other facility in Berkeley was open year-round to women for lessons or for recreational swimming. It is clear from the plan

Left: First- and second-floor plans, Berkeley Women's City Club, 1929–30 (now the Berkeley City Club)

Below: China designed by Morgan for the Berkeley Women's City Club

that the 25-by-75-foot pool (labeled "plunge" by the architect) was to play a major role in club activities, since it was given the entire stretch of the building's east wing. Every aspect of pool life was considered and planned for: changing, swimming, watching, sunning.[11] Morgan's dressing rooms shine in comparison with most of the mildewed dungeons set aside for this purpose. The turquoise-tiled pool is naturally lighted by tall leaded windows; five triple-arched windows on the east side look onto a garden. Originally there was a skylight that opened to decks for sunbathing and table tennis; this has now been roofed over for a tea garden. A spectators' gallery runs the length of the south end. The use of ornamental lanterns designed by the architect makes swimming there an evening festivity as well as a daylighted one.

Berkeley Women's City Club, with detail of fireplace

The ultimate Arts and Crafts structure, a consummation of the movements' fundamental desire to build in harmony with nature, can be seen in "the Hearthstone." Built in 1928 in a clearing at the Dyerville Flat redwood grove in Humboldt County in northern California, it consists of a huge rough-stone square chimney. On each side is an open fireplace, with redwood pillars set in concrete benches supporting a shake roof. A log marker is inscribed: "California Federation of Women's Clubs Grove presented to

Four views of the Berkeley Women's City Club. The sculpture at upper right is by Clara Huntington Perkins, who commissioned a house from Morgan in Los Gatos, 1919–20

the State of California that these trees in the coming years shall minister to the destiny of mankind.'' The project was begun in 1923, spearheaded by Dr. Mariana Bertola, president of the Federation of Women's Clubs. She had been the Mills College physician when Morgan was building on the campus there and had commissioned Morgan to build two houses in 1907, one to serve as her office and the other as rental suites in San Francisco. It is not surprising, therefore, that the group urged Morgan to design this monument commemorating the women's successful effort to save the redwood grove. By raising $50,000, they had managed to preserve about a thousand of these sequoias with heights averaging 350 feet and diameters of 15 feet or more; they purchased a tract through the Save-the-Redwoods League and lobbied to put through a state bond issue for matching funds, thereby doubling their effectiveness.

Morgan's monument symbolizes both the untouched nature of the forest and the federation's scrupulous protection of this heritage. It remains a

Pool, Berkeley Women's City Club

The Hearthstone, Dyerville, 1928

functioning campsite for visitors to this one hundred acres of virgin redwood along the south fork of the Eel River. The dignity of the design and its human scale in the midst of such magnificent natural growth embody the Crafts ideal of creating structures appropriate to their sites.

Women's clubs created a network of activists who were eager to work for a better environment and for humanitarian goals. When their programs required architectural skills, their members were delighted to find and to hire a sympathetic woman architect. Their commissions were often for buildings new to the architectural profession, meant to serve the diverse needs of women's associations of all types. General and specialized hospitals also posed new design problems, as did the increasing demand for physical education for women. Morgan's sympathies were engaged and her imagination fired by these varied social needs brought to her attention by a network of women clients.

6

COTTAGES AND MANSIONS

Many architects, men or women, devote a great part of their professional lives to domestic architecture. Julia Morgan was no exception, and dwelling places constitute a major element of her oeuvre. She designed houses at the very outset of her career, beginning with an addition to a house in Fontainebleau, which gave her her first practical experience in building after her studies at the Ecole. Her first commission in America came in 1902: a modest Crafts-style faculty house at the University of Missouri in Columbia, where Mabel and Frederick Seares, friends of hers from Berkeley and Paris, taught in the astronomy department. Unfortunately, only two dim snapshots remain to indicate the charming interior, with its built-in bookcases, fireplace, and wood paneling, as the house was demolished to make way for campus expansion shortly after the Searses left for brilliant careers on the West Coast.

Morgan's first commission after her certification in 1904 was for an apartment house in Berkeley for Annie Caroline Edmonds, an 1882 Berkeley graduate who taught mathematics and German in the local high school. The redwood-shingle structure with side entrance is subtle and sophisticated for such an early work, clearly demonstrating that Morgan knew what she was about. The apartment building remains intact, with no significant changes.

Determining the source of commissions for a young architect is always interesting, although not always easy, as is the case with Morgan. After soliciting the obvious family members and schoolmates, she obtained clients through her acquaintance with business and professional people in Oakland and in the fast-growing community of Berkeley. She soon gained a reputation for careful work, for on-site supervision of every step of construction, and for the ability to convert to positive effect any problems she encountered (a skill she always credited to Bernard Maybeck). Her primary weakness in domestic architecture was a lack of boldness in design, but that was what pleased her clients and attracts many admirers today.

Opposite: Foote house, North Star Mine, Grass Valley, 1905, with Arthur and Mary Foote

A selection of Morgan's houses in the Arts and Crafts style makes it clear that her best examples rank with the more celebrated ones designed by her contemporaries. Her efforts at economy and simplicity created uniquely satisfying buildings. She apparently never thought in terms of a set model to be followed but gave primary attention to the site and to the needs of her clients. One of Morgan's first significant domestic commissions in the style was a house built in 1905 for Arthur De Wint Foote, manager of the North Star Mine in the gold country near Grass Valley. The site selected, a knoll in a wooded area just above a flowing stream, provided a setting of great beauty and an appropriately commanding position for a house that was to cover 18,000 square feet and cost $23,000. Foote's diary of the period notes when Morgan first came up to walk over the site and mentions her visits during construction, but he says nothing about how he chose the architect or the extent to which he and his wife, painter-illustrator and author Mary Hallock Foote, were involved in building the house. The nearby Empire Mine had a house designed by Willis Polk about ten years before, which indicates that at least some landowners in the area were cognizant of Bay Area architecture.

Rear of Foote house, seen from east entrance gate

The Foote house creates a massive first impression: rough-cut quarry rock (containing a high proportion of quartz) forms the first floor and veranda; heavy columns are surmounted by a redwood-shingle second floor beneath a low-pitched roof. The apparent simplicity of these strong, straightforward elements masks a complex relationship to the site. The veranda and protecting stone terrace overlook the stream and the valley below, and because the brick footpath leads to the corner rather than directly to the front, the visitor's first view is one of two sides of a building that seems to have grown among the evergreens. The U-form plan features two sleeping porches, one along the porch in front and the other within the sheltered patio, whose massive stone columns along the sides support a pergola. The wide overhang of the roof in the rear is broken at each side to allow maximum light to the upstairs windows and to provide visual interest. Eyebrow ventilators on the inner sides of the U repeat the shape of the breaks in the roofline, exemplifying Morgan's skillful use of details to reinforce overall form.

The main entrance leads into a hall that serves as reception room; it is paneled in wood, as is the rest of the house. Structural elements provide the

major source of interior interest. A clinker-brick fireplace with semicircular opening makes a simple focal point and links the reception room to the sitting room, which features another fireplace from the same chimney. The windows show the variation of size and shape that is characteristic of the Crafts style, as is the continued use of local materials. Built-in features included inglenook seating hinged for wood storage, bookcases, buffets, and (on the second floor) bureaus and broad windowsill seating. Shutters helped mediate the bedrooms' exposure to heat and cold. The Foote house is one of a series in which Morgan worked out ways to integrate geometric forms and simple local materials into a sense of natural wholeness that is as fresh after eighty years as it was during construction.

Morgan also did a number of modest cottages in the Arts and Crafts style. Early examples can be chosen from those she built on speculation in Berkeley, both before and after the earthquake. A variety of related designs emerged during the following years, when doctors, dentists, professors, and

Clockwise from top left: Looking from sitting room through hall to office; two views of sitting room; and dining room

Orsamus Cole house under construction, Berkeley 1906.

The Coles bought a bay-view lot in 1905 for $6,000 and hired Morgan to design the house and gardens. Construction was almost completed by April 1906 (at a cost of $8,000) when the San Francisco earthquake delayed matters by making glass for the windows unobtainable. The family was able to move in by October and occupied the house until 1922, when it was sold to close relatives, Albert and Helen Kindt, who lived there until 1946. Mr. Kindt was the owner of the Sartorious Ornamental Bronze and Iron Company in San Francisco, which was a supplier to San Simeon.

lawyers turned to Morgan for well-designed and inexpensive residences. These include cottages north of the campus in the newly developing area of Marin Avenue and several pairs of houses near the south campus that used a common driveway. All were constructed of redwood—some shingled, some combined with board and batten, the most economical material available at the time—and most followed a simple axial plan around a hall and staircase. Some had bay windows, some had a band of casements, some had corner windows where the view was an attraction; all included simple balconies, pergolas, and sleeping porches.

A pair of cottages on Etna Street built for Louise Goddard in 1905–7 have corner windows flanking the chimney, reputedly because the architect said that some people enjoy looking at a fire on the hearth and watching what goes on outside with-

Goddard cottages, Etna Street, Berkeley

North and south elevations, west Linforth house, Derby Street, Berkeley

Opposite, top: East elevation, west Linforth house

Opposite, bottom: West elevation, west Linforth house

out changing position. Two redwood-shingle cottages built on Derby Street for Edward and Ivan Linforth in 1907 share a driveway and yard but are otherwise dissimilar. One doorway has classical details and a wooden arch that would never have won approval from a *Simple Home* advocate opposed to using wood in a way counter to its natural inclination. The second Linforth house is of the utmost simplicity, with board and batten for the second floor; parallel eaves and brackets added above the bay supply a touch of elegance. The most important elements of both these cottages are their functional plans and the easy way they merge into the tree-lined street, their common driveway and side entrances making a rhythmic pattern. For many years Thaddeus Joy of the Morgan office lived with his family in one of another pair of cottages on Derby Street, also built in 1907. These two cottages had equally close relations with the street, as well as similar but not identical side entrances, gardens, and views of the East Bay.

A year later Morgan built a house at Ojai, a town south of Santa Barbara that had attracted well-to-do members of the middle class seeking a simple life—artists and craftsmen, mystics, theosophists, retired industrialists. Her Ginn house (1907–8) seems to grow out of the rocky soil, with the deep-set rough stone windows, massive chimney, and heavy square pillars placing it firmly on the site. A horizontal band of casement windows under wide eaves makes the house parallel to the earth and sensitive to the shadows at different times of day. A sleeping porch and open terrace recall the North Star Mine house, although the plan, with one wing at a right angle to the other, is more like that of Greene and Greene's Gamble house in Pasadena, built the same year.

A clear example of an urban Crafts house is one in a distinguished area of Pacific Avenue on the Presidio in San Francisco, a neighborhood with houses by Bernard Maybeck, Willis Polk, Ernest Coxhead, and other prominent Bay Area architects. Morgan built a redwood-shingle house here in 1908 for Aurora Stull, whose daughter Florence had been a classmate of Morgan's at the university in 1894. Morgan created a geometric design that is symmetrical and ordered, composed to fit the streetscape and to take advantage of the site. With no sign of a pergola or any other facility for outdoor living, this is a restrained and decidedly urban townhouse, though profiting from a woodsy view of the Presidio. Central steps open to a hall lead-

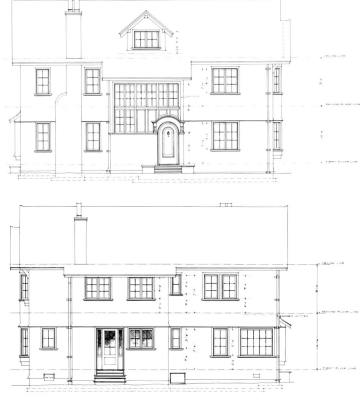

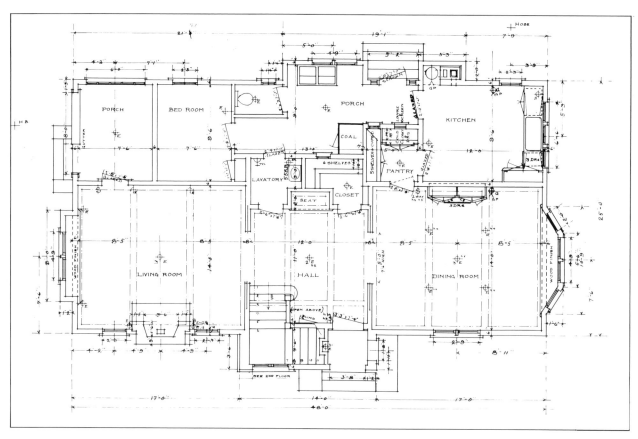

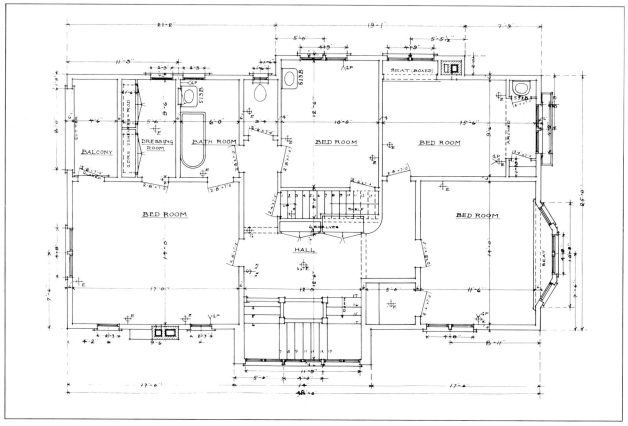

ing to reception rooms at the front. The interior of the house is paneled in walnut and gum, all quite formal and meticulously crafted, with fireplaces in the major rooms. Large windows with a window seat span the living room, which runs the entire width of the house, providing a spectacular view of the Golden Gate. The dining room is set off by sliding doors, usually left open, and it has a built-in china cabinet with leaded glass next to the fireplace. The rooms on the upper floor, originally four bedrooms and a bath, are also paneled, with built-in furniture in every room (additional bathrooms were added when the house was remodeled after World War II by architect George Livermore, the grandson of another Morgan client). The restrained discretion of Morgan's design means that it lacks the dash and drama of the asymmetrical windows, unorthodox details, and contrasting scales that Maybeck and Coxhead exploited only a few blocks away.

Drama emerged eight years later when Morgan built a mountaintop home near Fremont for the Starr family, for whom she also designed two other houses in Piedmont. Approached by a four-mile road winding up to its lofty site through a ranch gate and past tennis court and pool, the house is breathtaking. Two wings embrace the summit of the hill, joined by a stone-pillared loggia-veranda (now glazed but originally open) that looks out over the hills to the San Francisco Bay. Morgan used rough stone quarried from the site as a foundation, shaped into a solid wall and chimney by Italian workmen accustomed to fitting stones without mortar. Shingle was used for the main body of the house, which is essentially on one floor. The plan is more a butterfly than a U, with the veranda linking the public spaces with the private. The living room has open trusswork with unusual cutout shields where the roof supports meet, and the walls are of wood with battens of a sculptured thickness. The double doors are decorated with star motifs in honor of the family name.

Another dramatic Crafts building by Morgan is at the edge of domestic architecture. C. C. Moore, the president of the Panama-Pacific International Exposition of 1915, had a country place in Santa Cruz on Monterey Bay. The year before the exposition he asked Morgan to remodel the main house and to build some guest houses and an "entertainment casino" on the grounds there, as he planned to entertain widely and wanted to have the

Opposite, top: First-floor plan, west Linforth house

Opposite, bottom: Second-floor plan, west Linforth house

Top: Workers laying stone foundation, Starr house, Fremont, 1916–17

Bottom: Dining room, Starr house, Piedmont, 1938–39

best possible facilities, with private golf course, a yacht in the harbor, and luxurious amenities close at hand. Working in redwood and minimizing the disturbance to the site, she managed to convey to visitors that they were staying in a kind of wooded paradise. Dorothy Stone Wolff, who was a classmate of Moore's daughter, Josephine, at the Katherine Delmar Burke School in San Francisco, often visited the casino:

> It was a very attractive large rustic building with a wide porch, with an overhang on two sides, one of which was covered with purple bougainvillea. This side faced toward a beautiful fountain which was constantly splashing, with a delightful sound effect.
>
> The "Casino" consisted of a large recreation or game room with a huge stone fireplace. There were restrooms included. In the room was a pool table, a klondike table [a card game], a piano and card tables.
>
> There was another building, that Julia Morgan designed, to replace the old ranch house that was on the property, originally. It consisted of a large dining room and lounge on the main floor with bedrooms upstairs. Adjoining the daughter's was a delightful sleeping porch. . . .
>
> Julia Morgan also designed the guest cottages, each having two bedrooms and two baths opening onto porches. They were unique and very artistic.[1]

The casino was reported by the local newspaper to be 50 by 90 feet, with an immense stone fireplace in the 30-by-50-foot main room which had a billiard table, a piano, and a screen for moving pictures. Its roof was decorated with a long copper flower box, which proved difficult to engineer properly. Clerestory windows admitted daylight, which was somewhat obscured at ordinary window level by the wide overhang and by the splendid veranda on three sides. Early photographs of the interior show a Victrola with a large horn and three copper lamps by Dirk Van Erp, who had a copper shop in Oakland until 1910, when he moved to San Francisco. Several other early Morgan interiors were photographed with these special lamps, almost

Moore entertainment casino and verandah, Santa Cruz, 1915

as much a favorite of hers as the Chinese parchment ones that she and Maybeck both ordered through a Chinatown merchant.

Two women physicians, Dr. M. L. Williams and Dr. E. L. Mitchell, had Morgan build them a redwood-shingle cottage on a steeply sloping hillside lot in Berkeley. It appears from the street to be one story, symmetrical, its porch exactly centered, with the building covering most of the lot. To the right is the entrance to the porch and to the built-in one-car garage (innovative for the period), its door ornamented with a Celtic design on each of four panels. The porch has wooden bungalow columns, with the front door and the small adjacent window decorated with cast-iron versions of the same Celtic pattern. An ample bay window of three twelve-panel sections illuminates the doctors' office at left. Compact and utilitarian, the cottage was obviously intended for a servantless household, for the garage opens directly into the kitchen which directly adjoins the dining room, without the separate pantry that was usual in a more formal ménage. The wide entrance hall leads past the office with its own bathroom to the living room, which has four-foot windows and flower boxes at either side of a large fireplace; there is a deck with glazing at one side, and bookshelves line the remaining walls. Brilliant views of San Francisco Bay seem to enlarge the living room and the adjacent dining room. A change of scale from living to dining room is established by the shift from the high handcrafted open trusses and supports of the living room to the dining room's comparatively low ceiling and doorway, which are set off by brackets that give the feel of an alcove to the dining area. The latter, glazed on two sides, has a glass door at the back, which directs light to the steps leading to the floor below.

Downstairs are two main bedrooms, brilliantly daylighted, one of which is further warmed by a fireplace. On the side toward the street is a separate study, or office, and another spacious bedroom and bath. A third floor down has one more room and storage space. Morgan used a reverse plan and an

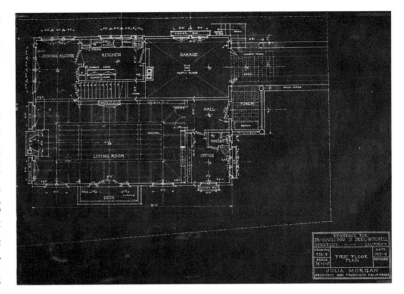

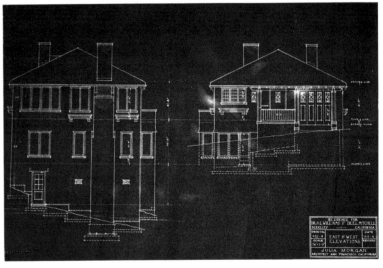

First-floor plan, Williams and Mitchell house, Berkeley, 1915–18

East and west elevations, Williams and Mitchell house

almost upside-down arrangement on a marginal site to create a light-filled house that has served for nearly seventy-five years as a snug, delightfully comfortable shelter, modest and horizontal from the street, brilliantly vertical at the hillside. Presently occupied by a Berkeley professor, only the third owner, it has been maintained almost unchanged since 1915.

An urban house that transformed simple Crafts origins into sophisticated, even daring design was built in San Francisco in 1916–17 for Mrs. Horatio Livermore. The Livermore family, prominent in San Francisco and in the Livermore Valley to the east, had large landholdings, including a family farm at the summit of Russian Hill in the city. Russian Hill Place, between Vallejo and Florence streets, was a private enclave with several notable houses. In the 1890s Willis Polk had built a house for himself there and remodeled the original Livermore house of 1860; in 1916 he built four houses for the Livermore family. Helen Livermore, for whom Morgan had built a house (Montesol) on the family ranch in the Livermore Valley, commissioned her to design a pied-à-terre at the edge of the family compound. As built in 1916–17, it was a two-story rectangle, with hall, bedroom, bath, and living room on the main floor, and stairs leading down to the dining room and kitchen. In 1927 and 1930 Morgan added an L-shaped addition to the uphill side, with another bedroom, bath, and study space; but it is still a small house (even after a 1981 addition by Livermore's step-grandson, Putnam), immeasurably enlarged by its views. Simple and vertical in plan, designed for a special kind of city living, it seems to be only tenuously connected to the city by a footbridge. Its large circular windows set in great

squares are a reminder of the Panama-Pacific International Exposition's YWCA Building, from which Morgan salvaged them (according to family legend). The only decorative touch in an otherwise austere exterior, these windows emphasize the significance of the outlook for which the whole building was planned.

Quite a different kind of structure was designed by Morgan in 1925 for one of her favorite workmen, Swiss wood-carver Jules Suppo. Suppo refused to leave San Francisco and his family for commissions at San Simeon and Wyntoon, so Morgan arranged for him to do the work in the city and ship it to the sites. She designed a two-story house for him on Polk Street, with the ground floor serving as shop and workroom; the apartments above (later enlarged by a penthouse) were entered by a separate door. The two doorways gave Suppo an opportunity to flaunt his wood-carving skills. The door to the shop shows consummate skill in combining a frank advertisement at the bottom with densely carved figures inhabiting the sea, the forests, and the skies, the whole surmounted by an ornamental presentation of Suppo's name and business under a basket of flowers. The other door, of matching wood, has more restrained, classical ornamentation—above the door are flowers and fluttering birds perched on a dish of fruit. A balcony

serving three tall windows with ornamented shutters has richly carved spindles and corner pieces, while the brackets are in the form of childlike figures biting into the fruit. Just under the cornice is a classical frieze featuring the shields of Switzerland and of Suppo's canton. The whole building is a Crafts gem, an affectionate tribute to a fine artisan.

In 1940 Morgan built a retirement cottage in Carmel for two married physicians who had been at the university with her as undergraduates. The Doctors Pope owned a lot overlooking the Carmel Mission, and here Morgan placed a horizontal cottage of redwood, composed largely of windows and a glazed doorway, with rich plantings protecting its privacy. Overhanging eaves provide shelter from the strong sun. Corner windows and double casements make it light and airy, while ingenious built-in furniture helps make it easy to care for. Bleached redwood interiors throughout carry out the feeling of light-

Pope house, Carmel,
1940

Playter house, Piedmont,
1907, main entrance

ness, while the open ceiling construction, with beams going the length of the living room, gives a sense of spaciousness. The brick fireplace has bleached redwood trim and mantel. When she built this house, Morgan was staying at her own studio-cottage in Monterey, and she walked to Carmel and back to supervise the construction, saying that she "needed the practice in walking" after a bout of labyrinthitis.

Since the Arts and Crafts movement had originated in England, it is not surprising that American architects working in that style became familiar with English architecture of the Renaissance and Tudor periods, which William Morris and his followers had studied with such interest. Late English Gothic, Tudor, and Jacobean forms were part of a design vocabulary that was almost as familiar to Americans as the archaic prose of the King James Bible. In approaching the buildings that Morgan designed in an English manner, it is important to recognize that there is no such thing as a unified "English style." Her eclecticism, with its free blending of diverse architectural precedents, is comparable to that of Edwardian English architects, whose building in the "Free style" was widely published in architectural magazines available in Paris, New York, and San Francisco.

A house built on a hillside in Piedmont for the mayor's daughter, Char-

lotte Playter, in 1907, blends equal elements of Crafts and English styles. The plan is L-shaped, with a pergola enclosing an interior patio that can be entered from the dining room, the living room, and the glazed terrace at the end of the cross axis. The two-story bay window of the staircase is the chief decorative feature on one side, while the downstairs bay of the hall alternates with an upstairs bay under a smaller gable, forming a rhythm continued under the low-pitched main roof. Eyebrow windows on each side carry out the curves of the windows on the two floors below. The chief decoration inside the rooms comes from structural elements such as windows, ceilings, and doorways. Gardens (now supplanted by a tennis court and pool) originally sloped away toward a brilliant view of the East Bay, which constituted a primary part of the setting and provided the reason

Built-in window-seats, Playter house

Back view, Playter house

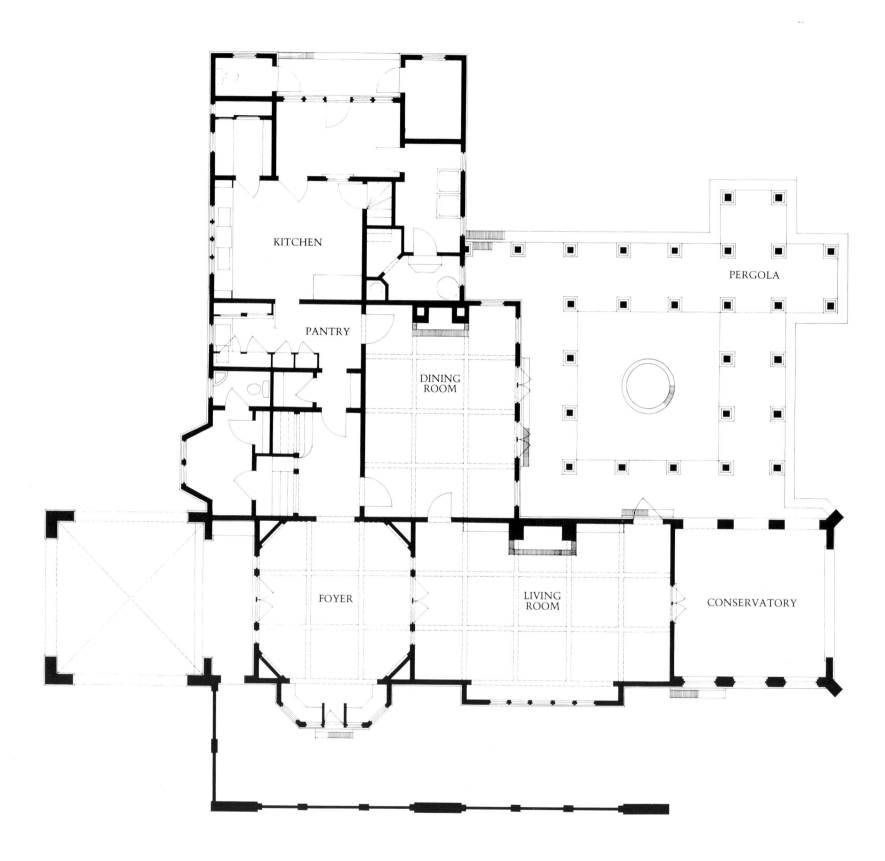

KITCHEN

PERGOLA

PANTRY

DINING
ROOM

FOYER

LIVING
ROOM

CONSERVATORY

for the extensive glazing. Size, site, and unusual style made this an important Californian house. It was reproduced in the *Portland* [Oregon] *Architectural Club Yearbook* in 1909 and was part of the club's second annual exhibition; it also appeared in the *Architect and Engineer* of April 1909—atypically wide exposure for work from the Morgan office. The house compares with C. F. A. Voysey's own house in Herefordshire (1901), while the entrance recalls that of Farmer's House (1898), in Perthshire, by James MacLaren.[2]

For domestic architecture the "half-timber" was the most familiar English style. Fifteenth- and sixteenth-century half-timber houses were usually made on a foundation of brick or stone, with strong posts measuring about 6 by 8 feet placed on oak sills; the extra strong corner posts were sometimes made from a tree trunk, with the root end upward. Crossbeams rested on the timbers, which were the basic load-bearing element. Walls were made of wattle and daub (also known as stud and mud)—a weaving of hazel rods or interlaced willow that was plastered flush with the timbers using a mixture of clay and straw or lime and cement; later infilling was often brick. The timbers were sometimes tarred, sometimes left to weather, in either case strongly contrasting with the relatively light-colored infilling.

Half-timbering with brick or stone began to interest northern Californian architects after the supplies of inexpensive wood were depleted, and especially after blocks of frame houses were consumed in the Berkeley fire of 1923. It also appealed to architects and clients who wanted homes that would evoke a stable past far from their own technological age. Morgan began to work in stucco and brick with the same enthusiasm and skill she had earlier shown in her use of redwood. For major institutional buildings she often used reinforced concrete for the framework, with brick facing in some cases; most English architects of the period did the same. Morgan's

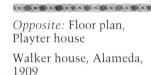

Opposite: Floor plan, Playter house

Walker house, Alameda, 1909

work has been compared with that of Voysey; both architects did look back with pleasure on traditional English country structures, freely adapting design elements from them.

Morgan turned to the striking visual effect of the half-timber style for some of her most remarkable dwellings, ranging from sumptuously paneled great houses to spare cottages. She generally used half-timbering as geometric ornament rather than essential structural support. One example is the large house that Morgan designed in 1909 for George L. Walker in Alameda, near the East Bay.

Detail of carved-oak mantel, living room of the Clark house, Berkeley, 1913

Detail of carved-oak mantel, library, Clark house

A brick first floor supports the building. The second and third floors, under two main gables and two smaller ones, are made of stucco, with decorative half-timbering adding verticality and visual interest. The balcony above the entrance, shaded by a gable, rests on heavy brackets. Interest in the roofline is supplied by a twin-peaked gable on each side, which surmounts a three-sectioned opening with side windows parallel to the gable roof and two casements at the center. A double string course runs just above protruding brackets between the first and second floors, while the second-floor corner posts are playfully carved in rounded abstract forms that are echoed by the copper drain spouts. The half-timbering was clearly used to carry the eye along the design.

The Richard Clark house of 1913 is another example, the main floor being of brick, with a modified Tudor arch in front of the doorway and repeated in the door frame and on the carved wood of the door. Additional carving in the triangles formed by the top of the arch and the cross-beam prepare one for the richness of carved details within. The second floor, made of plaster, has banks of windows, an iron balcony in the front, and sleeping porches at the side (subsequently enlarged and enclosed). The entrance hall—of such impressive proportions that it is really a "living hall" —is richly paneled in oak, dominated by a square staircase with deeply turned balusters that continue along the wide landing and the galleries of the upstairs hall. Morgan gave free play to her love of complexity in the wood-paneled living room, dining room, and library, all of which have fireplaces with elaborate mantels. The living-room mantel is carved of oak, showing acorns, leaves, birds, and squirrels; another has classical details; brackets in the hall and on yet another fireplace, in the library, repeat the Tudor rose. The dining room, paneled to the ceiling in square oak modules, has an ornate fireplace and two inset cabinets. This fine house became a sorority then a student cooperative-housing facility without entirely losing its elegance.

Unique in Morgan's work is a building constructed to suit a client's image of English architecture. James L. Lombard applied to Morgan's office with a turn-of-the-century English watercolor by Young and Mackintosh, of Croydon, England, showing a large house with sagging roof, half-timbering, and gables, which he wanted Morgan to re-create for him on a whole block that he had acquired in Piedmont. She replied that she had never designed or built anything from a picture, as she regularly began with the plan, but that it might be interesting to see what she could do with it. The finished house (1915) does indeed resemble the watercolor, which hangs in the place

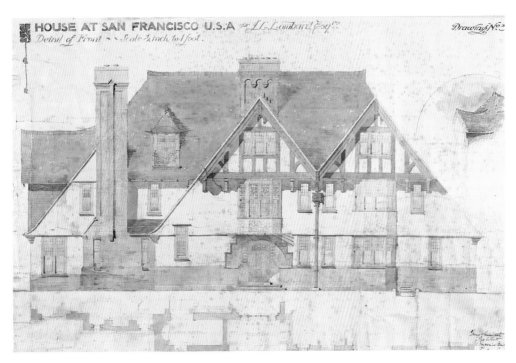

HOUSE AT SAN FRANCISCO U.S.A *for J.L. Lombard Esq.* Drawing No. 2
Detail of Front — *Scale ½ inch to 1 foot.*

Watercolor by Young and Mackintosh, of Croydon, England. This was the source for the Lombard house.

Lombard house, Piedmont, 1915

of honor in the living room. The living room and dining room are distinguished by ornamental plaster ceilings, examples of an art now priced almost out of existence. The house is most impressive for its siting and for the formal order of the spaces. Incised in its brick wall is "Harrow Manor," and the knocker on the master bedroom door is in the form of the lion crest of Harrow School in England, the client's alma mater.

Some other urban mansions by Julia Morgan (including the Wells house in Oakland, the Rosenberg house in San Francisco, and the Thelen house in Berkeley) deserve attention as examples of her English style. The Charles B. Wells house (1910–11) takes up a whole block on an acre in Oakland. Placed on a hill overlooking the East Bay, the building is massed so that almost every room faces the water. The Wells family is said to

Top: Dining room, Lombard house

Bottom: First-floor landing, Lombard house

Right: Wells house (Red Gate), Oakland, 1910–11

Gumwood stairway and hall, Wells house

Plaque, Wells house

151

Entrance, living hall, and first-floor plan, Rosenberg house, San Francisco, 1917

have claimed to have come from an English estate called Red Gate, which became the name of their new house. Of brick originally red and later painted gray, the gates, walls, and terraces extend the reach of the house. Decorative ironwork at the entrance and four balconies harmonizes with the design of the mullions in the living-room bay, while a Palladian arched doorway with stripped-down columns leads from the dining room to a wide stone terrace. The molded paneling throughout the house (some now unfortunately painted white) has the elegant proportions associated with Georgian English buildings, although there are Mediterranean aspects in the arches and the ironwork balconies show Italian influence.

In 1916 Abraham Rosenberg, who had made a fortune in dried fruit in the Fresno area, commissioned a Pacific Heights mansion that is still one of San Francisco's fine houses. The concrete structure timbered with redwood has a side entrance from a brick terrace. The Tudor arched doorway has stone pilasters that continue across the arch as ribbing. The downstairs windows, framed in timber, are mullioned, while on the second story a bank of windows following the corner above the entrance is framed by arches that repeat the line of the doorway. In the reception hall—an exceptionally ele-

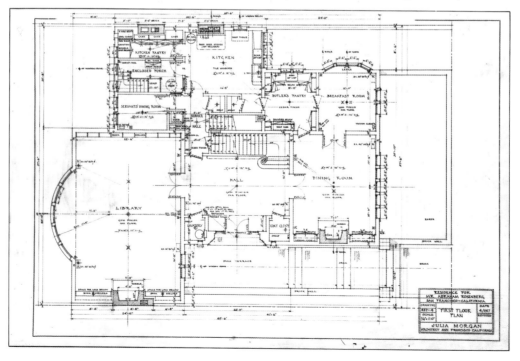

gant space paneled and beamed in gumwood that is larger than most living rooms—one can see through the dining room to the garden. The original gleam of hardwood floors complemented by the richness of Oriental rugs has been smothered in contemporary carpeting. The house served at one point as a Nepalese consulate, functioning easily in that semiofficial capacity; it is now a private residence again.

Perhaps the most nearly pure neo-Georgian example in Morgan's work is the Elliott house of 1920, built for a daughter of Elizabeth Glide. It crowns the hill at the south edge of Berkeley, overlooking the East Bay, with its brick, gables, and entrance deliberately recalling the Georgian style. Commodious and symmetrical, with the perfection of detail so dear to Morgan, it looks ready to face another sixty-some years with firmness and propriety.

Elliot house, Berkeley, 1920

Goodrich house (Hayfield House), Saratoga, 1920–21

Another type of English house, this one in the country at Saratoga, was commissioned by the Chauncey Goodriches. Clearly a Californian version of what was understood as an English country house, Hayfield House (1920–21) is of concrete with redwood trim. Approaching by a sinuous lane that follows a brook through a pear orchard, one encounters a great spread-out form gathered under a low-pitched green-shingle roof, with gables and windows at second-floor level. A wide tiled veranda flows around three sides of the U-shaped structure. At the back, set into the grass, is a low turtle fountain by Jo Mora, a sculptor who worked with Morgan on several occasions but is best known for his reconstruction work at the Carmel Mission.

West side of Stewart
house, Benbow Valley,
Garberville, 1926

The original plan shows all the downstairs
rooms opening to the outdoors and has the main
entrance on the patio side, which is confirmed
by the location of the reception hall and staircase in that wing. During construction, however, Mr. Goodrich asked Morgan to reroute the
driveway and entrance paths (at first of Yosemite
stone, then of redwood squares, both too uneven
for modern demands) to the center of the long
living room. The upstairs rooms are all on the
north (or patio) side for summer comfort, and
they are also equipped with sleeping porches.
The front, facing the distant Santa Cruz mountains, is composed of sitting
rooms, sewing rooms, a library, and the housekeeper's headquarters. A separate gardener's cottage, cook's and laundryman's quarters, stables, and garage are just beyond the swimming pool and garden at the rear. The living
room, like all of the downstairs rooms, is sheathed in Tiffany plaster, a
finish of remarkable durability and attractiveness, which works well with
the sandblasted redwood trim, beams, and murals. Iron chandeliers designed
by Morgan have an appropriately rural yet elegant simplicity. Touches such
as the carving of the dining-room mantel and sides of the fireplace to carry
out the motif of the huge heirloom sideboard indicate how closely the architect worked with her client.

Morgan was commissioned in 1926 by San Francisco hotel owner Margaret Stewart to build the first element of what was to be a summer-winter
resort on Lake Benbow, near Eureka in northern California. Only Stewart's
house and a nearby hotel ever materialized, constructed in half-timbering
above brick. With sun porches and sleeping porches ready for any climate,
this large house on the lake represented the client's dream of a Scottish
manor. There is a guesthouse and garage with service apartments above,
while the story-and-a-half living room of 820 square feet was planned to be
used as a Christian Science reading room. After a prolonged period of neglect, the house has now been carefully restored, and it is greatly cherished
by its current owners.

Morgan may not have been at her best in the English manner. The
weaknesses in her buildings in the style derive largely from her tendency to
remain too close to historical antecedents and to the preferences of her
clients. Her least imaginative clients preferred a "hominess" that could
verge on the sentimental, something quite foreign to Morgan's nature. According to Walter Steilberg, Morgan most admired Charles Adams Platt's
houses, which were English in origin and straightforward in design.[3] The
English style did offer her an opportunity to develop strengths in areas she
particularly enjoyed: she lavished richly detailed ornament on her interiors
and indulged in a free play of geometry in designing her half-timber work

and interior paneling. None of Morgan's houses could be thought of as a copy of English architecture, but clearly the vocabulary appealed to her. She adapted it to New World sites and society, using motifs and materials of English origin with freedom and occasional originality.

Morgan's houses in the Spanish or Mediterranean style are many and varied, located as far north as Chico and as far south as the Los Angeles area. She was certainly not the principal exponent of the Spanish style. Tribute for that is regularly paid to Bertram Goodhue and Carleton M. Winslow, especially for their part in the Spanish-Colonial revival after the San Diego Exposition of 1915, and to George Washington Smith and his associate and successor, Lutah Maria Riggs, of Santa Barbara, for their work in that community. They all devoted most of their careers to building in this mode. For Morgan, however, the Mediterranean style was always just one of several possibilities at the time of any commission; her eclecticism and her experience with many forms and materials made a wide choice available to her.

During the early period of her professional life Morgan developed what would be a lifelong interest in designing reinforced-concrete buildings, based on her experience on the Berkeley and Mills campuses. The commission to build a residence in that material for Lewis A. Hicks, whose company had supplied the concrete for the Greek Theater, came only about a year after the dedication of the Mills Campanil. Concrete was then a radical material for residential use, for in those pre-earthquake years no one had yet recognized its advantage of seismic stability. Hicks had a site on Piedmont Avenue, a prominent Berkeley street just southeast of the campus. He wanted a house suitable for the family of a business executive who was also a member of the Sierra and Hillside clubs, and he asked for a wood-paneled interior with fireplaces at the heart of the living and dining rooms. Morgan's plan for the two-story house is symmetrical, with a recessed entrance marked by four concrete columns between two massive square bays. The roof is flat, topped with ornamental openwork in cast stone matching that on the balcony, which extends the width of the columned entry—all features of strong horizontality. The porte cochere at the north side once led

Hicks house, Berkeley, 1906

to a substantial carriage house, and a circular drive with an island of planting interposed nature between house and street while emphasizing the basic symmetry of the design. There were originally four large bedrooms upstairs. Extensive remodeling of the second floor and of the exterior, with garages dug out of the driveway and garden, has made the house almost unrecognizable today.

Another early example of Morgan's work in the Mediterranean style, known only through Steilberg's photographs and the memories of a

Your room

son who lived there, was the residence of E. L. Brayton (1909) in Oakland. Edward Lacey Brayton was a hydraulic engineer with political aspirations; his wife enjoyed entertaining and participating in various cultural activities, particularly the Little Theater movement. Morgan designed for them a house of reinforced concrete, costing $13,600, with two stories and twelve rooms planned around an enclosed courtyard. The ornate ironwork decorating the stairway at one side continued around balconies supported by massive square concrete pillars; these were linked by wide, almost flattened arches, whose lines met to suggest capitals. Plants, a low fountain, and grassy space made a cloister of the center of the house, with the balconies extending this indoor-outdoor living to the rooms upstairs. The Braytons later also commissioned Morgan to do a smaller summer place in Pebble Beach, which features tall arched windows around an open courtyard with fountain, but the Oakland house was their showplace. It offered Morgan a significant opportunity to try her hand with a free, exuberant use of concrete in designing a house for expansive California living in an urban setting. Unfortunately, the house was demolished when the growth of the city overtook it after Brayton's death.

In the same year, 1909, Morgan built another, quite different Spanish-style house on a hillside in San Rafael overlooking the San Francisco Bay. For the Cary Cook family she designed an essentially one-story concrete house under a low-pitched red-tile roof, with a central courtyard entirely open. The entrance, where horizontality is most marked, has a flattened arch midway between two chimneys that serve as bell towers. Through the hall paved with large square tiles is the high

Left, top: Cook house, San Rafael, 1909, under construction

Left, center: Entrance, Cook house

Left, bottom: Rear view, Cook house

Above: Detail of interior court, Brayton house, Oakland, 1909

Opposite: Chickering house, Piedmont, 1911

arched entrance to the courtyard, which provides protection from the Bay Area's often chilly weather and makes outdoor living possible for most of the year. The rectangular house is one room deep all around, with an open arcade like a cloister on two sides; glazed arcades shelter an interior hall on the other two sides. Taking advantage of the sloping site, with its sweeping views of the water, the Cook residence is a fine example of the "villa style" that seems perfectly Californian, although it would also be at home along the Mediterranean.

A house designed in Piedmont for Allen Chickering in 1911 resembles Andrea Palladio's Villa Pisani (1552) at Montagnana, Italy. The columns marking the entrance and the balcony above it follow Palladio's design, but Morgan's balcony is characteristically of delicate ironwork, filtering the light, whereas Palladio used low balustrades. Her broken pediment, smaller and ornamented within, is directly over the entrance, erupting into the balcony to make a geometric effect different from that of the more severe perfect triangle of the Villa Pisani. Morgan's frieze, ornamented only by disks, is a much-restrained version of the original and extends over only the porch third of the house. At the side wings French doors open onto small balconies with curved iron railings. The openness of the downstairs windows, photographed in 1918 with colorful awnings, is Californian in style.

A hilltop country place designed by Morgan in 1919–20 for Clara Huntington Perkins at Los Gatos was called "an Italian house" when it was published in *California Southland* in that year, although it could easily be categorized as Mediterranean. Los Gatos is in the foothills of the Santa Cruz mountains, which are often declared to resemble the landscape of Italy's hill towns near Florence. The site likely suggested an Italianate design to the architect and to her client, who had lived much of her life in Europe. The approach up a long curving driveway gives importance and some mystery to the building at the summit. The editor of *California Southland*, Mabel Urmy Seares (who had been Morgan's second client, in 1902), wrote of the olive trees and the vineyard and the live oaks all around, with

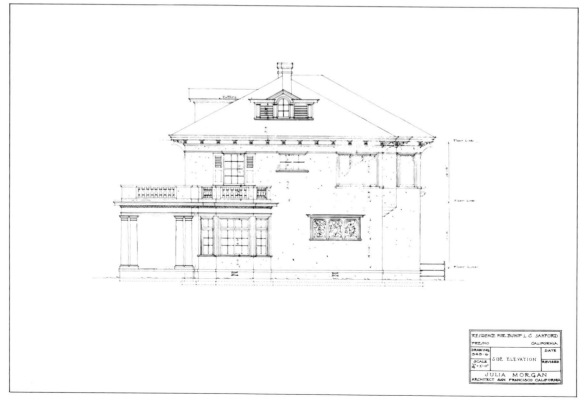

The Right Reverend Louis Childs Sanford, Episcopal Bishop of the San Joaquin Missionary District, was the client for this house built in 1912–15. (Mrs. Sanford was a Mills College graduate and may have met Morgan in connection with the architect's work on campus.) The exterior of the house, flanked by a pair of tall old palm trees, is of dark shingles with stick detailing. The several bedrooms with a large bath at the end of the hall were planned to provide hospitality for visiting missionaries as well as a home for the bishop and his family. The stairway has two sections, as was common in large houses; one begins

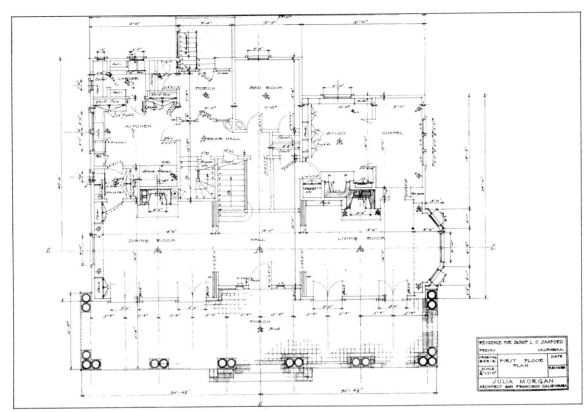

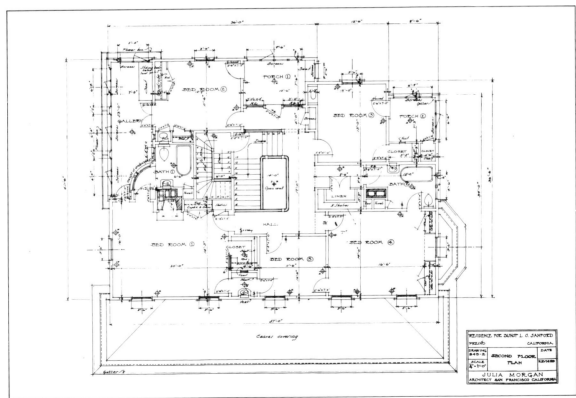

in the pantry area then joins the entry flight at the sunlit landing. The Frank Oneto family purchased the house in 1944 from the bishop who succeeded Sanford, and they have made only minimal changes (kitchen remodeling removed the built-in breakfast table and benches). The chapel is now used as a library; only the carved-wood biblical inscription in Hebrew set into the bricks above the fireplace recalls the initial purpose of the room lined with oak bookshelves. Originally the house was out in the country in the midst of vineyards, but the city has now grown up around it.

Entrance, Perkins house,
Los Gatos, 1919–20

Opposite: House
remodeled by Morgan for
her own use, San
Francisco, c. 1925

"glimpses of the valley between them. Sleeping porches abound. Stone steps and fascinating places for wall fountains and pools make every foot of the place interesting and unite the house with the hill and to the whole outlook in a way which makes the lover of California happy and gives hope that we shall emerge from the debris of Eastern ideas with which the state has recently been flooded and have on our hills at least, some real California homes."[4] The caption below the photograph of the Perkins house calls it "an example of what California demands in adapting Italian architecture to its landscape."

This one-story house, comprising 5,000 square feet, cost $90,000 to construct in 1919–20. One enters through an open court with an Italian garden bordered by a columned loggia; a massive paneled front door opens into a long vaulted hall that connects the two wings. All of the ten rooms have wide-plank teak floors; each major room opens to the outdoors. Leaded-glass arched casement windows have handmade copper fixtures. The living room has a 16-foot-high teak ceiling and a huge Carrara marble fireplace, both brought by the client from Italy. Clara Perkins was a sculptor (a high-relief panel by her decorates a garden in the Berkeley City Club) and the adored adopted daughter of the railroad magnate Collis P. Huntington. She was also a friend of Morgan's and considered herself to be a real collaborator on what she pictured as a Renaissance hillside retreat for a former princess (she was divorced from a fortune-hunting German prince) seeking privacy.

Some of Morgan's Italianate designs were achieved by remodeling. When her mother's illness made it impractical to keep up the family house in Oakland, in the mid-1920s Morgan bought two Victorian two-story houses (with attics and basements) on Divisadero Street in San Francisco, remodeling one into an apartment for herself plus two apartments to rent. The second house, actually a rusticated stone foundation and "piano nobile," became a kind of Italian villa, which she rented after taking off the two top floors in order to give more light to the apartments. In 1915–16 Morgan had made a similar alteration for David Atkins, an importer of artworks, whose daughter, Avesia, was a draftsperson in Morgan's office. In this adaptation Morgan removed the upper floors of a Victorian house on Green Street in San Francisco, changed the fenestration to three tall arched windows in the center, and added an ironwork balcony over the front arched entrance. A wide frieze under a projecting cornice banded the whole, while the low-pitched symmetrical hipped roof works as a pediment for the facade.

After a prolonged motor trip through Bavaria and Austria with her sister, Emma, Morgan returned home in 1932 with an increased interest in the architecture of that region. One house in that style was built for Else Schilling, a friend of Morgan's from the time Schilling had served on the board of

the YWCA in San Francisco. Like her father, August Schilling, she was Morgan's client for an apartment building in that city in the late 1930s and possibly for a cottage on the family estate in Woodside as well. She also wanted a summer house on Lake Tahoe, on wooded lakefront property at Bow Bay. She showed Morgan some paintings of houses in the part of the Tirolean mountains between Bavaria and Austria where her family had originated, and these became the inspiration for her summer house (1939). Its steeply pitched roof echoes the shape of nearby trees and mountains. The Lake Tahoe side of the building is primarily glazed, with a sheltered patio for outdoor dining in summer. Downstairs there are commodious paneled public rooms for entertaining and for service; the second floor consists mainly of two rooms and a bath, plus maid's quarters. The large living room with stone floors, massive fireplace, and high ceiling with open trusswork recalls an Austrian hunting lodge, and the shutters and interior friezes are decorated with some romanticized Austrian hunting scenes painted by Doris Day. Near the house, on part of Schilling's 400 feet of lakeshore property, are a wooden

Front view and living room, Schilling house, Lake Tahoe, 1939

tent floor and a separate guest cottage. When young nieces and nephews came to visit, they were delighted to stay in the tent, while other guests were put up in the cottage, an arrangement that recalls the pattern set at Asilomar and carried on in more lavish style at San Simeon and Wyntoon (the arrangement may have derived from Adirondack lodges of the nineteenth century). Else Schilling's place was a special kind of house built for a woman with pronounced tastes, and Morgan achieved a romantic, fairy-tale atmosphere while keeping the design simple, functional, and suited to the surrounding woods and mountain lake.

Clients appreciated and enjoyed Morgan's houses because she considered their individual needs and tastes before she drew the plans. When a Berkeley

Williams house, Berkeley, 1928, with detail of entrance. This now serves as the residence for the vice president of the University of California.

professor asked her to build him a house just like one she had designed for another professor, she reportedly asked him if he was exactly like his colleague; his inevitably negative reply led to a house shaped by his own choices.[5] If Morgan sometimes yearned for greater scope for imagination than domestic architecture generally provided, she was to fulfill that yearning in commissions for one California family, the Hearsts, who provided her with a lifetime of challenges.

By examining in detail a palatial dwelling designed by Morgan in 1928, chosen for its beauty and present fidelity to her original intentions, one can begin to understand how well she met the needs of her clients and how her solutions relate to contemporary patterns of living. The large, blocky, concrete house on Claremont Avenue in Berkeley was designed for Seldon and Elizabeth Glide Williams. It makes a first impression of formal symmetry, with seven tall shuttered windows evenly spaced across the second floor. The iron-grilled balcony over the wide front door and the broad windows recall the Mediterranean style, as does the red-tile roof.

Quoining punctuates the corners, while the wing to the west (at right) has Venetian Gothic windows on all three exteriors.

When the heavy front door opens, it seems to invite a procession: the spacious living hall, with its glow of dark wood and Oriental carpets, leads the eye up to a landing, where a great window with Gothic tracery and crowned by a large della Robbia wreath brought by Morgan from Florence looks out on a garden courtyard. A glance back to the front door reveals a wrought-iron gallery at the landing above, a broad expanse with heavy carved doors opening to the living and dining rooms, and an arched entrance into a library. Ornament is pervasive: even the radiators, set into the walls, are masked

Living hall, Williams house

Carved living-room doors, with view into dining room, Williams house

Top: Library, Williams house

Center: Cast-stone radiator screen, second-floor hall, Williams house

Bottom: Moorish window, second floor, Williams house

by large cast-stone screens. A Moorish window gives an exotic touch as it lights the stairway upstairs. Off the hall is a series of guest bedrooms separated from the service wing by a glass-paneled door. At the front of this floor is a large room with balcony and its own bath, while the west wing is like a separate apartment, with two oversize bedrooms (one with a splendid fireplace), a dressing room, two baths, a small but efficient kitchen, and a glazed sitting room that must have been planned as a sleeping porch.

Downstairs, both living room and dining room have similar friezes of gumwood cut to resemble a stencil. The walls are plaster, painted to harmonize with the fresco around the front door. A small hidden closet near the door receives mail from a slot outside. The east wing, for kitchen and service activities, includes a brightly daylighted breakfast room with stenciled frieze and patterned marble floor, facing the garden. In position this corresponds to the west wing's wood-paneled library-study, which connects with a marble-floored conservatory that also has doors opening to the living room and to the garden; the conservatory's wicker furniture underscores the indoor-outdoor relationship.

The circulation in this building makes it convenient for moving and serving large crowds: refreshments might be served in the conservatory, for example, or out in the garden, where an Italianate fresco suggests the atmosphere of a cloister, reinforced by the use of columns. To paint this mural Morgan hired Maxine Albro,

Conservatory, Williams house

Frescoes by Maxine Albro, Williams house

Opposite: Decorative plaque, attached to the bottom of the flower box on the porch of the Tesheira house, Berkeley, ‸1913–15

an artist who became known during the 1930s for her murals in Coit Tower and in other public buildings in the Bay Area.

The only part of the house that has required recent alterations is the large kitchen, whose octagonal-tile countertops, wood cabinets, and huge old stove had to come to seem old-fashioned. It was remodeled with the latest restaurant equipment, including wide ovens suited to caterers as well as smaller ones for the individual housekeeper; the upper cabinets next to the windows were retained as models for the new construction. The furnace, boiler room, and some of the plumbing required the attention of the Rankin Plumbing Co., still run by the son of the man responsible for the original installation. Space for a wine cellar and storage already existed.

When they commissioned the house the clients were planning for an active social life, but Seldon Williams died after they had been in the house only a year or two. His wife retreated to the upstairs apartment, closed the rest of the house except for periodic cleaning, and almost never left it for the forty-two years until her death in her nineties. She kept the furniture covered and the house intact in its 1928 splendor during all that time, maintaining it with the help of a part-time maid and a gardener. Just before she died in 1970, she agreed to sell it to a committee of friends of the University of California for use as the vice president's house, with proceeds to go to a charity she favored. The original Italian furniture was still in place, and much of it was sold with the house.

It is a victory for historic preservation to have such a house continue to function as it was originally planned. Even the orientation is well suited to welcoming numerous visitors throughout the day, as Morgan's concern for light has given the morning sunshine to the breakfast room, library, and conservatory as well as to the entrance hall, while the large rooms for entertaining have the afternoon sun. Stately and comfortable, this is a house very close to the eye and hand of the architect.

JULIA MORGAN, ARCHITECT
Wᴹ L. BOLDT, Contractor & Builder
WILLIAM NOE, Foreman.
1914

7

⌐⌐

THE HEARSTS AND SAN SIMEON

Julia Morgan's involvement with the Hearst family spanned three generations. Her first Hearst-related architectural project began when she returned from the Ecole in 1902; her last ended in the mid-1940s. The family's commissions ranged from early additions to Phoebe Apperson Hearst's Hacienda at Pleasanton to the so-called Hearst castle at San Simeon. Newspaper buildings, such as the Hearst *Examiner* plant in Los Angeles and the office of the Oakland *Post-Enquirer* plus the remodeling of the San Francisco Hearst Building, were commercial projects given to Morgan, as were two radio transmission-and-receiving stations on the Peninsula near San Francisco. Phoebe Hearst's oldest grandson, George, also became a client of Morgan's when he arranged to have his Hillsborough house converted into a western version of the White House. The final William Randolph Hearst projects of the 1940s, never completed, included a lavish Mexican hacienda at Babicora as well as an elaborate beach house in Santa Monica for Marion Davies and a children's hospital in Los Angeles. All of these constitute only a fraction of the total output from Morgan's office, but they loom far larger in the public eye than do her YWCAs, women's clubs, churches, schools, offices, and residences.

It all began with Phoebe Apperson Hearst. Called "the Empress" by members of the Hearst Corporation, who were irked by her furious energy, and by the staid leaders of San Francisco society, who resented her presumption of cultural superiority, Phoebe Hearst was a woman who enjoyed wielding power. Proud of her family connection, however tenuous, with the venerable Randolphs of Virginia and backed by one of the great American fortunes, Hearst was not content to enjoy a moneyed life of leisure. Before her death at seventy-seven in 1919 she had established kindergartens in California and in Washington, D.C., founded schools and libraries in the mining areas developed by her husband, and helped the University of California, Berkeley, make good its claim to be the "Athens of the West." In addition to contributing funds for the Hearst Min-

Opposite: The Neptune pool, San Simeon, 1935–36

Phoebe Apperson Hearst, c. 1910

ing Building and a women's social center and gymnasium called Hearst Hall, she underwrote the university's departments of archaeology and anthropology and became its first woman regent.

Hearst had developed her organizational skills on a national scale. She cofounded the General Federation of Women's Clubs (1890); the National Congress of Mothers (1897, which became the Parent-Teacher Association); and the Travelers' Aid Association (1917). She was also active in the Episcopal church as founder of the National Cathedral School in Washington, D.C., and as benefactor of the cathedrals in Washington and later in San Francisco. Her patriotic efforts included assistance in restoring and preserving Mount Vernon as a national shrine. Her eagerness to help the new class of young working women led her to support the national YWCA, particularly in establishing Asilomar. She was also the women's representative for the Panama-Pacific International Exposition in San Francisco and the force behind the YWCA Building there.

Julia Morgan may have first encountered Phoebe Hearst as an undergraduate. The Hearst home adjacent to the developing Berkeley campus was a center for the extracurricular life of women students, a small minority in the 1890s. Here they gathered for musicales and tea parties, surrounded by the art treasures of an enthusiastic and well-traveled collector. If Morgan and Phoebe Hearst did not meet at this point, they surely met in the late 1890s, during the international competition held to choose an architect for a new campus plan at Berkeley. Hearst made several trips to Paris and Brussels, the headquarters of the competition, to oversee its progress. At the same time, she commissioned Maybeck to design Hearst Hall, a reception pavilion to be connected to her Berkeley residence, which would initially serve as a space where she could hold official receptions for the jurors and others concerned with the competition and later as a social center and gymnasium for women students. This was in 1897–98, exactly when Morgan was in Paris struggling to gain entry to the Ecole des Beaux-Arts. For part of that period Morgan had an apartment in the same building as the Maybecks, and she worked on the drawings for Hearst Hall.

It was inevitable that Phoebe Hearst would encounter Morgan in Paris, especially since she was the only woman student in the architecture section of the Ecole. Like all of Maybeck's "boys," Morgan received a stipend of $50 per month from Mrs. Hearst. A letter of February 16, 1899, indicates that Morgan was offered an even more generous subsidy, which she refused.

Dear Mrs. Hearst:

My mother's letter in answer to the one I wrote telling of your kind offer the night you left Paris has only reached me after a round about journey. I could not tell her exactly why you wished to help me, because you can understand that she would worry if she thought you, or others, believed her girl was working too hard. But I told her all the rest, and she is very grateful for your kindness and joins me in thanking you most sincerely. If I honestly thought more money freedom would make my work better, I would be tempted to accept your offer—but I am sure it has not been the physical work which has been or will be, hardest, for I am used to it and strong, but rather the months of striving against homesickness and the nervous strain of examinations.

Now my brother is here and a place is won at the B.A., really mine now it seems, the work ought simply to be a pleasure whether housekeeping or study.

Your kind words at the depot were so unexpected, so friendly, they gave and still give, more help than you can guess, and I will thank you for them always.

> Very sincerely yours,
> Julia Morgan
> February 16, 1899[1]

When Morgan returned to California and began working for John Galen Howard in 1902, she became a member of the design team for the Hearst Mining Building, an imposing and original structure finished in 1907. These characteristics made it a fitting memorial to Senator George Hearst. The senator had received little formal education, but he clearly had a genius for discovering valuable mineral deposits. He died in Washington, D.C., in 1891, when Morgan was in her first year at Berkeley, so it is almost certain that she never met him. Yet it was his fortune, derived from copper, silver, and gold mines and invested in millions of acres of Mexican and Californian land, that helped finance some of her most important commissions. That he had been astute enough to marry a young teacher determined to improve herself and the world around her reveals that George Hearst recognized values beyond metallurgical ones. He left a will bequeathing everything to his wife because he considered their only son, twenty-seven-year-old William Randolph Hearst, owner and editor of the San Francisco *Examiner*, to be a hopeless spendthrift. He was not entirely wrong.

After Senator Hearst's death, when Phoebe Hearst seemed to be planning to stay on in Washington, D.C., her son made lavish plans for an estate in Pleasanton, thirty-five miles east of Berkeley, which his father had planned to use for hunting and for breeding horses. Ignoring the fact that it was his mother's property, in 1895 William Randolph Hearst commissioned A. C. Schweinfurth, a young San Francisco architect, to build the Hacienda del Pozo de Verona there (the name referred to a massive stone wellhead he had purchased in Italy and installed in the Hacienda gardens). The following year Mrs. Hearst asserted her rights to the estate but retained Schweinfurth to continue the work her son had started. The architect's departure for Europe in 1898 and his sudden death on his return two years later meant that the project remained unfinished, although habitable.[2] At about this time Hearst managed to convince his mother that he needed capital to expand his growing newspaper holdings, and with $7.5 million from the sale of her Anaconda Copper stocks, he set out to conquer New York. With the purchase of the *New York Morning Journal*, he was on his way to building a newspaper, radio, and film empire.

In the meantime Phoebe Hearst's social ambitions became more elaborate, and she turned her attention to developing the Pleasanton property as a place to entertain not just family and friends but also beneficiaries of the various good works in which she was involved. This included YWCA leaders and all the women students from Berkeley, as well as faculty members. She called on Morgan to complete the Hacienda complex, a commission readily accepted by the young architect, who was eager to leave Howard's office and begin work on her own. Contradictory accounts and the absence of records make it difficult to be sure exactly what Schweinfurth and Morgan each contributed to Pleasanton, but Morgan did carry on the project from 1903 through 1910. Phoebe Hearst already owned a castle built by Maybeck on a ranch at Wyntoon, near Mount Shasta in northernmost California. She also had an apartment in the Hearst Building in San Francisco and a house in Berkeley. She wanted, however, to develop the two thousand acres of the Hacienda as an accessible outpost, mild in climate, where she and her guests could indulge in diversions such as swimming, riding, tennis, and other sports, with musicales and dancing in the evenings. The enlarged and embellished Hacienda became her social center.

The Hacienda was set in an ideal spot, above the Livermore Valley but still protected by hills, with no fog and no wind to disturb the pleasures of the country. Schweinfurth's original plan as shown in *American Architect*, May 2, 1896, provided a great square, 150 feet on each side, built around a courtyard with the wellhead at the center of plantings. The grand entrance to the hall was through a porte cochere. The main social rooms (dining room, library, billiard room) spanned the front, while the other three sides were devoted to a bowling alley, seven guest apartments, and nine servants'

Hacienda del Pozo de Verona, Pleasanton, 1903–10, seen in the early 1920s

apartments. The central block had two stories above for the family's apartments and two towers, while steps from the guests' quarters led to a bathhouse.

After Phoebe Hearst and Julia Morgan had worked for about seven years to improve and complete the estate, it included a banquet room and heated indoor swimming pool in one glazed addition, while a complementary addition at the other side led to a 40-by-60-foot music room with a 30-foot ceiling and windows described in the local newspaper at the time of sale as "constructed of an imported bottle-end glass in lead"; next to it was a ballroom with sunken gardens. All in all, the Hacienda had ninety-two rooms; on the hill behind it were garages, servants' quarters, recreation buildings, and stables. It is not clear how much of this had been planned before Schweinfurth left, but the completion of the plans alone would have been a challenge to any young architect.[3]

The swimming pools at the Hacienda were surely designed by Morgan. The interior heated pool, 20 by 40 feet, was spanned by wide arches, with windows on three sides. It was built into the ground so that the entrance was a casual step down into a world of water and flowers. When the Castlewood Country Club purchased the property from William Randolph Hearst in the 1920s, they advertised the pools as a major attraction.[4] A fire in 1969 burned the main structures to the ground, leaving only the Boys' House (or Bachelor's Hall or Casa Bonita, as it was called by then). A new Castlewood clubhouse was built along lines similar to the old one in 1972, but little or nothing was salvaged of the original.

Although Phoebe Hearst also commissioned other architects (including Walter Steilberg and Willis Polk) for various projects, she always continued to be interested in Morgan, commissioning her to build the YWCA conference center at Asilomar and contributing to the Kings Daughters Home in Oakland. Hearst's death at the Pleasanton Hacienda in 1919 meant the loss of a valued friend and client for Morgan and, although she could not have foreseen it, a nearly lifelong commitment to the son.

Veranda of the Hacienda, seen in the early 1920s

For about twenty-five years William Randolph Hearst and Julia Morgan were engaged in the design and construction of two large-scale establishments as well as several lesser ones, in a collaboration of extraordinary magnitude. Morgan's affection and admiration for the mother developed into a genuine and respectful friendship with the son, which included an ability to enjoy his enthusiasm and his humor in what were often challenging moments.

Hearst had first engaged Morgan's services for a mansion planned in Sausalito, which was abandoned at an early stage of development when he moved to New York (only a retaining wall was ever built). He then commissioned her to do the Mission-style Examiner Building in Los Angeles, which was her most conspicuous commercial building in the Mission style and her first large project with William Randolph Hearst. Commissioned in early 1915 (Steilberg's *Architect and Engineer* article of November 1918 shows Ed Trinkeller's iron grille for the lobby and dates it April 1915), it was described by Hearst upon completion:

> What do I think of it? Why, it is well within the bounds of a conservative judgment to say that it is creditable to the city and to the newspaper which it houses.
>
> Miss Morgan, the architect, commendably accomplished the task of constructing a building that is thoroughly practicable, for all newspaper demands and which, I am glad to note, combines with its efficient qualities those pleasing traits reminiscent of an architecture which is identified with the beautiful and romantic history of Los Angeles and of California. I think she has accomplished the result happily and effectively from all points of view.[5]

The Examiner Building features wide Mission-style arches, expanses of white exterior surface, loggias, and skillful ornamental iron- and plaster-

Boys' House, the
Hacienda, c. 1910

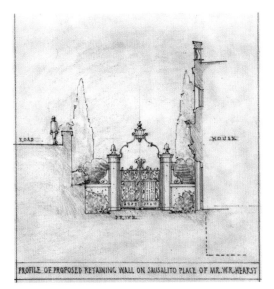

PROFILE OF PROPOSED RETAINING WALL ON SAUSALITO PLACE OF MR. W.R.HEARST

work. Built on a whole city block, it enjoys a scale worthy of Morgan's concept. The arcades were enclosed during World War II to make them safe during blackouts, but otherwise the building remains as built; it was refurbished in 1976. The interior, with its patterned tiled floors and ornate friezes, its great arched spaces with columns and trusses revealing the structure, flaunts all the romanticism of the exuberant Spanish-Mission style.

Discouraged by the political situation in New York, by 1919 Hearst was ready to move back to California to establish a home and a power base. In April 1919, the month of his mother's death, he came to Morgan's office in San Francisco. He was eager to build a place of his own on a hilltop at "the Ranch" at San Simeon, on the coast nearly two hundred miles south of San Francisco. We are indebted to Steilberg for the firsthand account of that late afternoon meeting in Morgan's private office. Steilberg admitted to having strained to hear Hearst's notoriously high voice saying that he was "tired of

Above, left: Retaining wall, Sausalito Place, 1912–14. Only the wall was ever built.

Above, right: Interior, Examiner Building, Los Angeles, 1915

Below: Early view of the Examiner Building

camping out and wanted something more comfortable on the Hill." He showed Morgan a book about bungalows and mentioned a "Jappo-Swisso bungalow" as a possibility. According to Steilberg, it was about a month "before we were going on the grand style." One of Hearst's first thoughts for the ranch, which he sometimes called the Enchanted Hill, was that its centerpiece must be the five-ton stone wellhead that he had purchased in Verona and placed at the Hacienda in Pleasanton. Other architectural

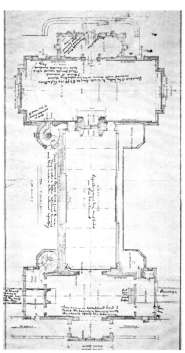

Early model for Main Building, San Simeon, marked "for mass, not for detail"

Early drawing of Main Building, c. 1923, with William Randolph Hearst's annotations

elements, along with paintings and other art objects, were subsequently brought from the Hacienda to the new Hearst headquarters.

Since Hearst was still living in New York and traveling a great deal, the project at San Simeon was designed in part by telegram and letter. This correspondence brings Julia Morgan out from behind her buildings and shows Hearst at his most charming, a devout amateur in the best sense of the word. Their collaboration was a close one, enduring a quarter of a century despite Hearst's mercurial temperament. They shared a heartfelt love of San Simeon that wove them together in an empathetic friendship built on the closest professional association. Steilberg would often see them sitting directly across a table from each other, talking, gesturing, making drawings, ignoring all other concerns as they concentrated on the work at hand. Records indicate that Morgan did not visit the ranch until August 9, 1919; she then went almost every weekend from 1920 through 1938, by which time she was also going to Wyntoon at least monthly. She continued on design and structural work until the corporation handling the Hearst money cut off funds and the "Hill Account" was formally closed, first in 1938, then finally in 1942.

When Hearst embarked on his San Simeon venture, he envisioned it as a place where he, his wife, and their five sons might spend most of their time, with additional guest bungalows to be built later. By August, Morgan had walked the site, had the rock analyzed, drawn up plans for the Main Building, and had a model constructed, partially based on the tower of the church at Ronda in southern Spain, a favorite of Hearst's. She had also discussed the guesthouses with him in order to plan the overall composition. She was by then considering what kind of ceilings to use in the "bungalows" and making arrangements to quarry rock from what would become the basement of the Main Building.

Although Morgan had already provided elevations and plans for four-room, two-room, and one-room bungalows with wooden ceilings, oak floors, plaster walls, and tile baths, a letter from Hearst in September said the bungalows should wait until the Main Building was finished. Then, on October 25, he wrote that he had decided to postpone work on the Main Building until after the next summer and that all effort should go to finishing cottages by then. Building the guesthouses first was more practical, since Hearst wanted to have a place to bring his family and to entertain, and he wanted it as soon as possible.

The cottages, no longer called bungalows, were each to have four bedrooms and a sitting room, and were to be sited exactly as Morgan had planned: on the ocean side, Cottage A, where Mr. and Mrs. Hearst were to stay; Cottage B opposite, across the esplanade in front of the planned Main Building; and the central Cottage C. These buildings were soon to be called Casa del Mar, facing the sea; Casa del Monte, facing the mountains to the north; and Casa del Sol, facing the sunset. The Main Building was to be the Casa Grande, although both architect and client continued to call it the Main Building and the cottages A, B, and C.

Letters and telegrams exchanged between New York and San Francisco in December 1919 deal with "cottage plans and notes." (Hearst wrote often about plans for a fourth and fifth cottage, one English and one Chinese, but only three ever materialized.) In one letter Morgan says that widening the court between the wings of Cottage B, making it practically the same dimension as the courts of the four-bedroom cottages, is not bad in itself, "only it leaves no variety in the mass." Morgan suggested that all three cottages be moved downhill in order not to obscure the view from the Main Building. On December 19 Hearst replied: "I have no objection at all to the houses being moved down the hill. In fact I think that is exactly what should be done with them. . . . They would otherwise cover a great deal of ground and shut out a good deal of view." And on December 31: "I have just received the location sketches of the houses and am very much delighted with them. . . . I would judge that we have placed them almost exactly right." His use of "we" is characteristic, as is his deference to her judgment.

In the same letter, discussing the style for the cottages, Hearst wrote:

The San Diego Exposition [1915] is the best source for Spanish in California. The alternative is to build this group of buildings in the Renaissance style of southern Spain. We picked out the towers of the Church at Ronda. I suppose they are Renaissance or else transitional, and they have some Gothic feelings; but a Renaissance decoration, particularly that of the very southern part of Spain, could harmonize well with them. I would very much like to have your views on what we should do in regard to this group of buildings, what style of architecture we should select. . . . I am not very sure about my architecture. . . . but after all, would it not be better to do something a little different than other people are doing out in California as long as we do not do anything incongruous? I do not want you to do anything you do not like.

And again, "Side elevation fine, rear stunning: however you are the best judge of that and I will leave the matter in your hands." Passages like these counteract any assumption that the domineering Hearst overwhelmed the reticent Miss Morgan.

The complex process of construction at San Simeon has been the subject of much speculation and false information over the years. The correspondence and the reports of people who worked for Morgan provide the most trustworthy picture of how the building progressed; snapshots taken by Morgan and by members of her crew document various stages of construction. Preparation of the site presented difficulties that might have been insurmountable for an architect not trained in engineering. The hilltop was five miles of winding path above the shore and 1,600 feet in altitude, with a steep grade rising from the harbor of the old whaling village of San Simeon. Only cattle trails existed, and roads had to be carved out of the hills before anything could be hauled up to begin construction. By November 1919 a labor camp with tents was established, and the hauling of gravel and sand had begun. Morgan determined that sand from the harbor could be used once the salt was washed out of it; later she had white sand brought from Carmel. A remarkably fine grade of concrete was possible with rock quarried from the site.

Morgan hired Henry E. Washburn of Monterey, who had worked for her at Asilomar, to supervise construction and the crew, which included ranch hands and men brought down from San Francisco. On November 21 the *Cleone*, a "very disreputable old coaster," set out from Oakland for San Simeon, carrying cement, nails, iron bars, roofing, a band saw, and a rock-

Early view of
construction equipment
at San Simeon

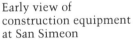

crusher. It docked at San Simeon on December 5, but by the time the material was unloaded, the rains had made the newly built and primitive roads so slippery that the trucks could not haul it up the hill. Roadwork had to take precedence, and more powerful trucks had to be found. Soon Morgan designed an enlarged pier at San Simeon, as Pacific steamships were too large to dock at the original whaling-boat wharf that Senator Hearst had earlier reconstructed. Collections of antique architectural elements and furnishings purchased at auction arrived from New York to be incorporated into the hilltop plans, so Morgan also designed a Mission-style warehouse; before the project was closed down, she had built an additional three galvanized-iron warehouses for Hearst's collections.

The pilot plan as drawn up by Morgan before the end of 1919 included the three cottages, a rose garden, a pool, and an esplanade in front of the Main Building. Cottage A was to have an open loggia looking to the sea, and all three were to be of a Renaissance style, not strictly Spanish. Morgan and Hearst incorporated some columns and other elements removed from the Pleasanton Hacienda before it was sold, but much of the work for San Simeon was done on site by carpenters, plasterers, stone casters, and skilled wood-carvers. Various delays plagued construction at San Simeon over the years, beginning in April 1920, when cement and lumber mills from Portland to Los Angeles went on strike. Men hired from cities

Warehouse in San Simeon village, 1926–27

Stone lions in front of the warehouse

were not willing to stay at the isolated site, especially when bad winter weather set in. Hauling 720 tons of concrete that first year was hard work, and the cement was slow to set during the rainy period. By the next year the crew's tents were replaced by wooden shacks, better cooks were hired, and a weekly moving picture was even provided. Morgan designed houses for the most important workmen and their families in the village or found places for

Above: Cowboy's house, San Simeon village

Left: Early construction at San Simeon, c. 1922

Opposite: Tower of the poultry-farm house, along the road on the way up to San Simeon, 1928–29

them to live in the nearby town of Cambria. The five modest houses, each different, that Morgan built for staff in the harbor area and partway up the hill are excellent domestic examples of the Mediterranean style. The poultry-farm house—residence for the men that Morgan hired as experts to raise chickens, pheasants, ducks, and guineas for the Hearst table—exhibits unique design features, including a bold tower and a walled courtyard. Nigel Keep (the tree man and later the gardener) had a Mediterranean villa at the waterfront, and the head cowboy had a smaller version nearby, while a more

expansive stucco house was allocated to the contractors, Camille Rossi (1922–32) and George Loorz (1932–40). The employees who stayed on were given a life interest in these homes when the complex on the hill was accepted by the state, and the homes are now held by the Hearst Corporation.

The crew of workmen varied according to available funds and, to some extent, the weather: winter camp (January–March) was always smaller. Morgan reported a crew of seventy men in 1920. In January 1922 she listed forty-four: six gardeners; three cooks; four truckers; five carpenters; eleven tilers and plasterers; fourteen concrete, fence, and road men; one office man. In January 1923 she had a force of thirty; in 1924, thirty-four; in 1928, seventy-five "plus twenty"; in 1929, ninety-three; and in 1931, twenty-five. A monthly payroll in 1929 totaled $9,940, plus $2,461 for the poultry farm and $1,378 for San Francisco office help; material costs added $13,311. Wages were good: a carpenter got $15 a day after 1920, when the going rate was only $10 elsewhere. Morgan wrote to Hearst on May 19, 1920, the "housesmiths, brick foreman, modellers, tile settlers all getting union city wages plus room, board and transportation."

On-the-job supervision was done by Morgan almost every weekend. She would leave her office late Friday afternoon and take the coast train for the two-hundred-mile trip down to San Luis

Obispo, often working on drawings in an upper berth, where she could have the most space. After an oyster stew and coffee at the depot hotel in San Luis Obispo, she would take a taxi (driven by the same man, Steve Zegar, over the years). They would cover what was then some fifty miles across the hills and up to San Simeon, arriving eight to ten hours after she had left San Francisco. She would work all day Saturday and Sunday, return to San Francisco by the Sunday night train, and go directly to the office on Monday morning. During the heaviest building periods she always had an office representative or two on site, very often Thaddeus Joy. He seemed to have had the talent and intuition to carry out her plans, without going beyond or falling short of what she intended. That her confidence in him was sustained for years is indicated by his being placed in authority at San Simeon at the height of the building there, and also at Beach House, under construction for Marion Davies in Santa Monica, which Morgan would occasionally visit on Mondays after her San Simeon weekend. It was at Santa Monica that Joy and several other workers contracted a debilitating illness attributed to drinking or swimming in polluted water. Joy was never really well again, but he remained on Morgan's payroll until his death in 1944.

That opportunities abounded for enterprising employees in Morgan's office is exemplified by the progress of the young Norwegian engineer Bjarne Dahl. He was first set to work constructing a ten-car garage for San Simeon; later he worked at Morgan's San Francisco office and on her YWCA projects in Fresno, Long Beach, Hollywood, Pasadena, and Hawaii, where he set up his own practice. Dahl recalls, "She trained me . . . we used to work until 10 or 11 o'clock every night, just she and I. If we got hungry, she'd take me down to different restaurants . . . the Oyster House or some Italian place. It was always a nice dinner, of course."[6] He often went with her to San Simeon, but the Monday morning after the overnight train ride back to San Francisco would find him exhausted and headed for home, while Morgan would go straight to the office to work on several other projects.

Morgan chose the superintendent of construction, who was responsible directly to her. Henry E. Washburn stayed until 1922, when he returned to his Monterey office. The one on hand the longest was her office engineer, Camille Rossi. He took command in August 1922 and had charge of the camp for ten years, until he was fired by Morgan, in a letter countersigned by Hearst, because he "began to think that all orders originated with him." Mor-

gan helped him get another job, and she then brought in George Loorz of Alameda, a young engineer whose work and character were above reproach. Warren McClure, an architect from her office, also supervised the outdoor work at San Simeon in later years.

As architect and supervisor of the burgeoning project, Morgan clambered over scaffolds, prowled around the extensive grounds, and bent over drawing boards in a primitive shack each weekend. When the buildings became habitable and guests began to outnumber workmen, Morgan would dine in the Refectory next to Hearst, but she rarely mingled with the Hollywood crowd. She was too busy checking on the craft workers and orchestrating the overall program. To Steilberg, Morgan bemoaned the loss of practically all the better workmen, who had left wood carving and tile work for factories during World War I and never returned to their crafts. To Hearst, however, she simply reported on the craftsmen she had found: "Washburn's carpenters are working on interiors" and "Van der Loo has worked hard reproducing antiques and plasterers wait [for him to finish his designs]." Edward Hussey, who had graduated from Berkeley with a degree in engineering, has told of doing the layout for a marble floor in one of the cottages, drawing various sizes of patterns on tracing paper four feet square. And then Morgan "just laid them down on the drafting floor and walked on them. That was the first time I had seen a drawing walked on to get the feel of it, but that was what she did in that case." Hussey added, "She never raised her voice or got angry but she was very particular in her work."[7]

In early letters to Morgan from New York, Hearst frequently referred to his wife's tastes and inclinations. For instance: "Mrs. Hearst prefers rose and gold valance for her room," and "Don't get wisteria, it is so ugly when not blooming. Bougainvillea is better. Mrs. Hearst and I are very fond of roses. We saw some beauties at the flower show in Paris." On February 14, 1922, Hearst wrote to Morgan that the cupid and scroll for the frieze in Mrs. Hearst's room "does not do its work as a transition member" between the ceiling of Italian Empire style and the purely Spanish window heads. A week later, however, he wrote, "I leave that matter to your judgment," a typical refrain. On September 20, 1922, Hearst wrote, "Mrs. Hearst and I feel that each bedroom should have its own bath. Divide up the baths or figure out something." Millicent Hearst increasingly wished to spend more time in New York City and on Long Island, where her charitable work had given her some prominence by the mid-1920s. But her husband's interests in radio and film, and particularly in comedienne Marion Davies, led to his concentration on California, with his social life revolving around Hollywood. Nevertheless, Hearst wrote to Morgan on March 11, 1923: "Mrs. Hearst and party arriving latter part of the month" (that may have been when Mayor James Walker of New York was a guest). And as late as March 31, 1924, he wrote: "Mrs. Hearst and children extremely anxious to have a swimming pool. Make Temple garden pool 8' deep for swimming purposes."

Major difficulties were caused from the beginning by Hearst's propensity to change his mind, usually wanting to aggrandize the project without adequate funds. He insisted on moving trees (even turning a large oak so that a branch would not disturb strollers), on creating a zoo with the animals roaming free and visible, and on raising the two towers of the Main Building to make room for a bedroom in each tower. Workmen were asked to move a fireplace from one side of the room to the other, then back again. All of these changes were made. Hearst recognized his weakness in a letter to Morgan dated March 18, 1920: "All little houses stunning. Please complete before I can think up any more changes." When asked if his many changes were exasperating, Morgan replied that they were often for the better and that they also made it possible for her to exercise her own "changeableness of mind." This she did during the design stage of the Gothic Study in the Main Building, for instance, by raising the roof several feet in order to have clerestory windows. She said that the limited height of the room had bothered her "at all hours," and Hearst cheerfully approved the higher roof, saying "the drawing looks surprisingly well."

Hearst's voracious acquisition of architectural elements and other art works is illuminated by Morgan's correspondence with Arthur Byne and his wife, Mildred Stapley (letters to her were addressed "Dear Julia," while she unfailingly called him "Mr. Byne" and signed her full name).[8] Both Byne and Stapley were ardent lifelong collectors of Spanish artifacts, who had been known to Morgan since her student days in Paris and her subsequent work with them for other clients. On September 3, 1921, Morgan asked Byne for detailed photographs of animal-bracket cornices at the monastery of Sanguesa in Spain, saying "Mr. Hearst has taken a great liking . . . and wants them for a house we are building here in California." Her next letter, of September 19, explains: "We are building for him a sort of village on a mountaintop overlooking the sea and ranges of mountains, miles away from any railway, and housing incidentally his collections as well as his family. Having different buildings allows the use of varied treatments, as does the fact that all garden work is on steep hillsides, requiring endless steps and terracing." In subsequent letters and telegrams Byne offered a rare Spanish collection, plus garden material, for $375,000. He once said (December 15, 1921), "Let me remark in passing that you are the only person who ever paid in advance for anything," and again (April 1923), "I have no right to ask this of you since you are so 'positively negative' as to a commission, but cash is necessary from Mr. Hearst. I have dealt with millionaires all my life (for better or for worse) and I know they don't like being spoken to in that manner, but it is the only way to buy at a low figure. Mr. Hearst has the habit of ignoring his obligations, [so] I am going to ask if you will present the enclosed bill." On September 7, 1923, Morgan wrote: "What we would like are ceilings, especially door trims, interesting architectural motifs—not so much furniture as objets d'art. We have three buildings completed

A 1925 view of the wellhead from Verona, which came to San Simeon via Phoebe Hearst's Pleasanton Hacienda, seen here with the east side of Cottage A in the background.

and one large one on the way but there are a number more contemplated." Then on May 7, 1924, she asked Byne to find a very fine, important stone cloister of any size, writing that "The place on the hill grows—and from a distance begins to assume the look of an old hill town. There is no effort to make the buildings themselves other than modern. They photograph badly, so I judge the actual charm is in the color—for the garden begins to be lovely in a sophisticated way."

On August 25, 1925, Morgan again wrote to Byne: "Mr. Hearst is going to erect a museum for the University of California [never built], and the cloister you have bought will in all probability be built into that building, as the idea is, instead of the usual formal exhibit rooms, to have the objects au naturel, otherwise to have the exhibits housed in rooms or about courts of the time and country to which the objets d'art, paintings, furnishings, etc. belonged. . . . But he does want for himself something really fine, Gothic, Transitional, or Renaissance, and I am sure that if you find something, expense would not enter. I imagine you are laughing, you and Mildred, when you get this request, but Mr. Hearst said last night 'You know we sent Mr. Byne a perfectly good set of pictures of possible looking patios and cloisters, and surely some of those Signors, Dukes, etc. are hard enough up to part with *one* of them.' I have in my charge something like

Cottage A, 1920–22

Entry court, Cottage C, 1920–22

four carloads of objects, the majority of which are small so that what we need are big things to use to make settings with. Enclosed check for $10,000 mentioned in cable."

In a later letter (October 6, 1925) sympathizing with Byne's difficulties in getting materials out of Spain, Morgan recalled the early years at San Simeon when almost everything had to be hauled fifty-six miles from the railroad over wretched roads. She added, "I look now at all the old medieval hill-top castles with a sense of fellow-understanding and sympathy with their builders—and so too grasp the nature of your physical (and moral) struggles."[9]

In the winter of 1919 models of each cottage were sent by express to New York and pronounced "charming and informative" by Hearst. Morgan wrote to him about two weeks later: "Enclosed is a suggestion for the court of 'A' which occurred to me yesterday as accomplishing two things—making 'A' seem much larger and more important by including all the areas in front of the house in the court, and making the entrance to this court at a point which allows of a psychological change, as the material one is chiefly the addition of the little wall at the ends and the change in the character of the pavement."

Each cottage had an entry from its one-story forecourt on the hill; both A and C had two stories below, cut into the steep hillside. In October 1919 Morgan had explicitly stated that "it would be pleasant to have a recall of

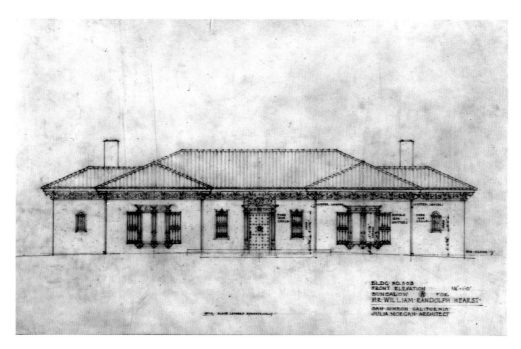

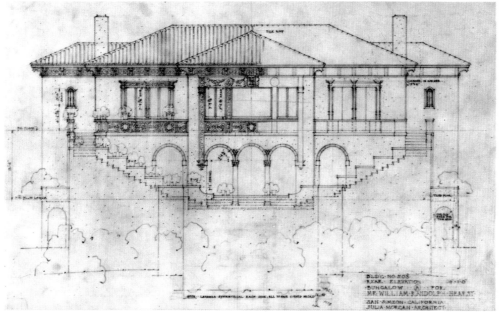

Top: Front elevation, Cottage A

Center: Rear elevation, Cottage A

Bottom, left: Main-floor plan, Cottage A, 1920. These plans were later revised so that each bedroom had a private bath.

Bottom, center: Lower-suite plan, Cottage A, 1920

Bottom, right: Plan of the suite on the lowest terrace, Cottage A, 1920

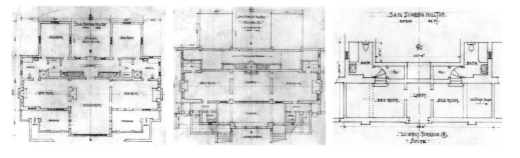

the character of the main building in the detail" of the cottages, and this idea was carried out in the designs. Each cottage was an independent building, but in placement and in detail each was also a part of a coherent whole.

The Main Building had originally been conceived with a medieval facade and a single tower, but in 1921 Morgan reworked the plan to include two towers. On February 5 she wrote to Hearst that "while standing at the point (A) yesterday and looking up imagining the towers, the fine 'looming up' effect grew on me—and the regret that few would see it often from this point. Then it occurred to me, why not make the guest machines [automobiles] stop and descend and the guests alight at a widened place in the road, and continue the steps on down. The machines could go on to the circular court and turn back—the baggage could go on around to kitchen turn —and a strikingly noble and 'saississant' ["gripping"] effect would be impressed upon everyone on arrival." Hearst noted in the margin: "Heartily approve those steps. I certainly want that saississant effect. I don't know what it is but I think we ought to have at least one such on the premises." (The steps were never completed, but a similar effect can now be experienced from the pool entrance.)

In April 1922 the decision was made to go ahead with the Main Building, and excavation proceeded through the spring and early summer, with the wooden forms for concrete up by August. Under Rossi's

Top: Early drawing for Main Building with only one tower, late 1919

Center: Early drawing for Main Building with two towers, 1921–22

Bottom: Front elevation, Main Building, 1923

Opposite: Front entrance, Main Building, 1922–26

supervision the crew forged ahead, with Morgan emphasizing the safety and fireproof characteristics of the fine reinforced-concrete work. Four stairway towers 24 feet in diameter were earthquake-proof in design, and deep basement walls gave a strong underpinning. Pouring stopped for the winter months at half the level of the first story, with the reinforced steel up to the second floor. On December 12, 1922, Morgan wrote: "The vista from the mezzanine floor scaffolding is superb and vast." She was then making studies for the main terrace pool and Neptune pool as well as for the Main Building. In her architect's report on December 9, 1925, she said that "San

Ceiling for Doge's Suite, third floor of Main Building. Central panel, *Annunciation to the Shepherds,* is by the School of Joachim Wtewael (Dutch, 1566–1638).

Opposite: Main Building, with unfinished south wing at right

Simeon may seem quiet but [Ed] Trinkeller is at work on the big grilles for the main room, [Ed] Milletin is on doorway trim and on San Sovino trim for vestibule, Lorenzi carving the bookcases of the library, Van der Loo on ceilings of library and vestibule, and last work of Doges' Suite; Rossi finished new stair extension of towers, [Jules] Suppo is on last panels of big frieze and kitchen wing cornice, chicken house man [Spengler] has arrived." Morgan concluded: "Am sailing tomorrow for Honolulu." It was a year later that the client brought his family to the Main Building for Christmas, and from then on, amidst constant enlarging and remodeling, it was a residence for a few months each year as well as an ever-changing museum in the eyes of both architect and client.

The Main Building, placed on the highest part of the site, was always planned to dominate the hill. Its dazzling white facade (cast in reinforced concrete and faced with stone) contrasts with carved teak and gleaming colored tiles. Spanish limestone figures from the late Gothic period stand out, their effect reinforced by the cast-stone ornaments created by craftsmen of the 1920s. A small quatrefoil-shaped pool is set back from the entrance; framed by benches and balustrades, it offers a place for the visitor to pause while examining the facade.

The high main story is outlined by a cast-stone balcony that extends all the way across the symmetrical front. The only front entrance is the elaborate main doorway, framed by sculptural elements, with a narrow window close to each side. The central portion is defined by ornamented Gothic

columns that are flanked by bare walls. Above the main central space are two more stories, with classical framed windows on the second, behind the cast-stone ornamented balcony, and curved iron balconies on the third. The central portion is brick with carved teak, under a low-pitched tile roof with a wide overhang. The tiled iron chambers of the two towers rise above arched windows screened with stone filigree. The towers are linked by a walkway that is faced in brilliantly colored tile and topped by a low-pitched ornamental gable of red tile.

On May 20, 1923, Morgan heard of some bargain teak from Siam available in a San Francisco warehouse; it had been ordered for the interior of a ship but never used, and the warehouse wanted to get rid of it. In response to her query Hearst wired Morgan to "accept teak immediately." Used to roof the towers and to ornament the balcony between them, the teak was called a "Maybeckian flourish" by Louis Schalk of Morgan's office, and Steilberg considered it too "Japonesque." Morgan may have been thinking of San Xavier del Bac in Tucson, Arizona, an eighteenth-century mission that features a dark, chiefly ornamental center between two white towers.

Once the visitor enters the oblong vestibule through the ornamental cast-iron doors, the plan of the Main Building begins to disclose itself. The immense two-story Assembly Room, about 80 by 30 feet, extends across the entire front of the building. From this magnificent space the walk through the building proceeds on a main axis through the Refectory to the morning room, where it intersects with the cross axis. The pantry and service area are located in the south or right wing; recreation in the form of a billiard room (originally called the music room) and a movie theater is offered in the north or left wing. As in a medieval building, stairs wind up in four corner towers, each with a diameter of 24 feet; for convenience a modern elevator was included in two other towers.[10]

When the visitor progresses from the vast Assembly Room to the Refectory, it is as though he had actually entered the Gothic period. This impression is intensified by the monumental proportions of the room, its height emphasized by the 28-foot stone mantel that stretches to the ceiling. Silk banners from Siena's Palio flutter overhead, directing the eyes to the ceiling, where life-size figures of saints carved from wood are placed in each of the

Opposite: Cast-stone figure, tower, Main Building

Above: San Xavier del Bac, Tucson, Arizona

Right, top: Walkway joining the towers of the Main Building

Right, center: Tile and ironwork along the walkway between the Main Building towers

Right, bottom: Carved teak, Main Building

Above: The Refectory,
Main Building

Right: Assembly Room,
Main Building

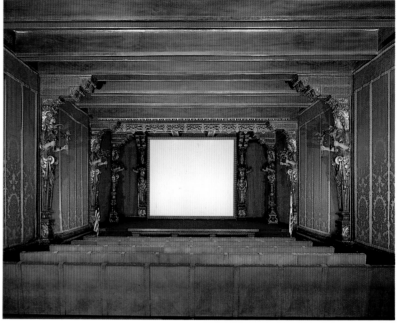

Billiard room (formerly the music room), Main Building

Theater, Main Building

coffered sections. Silver gleaming on the long table and sideboards, tapestries and choir stalls at the sides reinforce the late medieval atmosphere. Morgan worked out the first plan for this room in drawings in September 1919, using the proportions of the room and various objects to create a sense of verticality and expansion of scale when moving to the Refectory from the morning room and billiard room. As late as 1926 she was recommending to Hearst that "instead of bringing the large scale of the Refectory ceiling down, let's bring the scale of the mantels and stalls up." Stained glass had been planned, but Hearst wanted to see the California sky, so the colored glass was used in the Gothic Study instead (it was later replaced by windows that let the light in). The Refectory was said to be Morgan's favorite room, although she often told Steilberg that her favorite building or room was usually the one she had just finished working on.

The theater, reached through the morning room and the billiard room, is in some ways the heart of San Simeon. Although Hearst had shown films from the start—in tents, in Cottage A, in the Assembly Room (called the Social Hall originally), and then in the music room—by 1930 the largest room in the Main Building was ready for nightly film showings. Seating fifty in cut-velvet armchairs, it has walls lined with deep rose-red damask palace silk, creating a luxurious effect that paralleled the aim of designers of movie palaces all over the nation. At each beam along the sides is an oversize caryatid of cast stone, covered with gesso painted in gold leaf; these 1920s beauties carry bouquets ending in light bulbs. The effect is dazzling, evoking Morgan's elaborate competition drawing for a "Theater in a Palace" (see chapter 2), although the opulence of this version is somewhat subdued by the sterner rectangular form required for viewing the latest productions of the industry that supported so many of the guests and meant so much to Hearst and to Davies.

Both Morgan and Hearst were interested in having the best possible room for showing films, with a stage that could also be ready for impromptu amateur turns. The silver screen was built to descend through the floor to the bowling alley below, to make room for stage presentations. Good acoustics were the result of the wooden ceiling and beams, the rich upholstery of the armchairs, the heavy silk on the walls, the jutting beams, and the caryatids. A telephone by Hearst's chair provided instant communication with the projection room; if a film proved boring, an alternate could replace it without delay.

Letters between Morgan and Hearst during construction of the theater show that the concrete for what they called the Recreation Wing was poured by the end of December 1929; that in February 1930 he urged her to focus on finishing the theater; that she telegraphed him on March 1 about using the red damask from the Assembly Room for the walls and inquired as to his preference for columns or caryatids at the beams. By June the walls were ready for plastering while Theodore Van der Loo and Dien were casting the big caryatids. In July carpets and chairs were ordered, on August 22 the caryatids went up, and on December 15 Hearst wrote, "we will have ground floor perfect if we proceed with music room theater and projection booth." Morgan's own bedroom was above the music room, and one floor above was that of former reporter Joseph Willicombe, Hearst's secretary and right-hand man from 1922 to his retirement in 1944.

In the south wing is an immaculate pantry and a restaurant-size kitchen with the latest stainless-steel equipment, researched by Morgan. This was a hardworking part of a household that had to be ready to feed anywhere from two guests to a hundred, usually on short notice. Yet even here the ornamental brass-bird faucets and the tile trim around the sink show a light and decorative touch. The first two floors of the Main Building

Julia Morgan's bedroom, Main Building

Glazed porch off the Doge's suite, Main Building

are given over to public rooms, guest rooms, and service areas, with a library across the front on the second floor. The third floor and the tower rooms are private quarters, but no less museum pieces in their composition and furnishings. The many medieval and Renaissance ceilings throughout the building are suspended from the concrete, not bearing any weight themselves, and the entire building is both fireproof and braced against seismic disturbance. Fireplaces and mantels frequently came from Hearst's vast collection, but the stone or wood ceilings were often supplemented or duplicated by Morgan's artisans with a skill that defies detection. In some cases a whole painted ceiling or massive doors were created right on the hill in Morgan's little-known crafts center.[11]

There is a total of 127 rooms in the Main Building and guesthouses: fifty-eight bedrooms, forty-nine baths, eighteen sitting rooms, two libraries.[12] All are furnished with antiques and architectural elements—many original, many done on the spot. Hearst collected objects as diverse as Egyptian sculpture, Chinese and Greek vases, eighteenth-century silver, modern Swedish glass, and a few nineteenth-century paintings—all displayed in the various rooms along with clerical vestments and tapestries used as wall hangings and rare Persian carpets underfoot. In every room items from his lifelong collection are arranged to seem part of a comfortable environment. In the New Wing, furnished late, there are fewer antiques and grander bathrooms—one that is 36 feet long, all in marble, catches the eye of tourists.[13]

In an early letter to Arthur Byne (September 19, 1921), Morgan emphasized that the terrain and terrace were of great significance in creating the special charm of the Hearst estate. The success of the landscaping was largely due to the architect's efforts, encouraged and abetted by the client. Hearst began with admonitions to keep a great rose garden, then listed thirteen plants to be ordered (December 15, 1920), next demanded "yellow roses and purple jacaranda" (January 19, 1921), and by the next week (January 27, 1921) was proposing color schemes for each season. One of Morgan's tasks was to plant the garden, hire a force to maintain it, and as building designs increased and assumed more of her time, to secure a head gardener who could not only manage a crew but also anticipate what would be needed for luxurious plantings all over the hill. Water had to be piped for miles from mountain springs and topsoil brought from land down near the sea. Stories about the wonders of the gardens abound, from the universal delight at the flower arrangements in every guest room and the constant blooms at all seasons to the seeming miracle of an Easter morning when the guests awoke to see Easter lilies all over the hilltop, the garden crew having set out the plants during the night.[14]

Gardner Dailey of Morgan's office held the chief gardener's job for the first period, until Hearst's telegram: "Dailey do we not need." Then Morgan hired Isabel Worn, a distinguished horticulturist who had worked on the William Bourne estate, "Filoli," on the Peninsula. She, too, ran up against

South duplex suite, third floor of Main Building.

Hearst's changeable nature and was dropped. Next came a steadfast crew of gardeners under J. C. Heaton, until Nigel Keep, an Englishman hired as "tree man" in 1922, was put in charge of all the planting; a Portuguese man named Alfredo Gomes managed the greenhouses.

Morgan designed all of the outbuildings at San Simeon, from hothouses to kennels. A set of frame structures served as switchboard and newspaper offices under Willicombe and his staff, while telephones were placed not only in all the buildings but also along bridle paths and any other place Hearst might be likely to go. The smallest building, called the shack, was where the architect worked and where she conferred with Hearst on many

of her weekend visits. It has been preserved as an appropriate symbol of the ongoing character of the whole enterprise.

Perhaps Morgan's most unusual assignment at San Simeon was to design a zoo, with bear and lion pits, an elephant house, various shelters for grazing animals, and a giraffe house. The last was relocated close to the driveway after Hearst complained that people hardly ever saw the giraffes. In designing the animal shelters, Morgan would send Hearst a photograph of the roadway, with a tracing paper drawing or two to overlay it. With the keeper of the Hagenbeck Zoo in Hamburg as adviser, she devised concrete pits for the fiercer animals, with walkways over them and enough space, pools, and caves to make the animals both comfortable and visible. By 1939 Hearst had given the wild animals to the San Diego and San Francisco zoos, although miniature deer, exotic goats, and zebras still roam the ranch pastures with the cattle.

"The Shack," attached to the New Wing of the Main Building, where Morgan had her office

Sketch for an animal shelter, on tissue paper over photograph, c. 1927

The pergola was another original design by Morgan, recalling a nineteenth-century pergola at Amalfi, Italy, but longer. It encircles the hill for more than a mile, returning near where it starts at the Main Building. Made of concrete pillars with crosspieces cast in the shape of mythological figures, it is high enough for "a tall man with a tall hat on a tall horse" to ride through it (according to Hearst). Vines climb the posts; pomegranate and holly provide spots of color nearby.

Among the most flamboyant visual delights at San Simeon are the pools. From the start Morgan had planned a pool on a level just below the three guesthouses, between Cottage B and Cottage C. At first, it was to be clover-shaped, with a patio and palm trees surrounding it, merely an enlarged

Top: Julia Morgan with "MaryAnn," c. 1928—part of the San Simeon menagerie

Bottom, left: Animal pits, Orchard Hill, San Simeon, c. 1926

Bottom, right: Camille Rossi with cubs, San Simeon, c. 1930

version of many private pools for luxurious California homes. It was to be the largest of several decorative garden pools and was not exactly on axis with the Main Building, being shaped by the contours of the land. As plans progressed, this main outdoor pool, dedicated to Neptune, grew not once but twice: Hearst eventually had it extended to more than 100 feet in length, with a 345,000-gallon capacity. To give cohesiveness to the large form, Morgan had to design two semicircular colonnades of marble to encompass it. Hearst brought in the facade of a temple—a composite of Greco-Roman

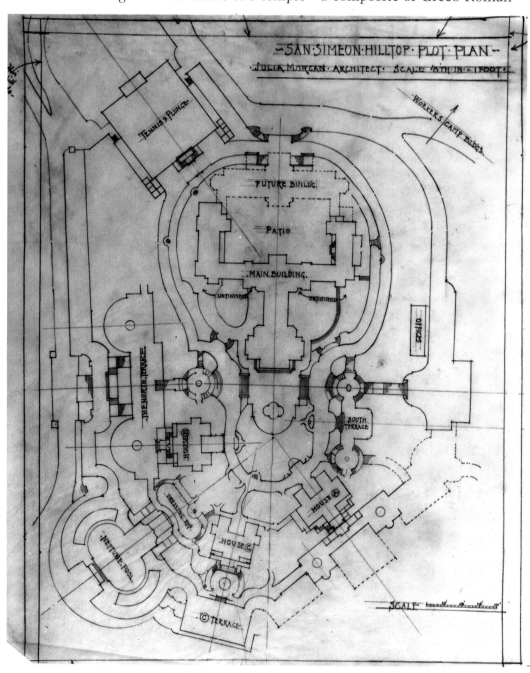

granite columns and a marble pediment, with a sculptured Neptune and two Nereids (not originally part of the pediment) at the center.

Opposite the temple is a raised square basin where sculptured mermaids and other sea creatures frolic below a Venus rising from the sea. The French sculptor Charles Cassou was chosen by Morgan to give his interpretation of the Neptune and Venus stories, and Hearst consulted him in Paris when the pool design was in the process of its final enlargement; Cassou's marble statues were not set in place until late in 1931. The basin lies between the arms of a double stairway guarded by lines of cypress trees; it is lighted by globes mounted on cast-stone duplicates of an original Greco-Roman boundary marker, imported by Hearst, which continue around the pool's periphery. Overlooking the pool is the Neptune terrace, in

Opposite: Plot plan, San Simeon, c. 1930

Top: View from Cottage A of the pergola, 1936

Bottom, left: First version of the Neptune pool, 1924

Bottom, right: Cross piece of pergola

Overleaf: Neptune pool, final version, 1935–36

whose foundations are seventeen dressing rooms, each with baths and full-length mirrors. The curves of this terrace form a counterpoint to the shape of the pool. Curved concrete balustrades continue the pattern and produce a late-afternoon play of light and shadow. Here on the terrace guests were served tea as they watched the sun set on the ocean five miles away, 1,600 feet below.

The engineering of the Neptune pool is as much a triumph as its aesthetic impact. On a site excavated from the steep hillside, the pool is hung by reinforced-concrete beams from the concrete retaining wall in such a way that a seismic movement would let it sway but not break. Water flows in from natural springs above, piped into two reserve tanks of tremendous capacity, one of 345,000 gallons, the other of 1,200,000 gallons. Below the pool is a large room housing a complex filter system based on the purifying power of sand and an electrical heating unit used to keep the water at a brisk 70 degrees Fahrenheit.

Hearst and Morgan were preoccupied with pools. In May 1925, at the time of the first enlargement of the Neptune pool, Hearst announced that he wanted a saltwater pool as well, either on the hill or nearer the ocean. Concerned about the potential cost, Morgan asked if a pool near the picnic beach might do. It would not, and by August 1926 Hearst suggested taking off the top of the adjacent "Chinese Hill" for a saltwater pool. By March of the following year Morgan was sending him "Tennis-Gymnasium Building" drawings and wall-facade studies for an interior springwater pool. He replied in April with "winter pool" ideas: "on Persian Hill with hothouse for palms, orchids, and ferns, to surround an indoor pool, glass dome and lattice windows—a loggia to serve tea or poi and a turtle—'South Sea Island' on the Hill, with sharks [April 24, 1927]." This was followed by a request for sketches of this hothouse, to be 120 feet square, with walls 20–30 feet high, a dome 15 feet higher, green glass, and gilded iron ribs; the north entrance was to have a lobby and dressing rooms. The handwritten letter, from April 1927, is signed "William Viollet-le-Duc Hearst, architect." Morgan answered on May 2, saying that she liked his "combination orchid-greenhouse and indoor pool—with plate glass partition for sharks!" The next week she reported that the steam shovel was making quite a hole in the tennis court–pool project, and by June 1927 the excavation was complete and construction of the forms had begun. Hearst hoped for a New Year's Eve celebration in the indoor pool, but bad weather and changes in plan caused delays. By 1930, when they were involved with

Above: Tennis courts on top of Roman pool, 1927–32

Below and pages 209–11: Roman pool, 1927–32

the artistry of the mosaic work for what they had begun to call the "Roman bath," they were still perfecting the filters, the heating, and the safety ladders. In December 1932 it was finally possible to celebrate that deferred New Year's Eve in the indoor pool, although the exterior of the building was never finished. That same year Hearst had urged Morgan to "please keep available those pictures of pools of southern France—we may want this kind at San Simeon Point," down near the harbor.

The Roman pool beneath the two tennis courts is lighted by skylights between the two courts, by tall windows, and by marble lamps with alabaster shades. Problems of engineering, on a hillside site, such a large, level pool (81 by 31 feet, with a uniform depth of 10 feet) with a flat, drainable place above it for tennis, led Morgan to bury one end in the ground. Handball courts were to be placed against the sides. The pool opens on one side into a 4-foot-deep wading pool encircled by a daylighted walkway, with rest rooms and dressing rooms built alongside. The pool itself is a luminous space lined with blue and gold (gold leaf fused in glass) tile. The effect is one of richly colored opulence, a veritable museum of a pool.

Hearst turned to Morgan for her expertise in constructing pools not only at San Simeon and Wyntoon, but also at his projected Hacienda in Babicora, Mexico, and even in Europe. When he was remodeling his castle in Wales, he sent Morgan a telegram on August 22, 1929, saying, "Please send Sir Charles Allom [one of England's leading architects] full details of Wyntoon pool sketch, including tile samples, to have a similar pool at St. Donats." On February 7, 1934, Morgan agreed to be consultant upon that project, writing, "I have 22 pools now in operation and have come to some quite definite conclusions—would willingly show full heating-filtering systems to Miss Head [Hearst's representative in London]."

One may marvel at the contrast between Morgan's sumptuous, artfully planned pools and her own virginal and ascetic life-style. She had spent her childhood summers at the modest Monterey Bay resorts of Santa Cruz, Capitola, and Pacific Grove, which provided

Pool at Hearst's castle in Wales, by Sir Charles Allom, who consulted with Morgan on its design

no precedents for her later lavishness. Although she remodeled a small house into a studio–retirement cottage for herself at Monterey, there is no evidence that she actually swam in the ocean or in any "plunge." By the same token, she almost surely did not frequent beauty salons, nor did she sunbathe; yet facilities for these activities were skillfully integrated with her pool designs at her YWCAs, her clubs, and at the various Hearst estates. Perhaps the pools express the exuberance of some alter ego, for in them we see a glorification of the senses that is rarely conspicuous in Morgan's other work. Grasping the inherent sensuality of the act of swimming, she momentarily cast off her inhibitions to create a series of exquisitely engineered stage sets for hedonism.

After walking through the amazing complex of buildings and landscaping at San Simeon, it is natural to wonder about the costs and the method of payment. Correspondence between architect and client makes it clear that financing was never easy and that it became part of the many nonarchitectural aspects of the work to absorb Morgan's energies.

As early as the first year of operation, money had become a problem. Morgan wrote to Hearst that she was charging him a 6 percent commission and that she was adding the cost of buying everything and doing contractor's work. She had spent $16,750 on a commission of $15,000. "Which would be better, charging a percentage that could cover expenses, or for your office to do the hunting out, buying, transporting, and checking? You know how I feel about San Simeon and so will understand that it is not a question of making a little more or less, but there is a real need not to go behind, and I know you would not want it." This letter of December 15, 1920, elicited a telegram: "What definite sum shall we add to the percentage to make satisfactory compensation for your work?" To this she replied on January 24, 1921: ". . . . the actual cash deficit over the 6% commission to December 1 is $1,780. If this is made up it will cover the costs of your work through the office to that date. If the loss had been caused by the architectural work I would not have spoken of it but it is due to the expense of 'running the job' as it were."

"Running the job" included hiring, firing, and settling disputes; arranging lodging, food, and working quarters for the laborers; making trips to interview specialists such as a cheese maker, a chicken man, gardeners, and housekeepers; procuring special plants and materials; creating various crafts centers on site; arranging transportation by ship, rail, and truck to the remote hilltop; building warehouses and cataloging objects to be incorporated in the project; checking on thousands of details; and satisfying the whims of artists and the client. That all this was taken care of by the architect was most unusual, but the physical remoteness of the site and the rare sense of partnership between architect and client in a venture cherished by both made it work out over a number of years, until Hearst was no longer able to command the funds needed to bring his visions to reality.[15]

George Loorz's letter to the Morgan office from San Simeon on October 9, 1935, provides a vivid image of Hearst's style:

> Mr. Hearst walked into the office in splendid spirits about five last night and we spent an hour of building and creating new projects. An airport on a hilltop above the fog was one. Oh boy, it would be an expensive project if it goes ahead. Sooner or later he will do something. In thirty minutes he moved the zoo, constructed new bear grottos and divided the present ones for cats. He levelled animal hill out here. We tore down the shop and lowered a dozen oak trees in groups of five, making tremendous concrete boxes, excavating under them and letting the trees right down into position. Moving one tree at a time is a big job, moving a close group of about five is still bigger. Anyway he laughed a lot and seemed happy so we will put it down as a successful interview.

In January 1921 Hearst had written to Morgan that he hoped she could complete the job quickly, but added: "Don't keep big crews, expenses should be kept down." And so it went for the rest of his life—grandiose plans and restricted funds. After more than three years of financial uncertainty during which bills were always outstanding (James LeFeaver of her office suggested the job was costing about $30,000 per month), Morgan wrote a long letter to Hearst on February 12, 1923, recommending more efficient payment procedures. Her last item was "that the architect be paid

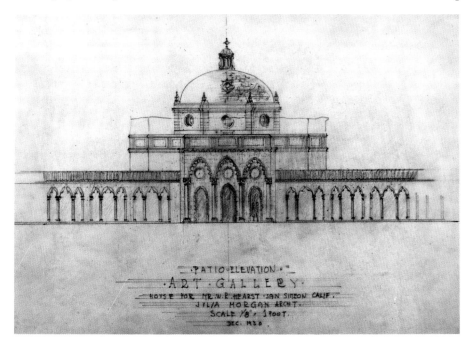

Proposed Great Hall, with art gallery and ballroom, for east wing, 1930. This was planned as an addition to the Main Building but never built.

each month the agreed percentage on the expenditures of the month—in order not to be worried for means to carry on the work." Then two weeks later, she suggested that a flat $25,000-per-month budget (to include 8½ percent for her staff) be allocated to cover crews, materials, and truckage. On March 9, 1923, Hearst telegraphed the *Examiner*: "Please deposit $25,000 April 1 and the first of each month thereafter, to be drawn against by Miss Morgan with the understanding that no more than that amount required monthly to cover operations on ranch, including material and architect's fees. Kindly acknowledge." The next day Morgan wired Hearst: "Think new payment arrangement will work for better prices and deliveries. Thank you very much. Will promise to keep within limit. . . ."

In a *New York Times* article of July 21, 1929, Duncan Aikman aptly compared the San Simeon business arrangements to those of an even grander age of patronage: "By a curious coincidence . . . the business system by which the building and collecting is done has been that used by the great Renaissance houses like Medici, d'Este, Visconti."

Morgan worked out this system under duress, and the accounts show the whole place to be a marvel of economy, considering the tastes and tendencies of the owner. Yet even with every kind of accounting effort she could devise, deficits and missed payrolls recurred throughout the 1920s and '30s. She had to telegraph for funds many times, once with a desperate message to Willicombe: "No March money, two payrolls unpaid." Her work for Hearst in the 1940s was hopelessly underpaid because she was so committed to the various projects in Mexico and at Wyntoon that she could not or would not see that his sons and the corporation had finally gotten such a grip on the old man's funds that construction had to come to a halt.

Morgan's invoices show that she made 558 trips from August 1919 to 1939 (when her attention shifted to Wyntoon), averaging about three weekends a month. She did not make much on her twenty-five years of work for Hearst—about $70,755. In answer to a request from the Hearst family's Sunical Land and Livestock Corporation, Morgan gave this breakdown—dated July 26, 1945—of San Simeon expenditures, 1919–42 inclusive:

San Simeon Village Buildings	$ 110,000
Animal shelters	40,000
A, B, and C Houses	500,000
Main Building	2,987,000
Neptune Pool, Temple, terraces, pavillions, dressing rooms, stairways, pool operation	430,000
Tennis Courts, Roman Plunge	400,000
Animal Hill, cages and arenas	35,000
General services: Water Line	25,000
Reservoirs	85,000
Sewers and Septic and Lighting	35,000
Temporary Construction	20,000
	$4,717,000

With the closing of the San Simeon accounts, both wings of the Main Building still remained unfinished, as did the patio-side walls and much of the planned landscaping. The bowling alley under the theater was equipped but still served as temporary storage space for ceilings and furnishings destined for the New Wing. Airstrip improvements had been outlined and begun but not finished. As for buildings planned but never even initiated, the Chinese Cottage was perhaps the most often discussed, but there was also the English Cottage and Cottage D (Casa del Cañon)—all were abandoned. Perhaps the severest loss in the eyes of client and architect was the Great Hall, or Gallery, which Hearst and Morgan had hoped would link the two wings of the Main Building to form an enclosed courtyard.

View from Main Building tower at twilight

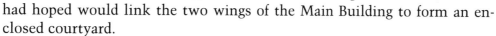

Hearst and Marion Davies spent two postwar years living in Cottage A, using a service area set up by Morgan so that they did not have to go to the Main Building for their meals. After Hearst left for the last time in 1947 (his health being so precarious that his doctors had ordered him to stay close to medical services), a skeleton crew of maintenance workers stayed on. Shops were run by the carpenters, plumbers, blacksmiths, and electricians, while the "dog man" Norman Johnson (who had served since 1932) kept up the splendid kennels designed by Morgan until Hearst's death in 1951. Norman Rotanzi remained the strongest link with the past even after the California State Department of Parks and Recreation took over in 1958; he served as grounds superintendent through 1987.

Two letters of June 1945 from Morgan to Hearst show her continuing concern for the preservation of San Simeon. The first (June 5) gives the precise formula for "waxing the statues." The second (June 13) deals with demothing the tapestries. Both letters bear Hearst's endorsement: the one says "tell Mr. Robinson to proceed exactly with this formula"; the other has a shaky "ok" in Hearst's hand.

In 1923 Bruce Porter, a poet, critic, and one of San Francisco's leading landscape gardeners, was asked to evaluate what had been accomplished so far at San Simeon.[16] His twelve-page report to Mr. Hearst ends:

> I was asked to put a fresh eye upon it and make a report of my impression. . . . That impression remains stupendous. The place is so perfect as it is—that nothing at all needs be done. What is done should be done boldly—and for bold effect, but with caution and discrimination dictated by a kind of reverence. . . . Just the right placing, the isolation, the way the thing 'fits' makes one ready to declare that this is the one unique romantic architectural event in America. . . . I found that in vision that shining group simply dominates the whole coast from San Francisco to San Diego.

Hearst commented on the report, "I agree with practically everything."

8

WYNTOON AND OTHER HEARST PROJECTS

Long before the San Simeon account was closed, in fact even before the Main Building was ready for occupancy, Hearst had turned his attention to fifty thousand acres he had inherited about fifty miles south of the Oregon border, in the shadow of Mount Shasta. The densely forested site at Wyntoon (according to legend that was the Indian name for the area) has a mysterious quality that is just as extraordinary in its own way as the Enchanted Hill at San Simeon. It had strongly appealed to Phoebe Hearst in 1889, when she visited her lawyer, Charles Stetson Wheeler of San Francisco, at his elegant version of an Adirondack hunting lodge on a bend in the McCloud River, designed by Willis Polk. Phoebe Hearst was so enthusiastic about "The Bend" that she eventually persuaded the Wheelers to lease adjacent land to her for a building to be designed by Maybeck. The resulting seven-story stone Gothic castle (1902) so overshadowed Wheeler's building that he agreed to sell her the whole acreage.

William Randolph Hearst and his family enjoyed summer visits at Wyntoon during his mother's tenure. After her death, even though he was preoccupied with his own extensive plans for San Simeon, Hearst liked to spend some time each summer in the invigorating mountain air, riding horseback through the wooded acres.[1] During the 1920s he was eager to share the memorable setting of his mother's art-filled castle with special guests. Yet this was no easy weekend jaunt from Los Angeles or even from San Francisco. Visitors could take a 9 P.M. ferry from San Francisco and make a connection with a Pullman train from Oakland; they could also take the "Daylight" train from Los Angeles, which arrived by seven in the morning. Both trains got the passengers as far as Dunsmuir, 3,000 feet up into the Cascades. From Dunsmuir a Hearst car picked up passengers for a drive a little more than half an hour long, going east into the mountains. These complicated arrangements were required until the mid-

Opposite: Bear House, Wyntoon, 1933–41

Bernard Maybeck's castle at Wyntoon, as seen on April 6, 1929. The castle was destroyed by fire in 1930.

1930s, when Hearst arranged for an airstrip only a quarter of an hour from the ranch. Once they got to Wyntoon, guests could be sure of plenty of horseback rides, croquet, and of course movies, but there was no pool until the summer of 1930, and little other entertainment was available. Hearst did not permit hunting, and there was no fishing because of volcanic ash in the McCloud River (a condition corrected in about 1940). The isolation was a barrier to some guests and a particular enchantment to numerous others, including the host.

The Maybeck castle burned to the ground during the winter of 1929–30, in a fire attributed to chipmunks' having eaten through electrical wiring. William Randolph Hearst made plans for rebuilding almost immediately, enlisting Maybeck and Morgan as architects. Drawings by Maybeck and by Morgan and a model done in the Morgan office show a medieval castle with two main towers, one of which culminated in a circular study at eighth-floor level. The fact that it was to have sixty-one bedrooms gives a sense of its scale. This grand scheme appealed to Hearst, but he finally recognized that the cost would be prohibitive and reluctantly gave up Maybeck's plan.

In the meantime Morgan had devised another approach related to the San Simeon complex. She designed a "Bavarian village" with three half-timber three-story guesthouses, each composed of four to eight bedrooms (each with its own bathroom), and two sitting rooms. These were to be placed around a large, grassy oval clearing in the midst of the forest, with the back of each house paralleling the river as it curved downstream toward the earlier River House.[2] Meals and all kinds of entertainment were to be offered in an elaborate central structure called the Bend (so named because the McCloud River turned at that point). There were three main areas: the "Bavarian village"; then, nearly half a mile down, the swimming pool, tennis courts, croquet court, and the Gables for dining and movies; and finally, another quarter of a mile below, the Bend. The site of Maybeck's original castle was close to the croquet court, nearer the Bend than to Morgan's oval with the new houses.

Top: William Randolph Hearst, Wyntoon

Center: Morgan's drawing for Wyntoon Castle, 1931 (never built)

Bottom: Model of Wyntoon Castle, 1930

The guesthouses, which seem more like small castles, are Bavarian-Austrian in style, a choice no doubt influenced by the landscape, with its steep pine-covered hills and tumultuous stony river. Hearst and Morgan may also have felt that Maybeck's Teutonic castle for Phoebe Hearst had caught the spirit of the place. Morgan and Hearst each traveled in Austria and Bavaria in 1931–32 (Morgan with her sister, Emma), the year after construction began, and their choice of the style may have been reinforced by a desire to transplant a fairy-tale world to safety in the California woods

Top, left: Houses at Wyntoon, 1933–41, front view

Top, right: Houses at Wyntoon, river view

Right: Overall plan of Wyntoon

at a time when Hitler's machinations were threatening the originals.

The effect of the "village" is Bavarian, but the symmetry of each building and the careful siting around the central green are more Beaux-Arts, a welcome antidote to the potentially cloying Bavarian style. Morgan's use of the local stone and wood is characteristically sensitive. The steep roofs feature many gables, chimneys, and bay windows accented by timbers; but the playful arrangement of forms, in counterpoint to the adjacent patterns of trees and river and mountains, gives a rhythmic quality to the whole design. As usual, Morgan brought with her a team of seasoned workers who were happy to follow her from job to job, as they respected her high standards, her fairness, and her appreciation of superior work. A force of artisans worked from her full-size drawings. For the shutters, murals, and other details, she called on her favorite painter, Doris Day, who had worked on the Chapel of the Chimes in Oakland. Ironwork and other hinges were the special province of Otto Olson, an Austrian who had also been part of earlier Morgan teams, at Asilomar and elsewhere. Jules Suppo did some of the wood carving in San Francisco, while two of his helpers worked steadily at the site. Edward Hussey worked as designer, when the Principia College project permitted, and George Loorz came to supervise whenever San Simeon work slowed down.

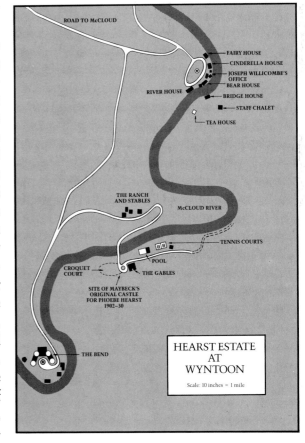

ROAD TO McCLOUD

FAIRY HOUSE
CINDERELLA HOUSE
JOSEPH WILLICOMBE'S OFFICE
BEAR HOUSE
RIVER HOUSE
BRIDGE HOUSE
STAFF CHALET
TEA HOUSE

THE RANCH AND STABLES

McCLOUD RIVER

TENNIS COURTS

POOL
CROQUET COURT
THE GABLES

SITE OF MAYBECK'S ORIGINAL CASTLE FOR PHOEBE HEARST 1902–30

THE BEND

HEARST ESTATE AT WYNTOON

Scale: 10 inches = 1 mile

Top, left: Seventeenth-century stone capital, Fairy House

Top, right: New stone capital, Fairy House, carved as a counterpart to the old one

Center, left: Doorway, Bear House, with hinges by Otto Olson

Center, right: Stairway, Bear House

Bottom, left: Fireplace, Cinderella House

Bottom, right: Fireplace, Cinderella House

Top: Ceiling carved by Jules Suppo, Cinderella House

Center: Carved-wood decoration by Jules Suppo, Fairy House

Bottom: Carved-wood paneling by Jules Suppo, Fairy House

The three guesthouses at Wyntoon were named Cinderella; Snow White–Rose Red or the Bear; and Angel, Sleeping Beauty, or Fairy. In the early 1930s Willy Pogany, a muralist from New York and Hollywood, painted scenes from the Grimm tales on the exterior surfaces of the first two. (These were repainted by his son in the early 1980s, in a style strongly influenced by Walt Disney.) Winter set in before he reached the third house, and he never returned: Angel House remains undecorated half-timber and has never been completely finished inside.

The most interesting of the three and the one most used is Bear House, where Hearst had his own living quarters. He and Marion Davies lived there during at least one winter of World War II because San Simeon was considered vulnerable to attack from sea and air; the cold winters were too much for their old dogs, as the pet cemetery attests. Almost every inch of the stucco exterior is given over to the portrayal of the Grimms' story of Snow White and Rose Red, the two lovely maidens whose kindness released the prince from his enchantment as a bear. The characters had first been portrayed by Day in an innocently folkloric manner. When Pogany came on the job from Hollywood, he expanded and enlivened the decorations, using local models and adding a pronounced eroticism: the blonde heroine now resembled Marion Davies, while the prince emerging from his bear enchantment had Hearst's mien.[3] The bear was a special totem of Hearst's and, of course, is also the California emblem. The murals, unfinished and somewhat faded, underscore the romantic atmosphere of the place.

Pet cemetery, Wyntoon

The recessed entrance to the Bear House has a tower-shaped overhang upheld by sturdy brackets from which hang iron lanterns. The carved wooden door with huge decorative iron hinges leads into a central hall with a stairway curving into the tower. Carved wood covers the vents and radiators (at Hearst's insistence the houses all have central steam heat, essential for comfort in that cold and snowy climate). In addition, a sixteenth-century Austrian fireplace with a faience mantel, which Hearst had purchased in 1913 from the collector Frances Fleming, was installed in the Bear House in 1934. Interior wood paneling and decorative elements are all made of the local soft fir and pine. Some of the carving is in high relief, with a flowing abstraction that creates a magically alive effect. In all of the houses, bathrooms with colorful tile were crafted by the Rankins of Oakland, artisans favored by Morgan.

Cinderella House is clearly identified by exterior paintings telling the

Right: River view of Bear House

Below: Tiled shower, Bear House

Below, right: Details of Bear House murals, painted in the early 1930s by Willy Pogany

Cinderella House, with
murals by Willy Pogany

Antler chandelier,
Cinderella House

Top, left: Fairy House, with seventeenth-century German fountain in foreground

Top, right: Entrance to Fairy House

Below: Bear fountain by Hanna Gaertner, 1930s

Cinderella story. Its symmetrical gables and turrets fit perfectly into the steep topography, carrying out the lines of mountain and forest. The high-ceilinged living room provides an impressive place for large gatherings of guests. The Hearst Corporation still uses it for occasional meetings, and various members of the family vacation there. The third house, never completed inside, was never formally named; in Morgan's drawings it is called Angel House and Fairy House. The layout of the three houses recalls the arrangements at San Simeon, although Wyntoon was to offer accommodations for sixty to one hundred guests, while at San Simeon ten to fifty was more the expected number.

Wyntoon was being developed by Hearst as a place to house his collection of Germanic art, several carloads of which were shipped there (some objects remain uncrated in Angel House). Stone mantels, porcelain and faience stoves, and antler chandeliers are part of the collection still on view. Integrated around the green as part of the design are various works of art, including a seventeenth-

Top: View from River House, looking down the McCloud River toward the Bend

Center: Bridge House (left) and River House, viewed from up-river, across from Bear House

Bottom: View of Bridge House from River House. Bridge House, designed by Morgan in the early 1930s to serve as a movie theater for Hearst's guests at Wyntoon, makes witty reference to Bernard Maybeck's original castle for Phoebe Hearst. Although only a "temporary" shingled tower with gabled sides, Bridge House recalls in its lofty angularity the far grander stone castle built in 1902 and destroyed by fire in 1930.

Opposite: Bridge House

century fountain from the castle of Buxbeim near Würzburg, which features a 25-foot marble shaft circled by Eros figures, and *Diana and a Fawn*, a copy by Paul Traverse of a contemporary marble sculpture by Paul Manship. At one side of Bear House stands a sculptured stone fountain, with bear and cub in the center of a basin carved with zodiacal figures. In connection with this work, made in Austria by Hanna Gaertner, Morgan wrote to Hearst on April 7, 1939: "It would be interesting if the sculptress could have the opportunity of seeing it as well as to 'unveil it.'" Morgan also refers to "such cruel treatment of her co-religionists, people of fine quality." Hearst wrote to Ambassador Joseph Kennedy to try to bring Gaertner to America, but the results, if any, of his attempts are unknown.

Next to Bear House, Morgan designed a modest shingled bungalow that served as a newspaper and switchboard headquarters whenever Hearst was in residence. Joseph Willicombe, Hearst's secretary for twenty-two years, and Willicombe's secretary, Jean Henry, ran what *Fortune* called the nerve center of the Hearst Empire. It resembled a Signal Corps operation,

Top: River House, which had been built before 1900, when Wyntoon still belonged to Charles Stetson Wheeler. According to a 1935 article in *Fortune,* William Randolph Hearst "plans to replace it with a great Teutonic structure which will straddle the turbulent river." Instead, Morgan remodeled it as an additional guesthouse.

Bottom, left: Fountain and small pool beside River House

Bottom, right: Tea House, 1935, with terrace for dancing

Opposite: Tea House, with boat landing

Top: The Gables, 1937, which burned in 1945

Center: The Bend under construction, mid-1930s

Bottom: Dining room, the Bend, c. 1936

with three operators on duty twenty-four hours a day. This building has now been remodeled for use as a dining room and kitchen for guests at Wyntoon. Across the bridge at a curve in the river still stands Bridge House, a "temporary" wooden building with a tower, which was used for showing the nightly movies to Hearst and his visitors while the next entertainment building, called the Tea House, was being planned to include a boat dock, a terrace for dancing, and space for games. The Gables, a stone and half-timber structure that could seat sixty dinner guests, was completed in 1937. It had a lounge that was also used for showing movies, pending construction of the large main building, the Bend, which was to be a reconstruction and enlargement of the early Wheeler house that had enticed Phoebe Hearst to the area. The loss of the Gables to fire in 1945, with its many tapestries and decorative arts, was a bad blow to Hearst and to Morgan.[4] A chalet was added in the mid-1920s for staff quarters.

The pool at Wyntoon is along the river, adjoining the tennis courts. Sheathed in blue-green marble, it was surrounded by floors of ornamental tile and marble, with dressing rooms at one end and at the other a special wide deck filled with sand two or three feet deep, for sunbathing on "the beach." Fortune magazine called the pool a "sylvan jewel" where "the chill mountain water is heated . . . a swimming hole perfectly appointed, which dazzles you as you come on it unexpectedly while strolling through the woods. An instructor attends at all hours, and outfits the guests with costumes. Men receive trunks and colored towels ten feet square."[5] The article pointed out that "The No. 1 Bathhouse is labeled 'WRH.' " The pool is now a ruin, abandoned for a newer one at the Bend.

Morgan's involvement in the Wyntoon complex from 1924 into the 1940s represented almost as great a part of her practice as San Simeon had, much of it concurrent with the latter. Her heart was clearly in the place, as it was in San Simeon, to the point that she wished to bring it to completion even without any remuneration for her own work. Her letters repeatedly reveal her enthusiasm for Wyntoon. On July 7, 1937, she wrote to him: "Wyntoon is at its best—tiger lilies out. Wild roses and foliage beautifully clean and fresh from late rains—houses too are cheerfully crisp and fresh." On September 9, 1939, Morgan wrote to him: "Anything else I can do for

Left: Two views of the Bend. The bottom view is seen through the arched doorway of Willis Polk's original building.

Below: Staff chalet, 1925

the rest of the year at Wyntoon, please allow me to do without any question of commission." Work on the Bend was still in progress during the early 1940s, under the direction of Warren McClure and George Loorz, from Morgan's office, who were working from her plans with slim funding from the Hearst Corporation. Construction had been halted and restarted ever since the late 1930s, but it seems to have wound down by November 18, 1943, when McClure wrote to Morgan, "Crew shrunk to 1 carpenter and a wood carver (Romolo) carving for Bend room." Finally, and reluctantly, Morgan turned her attention to other projects.

Back on the central coast, Hearst had earlier told Morgan to go ahead with the construction of a road to connect San Simeon to the valley across the mountains, where he was planning yet another splendid but isolated retreat. By 1936 Morgan had completed an elaborate hunting lodge to accommodate Hearst's romantic notion that his guests would ride horseback over thirty some miles to spend a night or weekend at Jolon (originally called the Milpitas Ranch), near the mission of San Antonio de Padua. A great reinforced-concrete Mission-style hacienda was erected,

Morgan at Wyntoon, after an ear operation left her face temporarily distorted. She wrote on April 19, 1933: "The face has not yet regained its normal form. For an architect, it is more or less embarassing [sic] to present so unsymmetrical an appearance."

with private apartments connected to large dining and assembly spaces and a powerful curved stairway leading to a spectacular second-floor room with an octagonal dome. A road and bridges were built across the mountains, but the rare excursions that were made to the lodge were usually by motor car, taking the longer but easier way around. The hacienda's thick concrete walls and massive stone colonnades surrounding a courtyard make an impressive sight, often mistaken by travelers for the nearby mission.[6] Although on a far grander scale, Jolon recalls the bunkhouse that Morgan built during the same period (but on a much tighter budget) behind

Above: George Hearst house and pool, Hillsborough, 1930–31

Below and opposite: San Francisco Hearst Building, remodeled by Morgan in 1937, with detail of grillwork

Senator Hearst's original ranch house at San Simeon. That bunkhouse is still used from time to time by ranch hands during roundup season and by sundry Hearst and Sunical employees.

A third-generation Hearst became a client of Morgan's when Hearst's oldest son, George, commissioned her to convert his house in Hillsborough, a few miles south of San Francisco, to a California version of the White House. To the existing structure Morgan added columns, wings, Palladian windows, and a circular driveway, plus a large pool. The effect was imposing enough to satisfy George Hearst's ambition of entertaining political visitors in style. Completed in 1931, this is another example of Morgan's ability to create a kind of stage setting, and the house, recently sold to its third owner, is still a showplace. There must have been an operatic instinct hidden behind her austere professional demeanor, something that responded to a similar chord in a family so often on stage.

Morgan's commercial commissions for the Hearsts included a major remodeling of the San Francisco Hearst Building in 1937, which entailed adding a spacious marble lobby and a decorative facade, along with improvements in office space and a radio broadcasting studio. She also built radio transmitting-and-receiving stations for the Hearst Globe Wireless Company.

Two of these "news-forwarding stations" were near San Francisco—at Bayshore, Redwood City, and at Cahill Ridge, San Mateo. A snapshot of the Bayshore station in 1936 shows a square stucco building with a tile roof and groups of four windows on each side of a three-panel door, set in the midst of flat, uninhabited land punctuated by tall antenna poles. Henry Bogardus, who was in charge of the station from 1936 to 1938, said it was "built like a battleship," snug and compact with everything functioning smoothly. The plan to extend the chain across the country failed because the needed frequencies could not be obtained, and the buildings fell to the advancing freeways of the postwar era.

The multistory Oakland Post-Enquirer Building of 1918 (demolished in the 1960s) was a commission that came through Morgan's Hearst connections, as it was a part of Hearst's media empire. Still another Hearst-related commission came in 1928 from MGM for Hearst's Cosmopolitan Headquarters in Hollywood. This project included a bungalow with a projection room and set as well as an elaborate

drawing room, sitting room, and bath that would be portable via two trucks.[7] Morgan worked it out in two parts, creating a structure not unlike later mobile homes. She favored the California Mission style for both the bungalow and the drawing room, but for the set Morgan designed an Art Deco fireplace that appeared in several films, including *Gertie's Penthouse Apartment*, a 1930s film that may never have been released (a photo of the set is in the Morgan Collection at Cal Poly).

Projection room, Cosmopolitan Headquarters, Hollywood, 1928

Site for the Babicora Hacienda, in Chihuahua, Mexico, photographed September 1, 1943

Julia Morgan was fortunate in having relatively few projects for which plans and drawings were made without any construction taking place. Most of these unbuilt projects were commissioned by William Randolph Hearst, whose dreams were not always consistent with his finances. It is difficult to comprehend that a figure as conspicuously powerful as Hearst, with inherited assets in gold, silver, and copper mines plus thousands of acres of land, could be genuinely and consistently unable to pay his bills without elaborate negotiation. Yet it was the Hearst Corporation that controlled the purse strings, and the corporation took a dim view of Hearst's grandiose building projects. Sometimes he was in such a financial bind that Morgan would refuse to take a commission or accept fees for work designed but not built. At the same time, she was scrupulous about protecting her contractors and craftsmen from being out of pocket. Several times during the San Simeon years she submitted her resignation because she couldn't pay her workmen, although her heart was clearly involved in the work. Hearst never accepted her resignation, and the Hearst Corporation came through each time with a pared-down budget.

Occasionally, political rather than economic pressures kept a Hearst project from being built. For instance, Morgan had prepared plans for a cabin, a hotel, and possibly a desert house on the South Rim of the Grand Canyon. The cabin was constructed in 1914, but a newly developed policy blocking private building in the park prevented construction of the hotel, originally planned for 1936. The cabin was taken over by the National Park Service in 1941 and finally demolished about 1950.

Events both political and economic combined to prevent the realization of Hearst's Babicora Hacienda in Chihuahua, northwestern Mexico. There was an adobe ranch house already on the 900,000-acre cattle ranch when it was purchased by Senator Hearst, but when his son decided to make it his southern headquarters, the plans were much aggrandized. The plans show a classical

one-story Spanish adobe structure with a large recreation room on one side and an indoor pool on the other, while thirteen bedrooms with baths flank the central patio. Servants were to live in another building. During World War II Morgan's letters to Hearst reported step by step on the difficult negotiations (her 1943 letters, with replies from Hearst, are the principal source for our knowledge of the Babicora project). She made several trips to Mexico City and to Babicora, arranging the purchase of materials (for the thirteen bathrooms, for instance) not easy to come by in wartime and hiring workmen to carry out the plans.

Hearst wrote on November 4, 1943, that "if there is a choice between monotony and expense, we will choose monotony. We have to. . . . The Company is paying so we have to adhere to the original estimate." And the next week he wrote, "We can build this house on the installment plan if necessary—get some of it finished in 1944 and the rest in 1945." After several more letters about the cost, including a suggestion to cut the number of bedrooms and baths to nine, Hearst wrote in December 1943 that if there were too many obstacles and expenses it might be better to abandon the project and secure a place in Cuernavaca, or "maybe sell Babicora and get a sugar plantation—let's get the information and come to a conclusion." Talk of Mexican confiscation of property held by foreigners reinforced the Hearst Corporation's reluctance to underwrite another expensive building project. And Hearst himself was conscious of his advancing age (in contrast to the often-repeated stories of his avoiding any mention of death). He wrote to Morgan on December 6, 1943, in connection with the difficulties of getting materials: "No one knows how long this war will last. Or how long I will last, for that matter."

By June 15, 1944, the project seemed to be indefinitely postponed, although still considered pending, for Morgan wrote, "the materials assembled are first class and should not deteriorate," and "I will send you in the next few days a roll of the full size details for record with this use in mind." Her drawings show that she was still working on the new hacienda as late as 1945. This project would have been a grand culmination of Morgan's experience in designing pools and great houses, but no structural work was ever done, beyond excavating the foundation, and her drawings and reports are all that remain of this final Hearst commission. In 1953, two years after

Drawing of proposed hacienda at Babicora, 1943

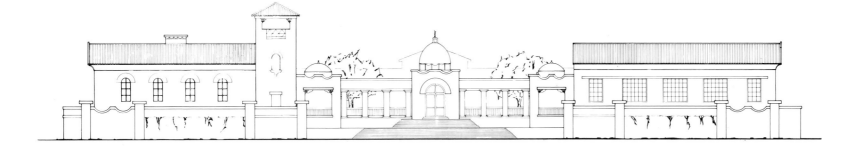

Hearst's death, the Mexican government bought the Babicora ranch for $2.5 million.[8]

Morgan's most important commission of the 1940s was the one perhaps dearest to her: the proposed Medieval Museum for San Francisco. This final unfinished project, which began at Hearst's behest, was the adaptation into a museum of part of a Spanish monastery, Santa Maria de Ovila, that he had bought and then had dismantled and shipped to a warehouse in San Francisco in 1931. It must be remembered that the revolutionary situation in Spain during the early 1930s meant that all buildings that had belonged to the Church were threatened and many were converted into houses and barns or demolished in order to make use of the stone for other buildings. It is easy to understand, therefore, that collectors such as Hearst and dealers such as Morgan's old friend Arthur Byne, who recommended that Hearst buy the monastery, were eager to save these buildings as works of art.

After Maybeck and Morgan's plans for a genuine castle at Wyntoon—which would have incorporated the monastery's refectory and most of its stones—had to be dropped for lack of funds, Morgan convinced Hearst that he should make a gift of the stones and her plan to the city of San Francisco. This would enable them to have a medieval museum that would ultimately surpass in its authenticity and in its collection the recently constructed Cloisters branch of the Metropolitan Museum of Art in New York. Morgan drew up sheaves of plans, the city government welcomed the gift, and a Golden Gate Park site was selected.[9] A model was carefully constructed under Morgan's watchful eyes by Cecilia Bancroft Graham, a sculptor whose work had been a feature of the 1939 Golden Gate Exposition at Treasure Island. (It was this exposition that named Morgan "California's Most Distinguished Woman Architect.")

Although Morgan was in her seventies, she was determined to build a museum that would be a source of pride for her city. The *San Francisco Chronicle* of May 22, 1941, published a sketch of the way it would look. *Architect and Engineer* ran an article in the July 1944 issue entitled "From Spain to California—Ancient Monastery to Rise Again." In readiness for construction the stones, each carefully numbered and crated with excelsior packing, were moved to the park, near the M. H. de Young Memorial Museum. Yet the museum was never built. Fires in 1941 and 1942, thought to be the result of arson, burned the crates holding the stones. Morgan and Steilberg relabeled the stones, but three more fires seriously harmed some of them, while others were scattered or used for the Japanese Tea House garden. After all the fires the enthusiasm of the city government cooled, especially as it was under pressure to save Golden Gate Park from what parts of the community considered encroachment by the museum. The 34-foot-high Gothic portal was set up in the de Young Museum in 1965, and the model by Graham is still in storage there, along with all the plans and correspondence, though it is most unlikely any use will ever be made of them.

Morgan's relationship with Hearst has been the subject of speculation by almost everyone who has been to San Simeon or has encountered other results of their collaboration. It is indeed uncommon for a client and architect to forge a bond as close as theirs was over some twenty-five years. The powerful, driving character of Hearst melted before the quiet authority of his architect. Humor and imagination strengthened their bonds, while the exhilaration of bringing fine plans to reality helped overcome the frustrating lack of fiscal stability. Disappointments were many, but there always seemed to be a new vision ahead.

9

▨▨▨▨▨▨▨▨▨▨▨▨▨▨▨▨▨▨▨▨▨▨▨▨▨▨▨▨▨▨▨▨▨▨▨▨

THE END OF A LIFE

To some degree every biography must end sadly, with the death of the protagonist. In Julia Morgan's case the sadness is deepened because her last few years were spent as a recluse who no longer cared to live after her working life had come to a close. Her most devoted clients had died, with Hearst's death in 1951 preceded by many others. Morgan lived to see the sweeping changes brought on by the International Style in architecture along with the complete discrediting of the Beaux-Arts training that had been so central to her aesthetic. In the new architectural canon the use of ornament and most historical allusion in design was scorned, even held to be dishonest. Morgan's high hopes for the San Francisco Medieval Museum as the crowning achievement of her many years of practice were doomed by events entirely out of her control. As for her office, there was no one to continue her practice, and no practice left given the turnaround in the philosophy of design and the state of the architect's health after she turned seventy-nine.

So it was that in 1951 Morgan closed her office in the Merchants Exchange Building, which had been the center of her practice since 1907. In that same year she asked for and received emeritus status in the American Institute of Architects. She saw to it that Otto Haake, the building superintendent who had always considered himself her friend, burned her files and blueprints and most of her office records, on the grounds that her clients had copies of their own material and no one else would be interested. In fact, no one was. Morgan brought home to her Divisadero Street basement her Beaux-Arts drawings and memorabilia and her files and correspondence with William Randolph Hearst.

Morgan had felt alone personally ever since the death in 1940 of her younger brother, Avery, for whom she had always taken responsibility. Her sister, Emma, although she visited Julia frequently, was absorbed in her own life in Berkeley. There were only two Morgan grandchildren: Parmelee's unmarried daughter, Judith, teaching in Los Angeles, and Emma's son, Mor-

Opposite: Julia Morgan, 1947 photograph from her passport

gan North, busy with his family and career. Most of Morgan's staff and her friends in construction had gone on to other work; her old coworkers Steilberg, Hussey, and Dahl have expressed regret at not having attempted to see her in her last years. Her cousin Pierre LeBrun had died, as had Chaussemiche, her mentor in Paris, who had visited her in San Francisco and whom she had seen again on a visit to Paris in the 1930s. His young daughter, who had followed in Morgan's footsteps at the Ecole and greatly admired her, had died in childbirth. The young women who rented apartments in Morgan's remodeled Victorian house were friendly and certainly fond of her, but they too had their own professional lives and preoccupations.

Travel, always a stimulating pleasure for Morgan, lost some of its savor when, on a 1947 freighter voyage to Portugal and Spain, she failed to return to the ship at the appointed time and was, as a consequence, not permitted

ashore at the next port. She began to recognize in herself the dreaded loss of faculties, something she was never ready to accept. When an expedition to her old haunts in Oakland ended in a mugging and hospitalization, the harsh realization of her limitations was borne in upon her. She returned to her apartment and engaged a nurse-companion from New Zealand who had no association with her earlier life. Aware of being very much alone in her world and also aware of her diminishing memory and physical energy, Morgan simply turned her face to the wall of her small bedroom, closing out the world. She did not emerge during the last four years of her life. Her two closest remaining client-friends, Else Schilling and Johanna Volkmann (both board members for the YWCA Residence in San Francisco), were discouraged from visiting, although they were devoted friends. Only the young women in her apartments and her faithful secretary, Mrs. Lillian Forney, were regular visitors.

When her death on February 2, 1957, was announced in Bay Area newspapers, Morgan was given recognition as a distinguished architect. The *San Francisco Chronicle* of February 3

Emma North (left) and Flora North (right) seeing Morgan off on a freighter trip around South America and to Portugal and Spain, her last major voyage

headed a two-column account with "Noted Architect Julia Morgan Dies After Long Illness." A month later a committee of Morgan's friends announced the establishment of the Julia Morgan Memorial Fund at the University of California, an endowment fund for the aid of architecture students. James LeFeaver, her engineer–office manager during the latter part of her career, was the spokesman in charge of fund-raising, which was launched by a gift of $10,000 from Miss Schilling and Miss Volkmann. Scholarship funds have since been pooled, so the Julia Morgan Endowment has not received any public recognition, but students of architecture over the years have been helped by the income. Since Morgan aided many other young people throughout her life with informal scholarships to preparatory through graduate schools this was an appropriate memorial.

Morgan's own succinct summation of her practice can be found in her answers to a questionnaire circulated by the American Institute of Architects in 1946, five years before she closed her office. The survey was intended to determine the number and kinds of architectural firms in the United States and probably also helped the Institute to direct large-scale postwar government projects to its members best able to handle such commissions. (Morgan indicated that she did "not wish to be considered for the *Register of Architects Qualified for Federal Public Works*.") Each architect was asked to list three projects each, in categories ranging from $300,000 to more than $1 million (which would have eliminated most domestic architecture). Morgan responded as follows:

NAME OF PROJECT	COST	LOCATION	OWNER
(a) Three Projects Not Exceeding Cost of $300,000:			
The Kings Daughters Home for Incurables		Oakland	
Ranch Administration Center (now [Hunter Liggett] Army Camp)		Jolon, Cal.	U.S.A.
Hollywood Studio Club		Hollywood, Cal.	Club
(b) Three Projects Costing from $300,000 to $1,000,000:			
University of Cal. Women's Gymnasium	$650,000.00	Berkeley, Cal.	University of Cal.
Honolulu Y.W.C.A.	$350,000.00	Honolulu, T.H.	Honolulu Y.W.C.A.
Berkeley Women's City Club	$350,000.00	Berkeley, Cal.	Club Corporation
(c) Three Projects Costing Over $1,000,000:			
San Simeon Development		San Luis Obispo Co. Cal.	Sunical
Wyntoon Development		Shasta Co., Cal.	Land & Livestock Co.

She also submitted photographs of a good cross section of her work, including the Chinese and Honolulu YWCAs, houses of various types, and several views of San Simeon. It was a record to be proud of.

Introduction (pages 7–17)

1. England had pioneered in the use of reinforced concrete, and France followed suit. Morgan was familiar with European examples of the technology to an extent unusual for architects at that time.

2. In addition Morgan maintained an interest in Chinese art that had originated during her student days in Paris, when the Trocadero Museum opened up a whole new view of the Orient. Walter Steilberg reports having found Morgan bent over efforts to reproduce Chinese calligraphy, and letters to Hearst show her enthusiasm for the plan to have a Chinese Cottage at San Simeon.

3. Morgan's house for Congressman Ralph R. Eltse (1915) is remarkable for its skillful avoidance of rectangular spaces, which made his wife uncomfortable. The stucco building hugs a rugged site in the Berkeley hills; it has been extensively remodeled, but the asymmetrical dining room remains as it was originally built, with no right angles.

1. The Early Years (pages 19–25)

1. Julia Morgan to Walter Steilberg, undated (written during World War II when Steilberg was in Alaska), photocopy in author's collection.

2. Morgan's first American ancestor had emigrated from Wales in 1636, arriving at Sandy Bay, near Gloucester, Massachusetts; he founded a long line in that state and in New Bedford, Connecticut, where Charles Morgan grew up. Other relatives included the Bill family (from whom Morgan got his middle name), who were prominent in Connecticut politics, and the Gardners and the Bulkleys (names given to Charles Morgan's third son), who founded important insurance companies in Hartford, Connecticut.

3. Charles Morgan to Julia Morgan, 1902, Julia Morgan Collection, Robert E. Kennedy Library, California Polytechnic State University, San Luis Obispo; hereafter cited as *Morgan Collection*. This is the principal collection of Julia Morgan's correspondence, photos, drawings, and memorabilia. Unless otherwise indicated, all correspondence cited in the text is from this source.

4. When Morgan received an honorary doctorate from the University of California, Berkeley, in 1929, a former grade-school teacher wrote to congratulate her: "You must have looked sweet at the happy moment, just as you used to look as a gentle eight-year-old child in Riverside [Grammar School] when all the prizes came your way."

5. Charles Morgan to Julia Morgan, April 16, 1896. That Morgan did not similarly distinguish herself in English is clear from a comment by Professor William Dallam Armes that her paper "The Value of the Study of Literature" contained "much good thought but [is] narrow in scope and not free from errors in spelling and syntax." Spelling was an art that Morgan never was able to master.

2. Ecole des Beaux-Arts (pages 27–39)

1. Julia Morgan to Aurelia Reinhardt, September 10, 1917, library, Mills College, Oakland.

2. Pierre LeBrun wrote to her in consolation, April 12, 1898: "We all feel that you have made a splendid fight for recognition against great odds and are proving how earnestly you must love your chosen art. But you must be careful not to overestimate your physical endurance. It seems to us that you are working too hard, & no one is there to notice it & warn you of the consequences. Several of the Beaux Arts fellows here have told me that the entrance ordeal is something tremendous. If you did not succeed in getting in they cannot at least deprive you of the proud position you have taken in the *annals of the Ecole* (Archtl Dept.) as the *first of your sex* to brave the terrors of their entrance examination. It appears to me that by attending the lectures, & by your atelier work & sketching & reading & the observation of things architectural all around you, you are doing about as well as if you were a full fledged member of the Ecole. Your whole life is full of the things that make for progress & development & an enlarged capacity for inspiration & the enjoyment of the inspirations of others, as you will only fully realize when you return to these scenes & look at them from your new vantage ground. It would be grand if, when your brother comes to Paris, you & he could make a good tour—*a leisurely tour of North & Central Italy* say, & see Rome, Venise [*sic*], Florence, and many other choice spots of earth that cluster so thickly there, where great artists & builders have expended their best efforts & left so generous and enduring a legacy of beauty. There is nothing so educating—so thoroughly fertilizing to the perceptive faculties as intelligent travels, and the aftermath is inexhaustible."

3. An interesting coincidence almost surely unnoted by either party is that 1898 also marked Ethel Mary Charles's success as the first woman architect to pass the examinations for the Royal Institute of British Architects (RIBA). Charles maintained her own practice in London during much of the time that Morgan was operating in San Francisco. Charles has remained generally unknown to architectural historians, although some of her drawings are at RIBA. Margaret Richardson, *The Craft Architects* (New York: Rizzoli; London: Royal Institute of British Architects, 1983), pp. 68–69.

4. Julia Morgan to Eliza Morgan, February 11, 1899.

5. Julia Morgan to Mr. and Mrs. Pierre LeBrun, July 31, 1898.

6. Jean-Paul Carlhian, a student at the Ecole just before World War II and later professor at the Harvard School of Design and a partner in Shepley, Bulfinch, Richardson and Abbott, in Boston, noted in conversation with the author how unusual it was to find *esquisses* preserved and that he knew of no other complete series of efforts toward any *projet rendu*, making the Morgan material especially valuable as evidence of the way students worked at the turn of the century. Morgan's Beaux-Arts drawings are in the Documents Collection, College of Environmental Design, University of California, Berkeley; hereafter cited as *Documents Collection*.

7. Brown's drawing, which Morgan kept with her Beaux-Arts material, is now in the Documents Collection. He was later to build a city hall in San Francisco and another in Berkeley, both with towers, although neither duplicated his Beaux-Arts exercises. Morgan's first major independent commission was the Mills College Campanil, a bell tower in no way related to her drawing at the Ecole.

8. Armand Guérinet, *Médailles des concours d'architecture à l'Ecole des Beaux-Arts: 4ᵉ année scolaire, 1901–1902* (Paris, 1901–2), plate 76.

9. Morgan's Ecole Competitions, in Chronological Order

NATURE OF COMPETITION	DATE OF JUDGMENT	REWARDS	POINTS
Second Class, enrolled Nov. 1898			
Sculpture	Dec. 23, 1898	Mention	1
Ornamental Drawing	Dec. 23, 1898	Mention	1
Drawing	Feb. 3, 1899	Mention	1
Sculpture	Feb. 3, 1899	Mention	1
Analytic Elements of Architecture	Mar. 9, 1899	2d Mention	1
Descriptive Geometry	Mar. 30, 1899	Mention	2
Mathematics	Mar. 31, 1899	Mention	2
Analytical Elements of Architecture	May 4, 1899	2d Mention	1
Drawing	May 30, 1899	3d Medal	1½
Projet rendu	July 6, 1899	2d Mention	1
Stereotomy	Aug. 4, 1899	3d Medal	3
Perspective	Oct. 20, 1899	Mention	2
			(enough for 1st class)
Projet rendu	Jan. 11, 1900	2d Mention	1
Esquisse	Jan. 11, 1900	2d Mention	1
Projet rendu	Mar. 8, 1900	2d Mention	1
Exercises in History of Architecture	Mar. 22, 1900	Mention	1
Projet rendu	July 5, 1900	2d Mention	1
Projet rendu	Aug. 2, 1900	2d Mention	1
Construction	Aug. 6, 1900	Mention	2
First Class, accepted Aug. 6, 1900			
Concours Godeboeuf: *Projet rendu—* Campanile	Dec. 24, 1900	1st Mention	1

Projet rendu— Museum for Seat of Local Government	Apr. 2, 1901	1st Mention	1
History of Architecture	May 14, 1901	Mention	1
Projet rendu— Lecture Hall for an Institute	July 16, 1901	1st Mention	1
Guadet competition: *Esquisse—* Scaffold for Church	Oct. 8, 1901	2d Mention	½
Drawing	Nov. 26, 1901	Mention	1
Sculpture	Nov. 26, 1901	Mention	1
Projet rendu— Vestibule the Length of a Building	Dec. 3, 1901	2d No. 2 Medal	1½
Concours Godeboeuf: *Projet rendu—* Stairway Balustrade for a Palace	Dec. 24, 1901	2d Medal	2
Projet rendu— Theater for a Palace	Feb. 4, 1902	1st Mention	1

3. The Morgan Atelier (pages 41–49)

1. The degree to which Morgan was involved in the Merchants Exchange Building before she moved her office there remains unclear. During the remodeling of the Trading Room in 1975–76, the original hall (where merchants of grain, hay, gold, and marine equipment met to barter their goods) was restored and reborn as the Chartered Bank of London. This brought new attention to Morgan's role in designing the decorative elements for the building. Otto Haake (the building superintendent and a lifelong employee of the Merchants Exchange) recalled that she was responsible for changing that large hall from an open place where traders actually brought their wagons to a more refined but still clearly maritime center where the captains sat bargaining at tables. She commissioned William A. Coulter, whose sketches of arriving ships appeared regularly in the *San Francisco Call*, to execute five 6-by-18-foot oil paintings of ships in various world ports, which she placed in arched frames around the room. Ships are also portrayed in eight lunettes 40 inches in diameter that fill the triangular spaces between the large murals and the archways on the opposite side of the hall. Details of the ornate brackets and coffered ceiling reflect a Beaux-Arts education, as do the massive columns faced in marble. Lighting fixtures and carved-wood details throughout the building are attributed to Morgan by Haake. Ansel Adams, whose father was one of the founders and officers of the Merchants Exchange, told the author that he recalled seeing Morgan daily when he worked there as elevator operator during school vacations, and he understood that she was responsible for the interior decoration of the building.

2. The procedures in the office and the quality of the atmosphere are well documented in taped interviews conducted during the 1970s with people who had worked in Morgan's office. This material, gathered by the Bancroft Library Regional Oral History Office, University of California, Berkeley, into two volumes entitled, "The Julia Morgan Architectural History Project" (1976), edited by Suzanne B. Riess, includes conversations|with|Walter|Steilberg, an architect and engineer of some distinction who had come to the office in the Merchants Exchange Building in 1910. Even after he left to work on his own he remained a close associate and friend as long as Morgan was in practice. He returned in 1931 to be her representative in Spain for the Santa Maria de Ovila project. Others interviewed include Dorothy Wormser Coblentz, who was with Morgan from 1919 to 1923, before working with Henry Gutterson and later on her own; Edward Hussey and Bjarne Dahl, who worked with Morgan in the 1920s; and Polly McNaught, who was in the office during the 1930s. There are also photographs and letters from several young women who became architects with financial and professional assistance from Morgan, such as Charlotte Knapp, Elizabeth ("Bessie") Boyter, and C. (Charlotte) Julian Mesic. Unless otherwise indicated, all subsequent quotations in this chapter are from this source.

3. That Morgan traveled fairly often and fairly far can be seen from the following list of her travels (this does not include her many trips to San Simeon and Wyntoon):

1872	November—to Brooklyn Heights, New York, for her christening (she returned for Emma's in 1874 and for Avery's in 1876).
1878–79	Spent most of year with mother and siblings in Morristown, New Jersey, and Brooklyn.
1896	March—to Boston, New Bedford, and New York, then to Paris with Jessica Peixotto.
1896	August—to Switzerland and Germany, with Jessica Peixotto and Miss Kalisher, a music student from San Francisco.
1897	July—to Chartres and Saint-Germain-en-Laye with the Arthur Browns and the Bernard Maybecks; August—to Luzarches for a month, to Bellefontaine, and back to Paris.
1898	November—four-day trip to Amiens with Avery.
1899	Summer—to Avignon, Genoa, Pisa, Florence, and Rome with Avery.
1902	Summer—to New York from Paris; to Oakland a month later.
1919, 1920	To Salt Lake City for YWCA commission.
1920–21	To Hawaii for Atherton YWCA commission.
1924	To Boston, New Haven, Ann Arbor, and Princeton to examine university museums in anticipation of the U.C. Berkeley commission.
1928	January 28–February 11—to Honolulu for commission.
1929	December—to New York City to see relatives and friends.
1931–32	To Naples, Germany, Austria, Florence, Paris, Holland, and Spain with Emma.
1935	To Acapulco via freighter, then through the Panama canal to Amalfi, Sicily, Venice, Siena, Florence, the English Lake District, and Stockholm.
1938	To Saint Louis for the Principia College commission. To New York, then to Sicily, Venice, Siena, Florence, and Switzerland.
1941, 1942, 1945	To Mexico for the Babicora project.
1944	To East Coast to see "dear faces in old bodies."
1947	All around South America then to the Azores, Portugal, and back to Los Angeles on December 11.

4. Walter Steilberg, draft for an unpublished article, 1969, Morgan Collection.

5. Adela Rogers St. John, interview with author, Atascadero, California, September 1975.

6. This letter, sent to Dahl in Honolulu, reveals a great deal about Morgan's character and working methods and is worth quoting in its entirety:

Dear Bj—

It was a relief to hear from you—I have thought of you three often—but as you say—the hours—days—months go so quickly.

I am returning the blueprints—think your design is improving—the chief defect being in not carrying scale well—This can be done by a little more care in keeping subdivisions of units, heights of like elements, etc. together by repeating of line or motif or glazing or what not.

I do hope the examination *was* successful,—it certainly was long enough, & with plenty of stress on the cultural.

I can't imagine the leper settlement work as anything but a great strain and worry—and am glad it is nearly over. The turn of the tide may be on us now —in any case it cannot be far off, probably will come very slowly over next winter and spring. What is needed is young courage and a realization that money in itself is but a small part of living, a means, not an end. I think the simpler living and a return to simpler pleasures is a healthful and worthwhile result, if the high level of wage and income is never reached again. I trust work will develope [*sic*] for you.

We have been fortunate in having enough to keep the old staff on until now —We all are going to have generous outings this summer, a couple of months each—and by then will know what to plan for next. No work actually in sight of any consequence. But this has happened before. TJ [Thaddeus Joy] is in bad shape still—is to have another rest period—the others and their familys [*sic*] happy.

Ed's [Edward Hussey] job [at Principia College] is completely closed down & I think he comes home with his family. He was much liked and appreciated at Elsah but the stocks and bonds with which the Bldgs were to be constructed fell so low that it seemed best to stop construction & mark time.

My own vacation will probably not come before next winter—as it will be necessary to watch for work as well as to do it.

& now to the most important—those pictures! What a young Hercules you and Eve are developing! and so good looking and jolly—We are delighted with him—and so glad to have the sweet glimse [sic] of Eve as well—Thank you both very much.

Your study idea is interesting and probably will fix periods etc in your mind. But I imagine what you need most is a freer design—a knowledge of the elements of various styles so that your hand rather than your mind will lead you into making more varied and interesting forms. You have a good sense of proportion and balance but you lack fullness & richness of expression. I'd suggest you watercolor & free hand draw (does that sound like familiar old advice?) never mind, it's just as true and as necessary—Why not try working in charcoal, making details of simple caps [capitals] ironwork, tile, large size on the wall, of vases, anything to call for decorative invention—as though your days & nights were not full enough already! Even if you can't afford "decoration," the practice will free your eye and hand.

Affectionate good wishes go with this to Eve & the young Bj and yourself,

from
Julia Morgan
May 29th, 1931

7. Bjarne Dahl, Bancroft Library Regional Oral History project and subsequent conversations with the author, 1975–87.
8. Albert Evers, interview with author, San Francisco, August 15, 1975.

4. On Campus, in Church, and at the Marketplace (pages 51–81)

1. After attending the Polytechnic Institute (MIT) and the Ecole des Beaux-Arts, Howard had worked in the H. H. Richardson office in Brooklyn and with McKim, Mead and White in New York. Appointed supervising architect at Berkeley in December 1901, Howard held that post until 1924; he directed the School of Architecture until 1927.
2. William Randolph Hearst to Julia Morgan, September 15, 1926, Documents Collection.
3. On the landing of the stairs leading to the library was originally a window (now unlocated) bearing the inscription "Margaret Carnegie Library." This came about because Susan Mills knew that Andrew Carnegie had offered a library building to any community ready to raise matching funds for books and personnel; she wrote to Carnegie saying that because their library had been designed by a woman architect to be used by women students she would like the building to be named for his daughter. A reply granting this favor as well as the funding was cordially and speedily sent by Mr. Carnegie. This seems to be the only Margaret Carnegie library.
4. Claiborne Hill to author, n.d.
5. Marian Simpson, personal communication to author, July 1975.
6. The photographs and insurance document, entitled *Trial by Fire*, are in the Morgan Collection.
7. A similar use of decorative letters is evident in the chapel at Asilomar and the Oakland YWCA.

5. The Women's Network (pages 83–127)

1. "The City Beautiful" is a term associated with Daniel Burnham and his plans for the Chicago World's Columbian Exposition of 1893. The aim was to have a beautiful city core that would include major public buildings united by architecture and by architectural spaces. Such planning was part of the turn-of-the-century efforts to re-form cities both politically and aesthetically. Californian examples may still be seen in Pasadena and in San Francisco.
2. Albro assisted Rivera on the following murals: *The Riders of California*, 1931, Luncheon Club, Pacific Stock Exchange; *Still Life and Blossoming Almond Trees*, 1931, Stern Hall, University of California, Berkeley; *The Making of a Fresco Showing the Building of a City*, 1931–32, San Francisco Art Institute; *Pan-American Unity*, 1940, Little Theater, City College of San Francisco.

3. Surprisingly, women's colleges and boarding schools seemed less eager to commission her services or those of other women architects. Scripps College in southern California was the only women's college started in California during Morgan's prime; she was not asked to design for it, despite her success at Mills. East Coast colleges for women, Smith and Bryn Mawr especially, embarked on building programs in the 1920s, but they did not commission women architects.
4. Helen A. David, November 1913 report, National YWCA Archives, New York.
5. Bjarne Dahl, Bancroft Oral History Project and conversation with author, June 15, 1980.
6. Julia Morgan to Nancy Woods Walburn, director of newspaper and magazine publicity, September 27, 1927.
7. David Gebhard and Robert Winter, *A Guide to Architecture in Los Angeles and Southern California* (Santa Barbara and Salt Lake City: Peregrine Smith, 1975), p. 403.
8. Hettie Belle Marcus, in Suzanne B. Riess, ed., "The Julia Morgan Architectural History Project" (Berkeley: Bancroft Library, Regional Oral History Office, University of California, 1976), vol. 2, p. 138.
9. Walter Steilberg, Morgan's engineer on the Heritage and on the Berkeley Baptist Divinity School of 1918, said that she had wanted terra-cotta trim on the latter, but her clients had preferred stone ornamentation. Morgan's love of color was not inconsistent with the English Free Style as revived in the early part of the century, notably by the Arts and Crafts architect Halsey Ricardo in England and by Charles Rennie Mackintosh in Glasgow.
10. Mrs. Edwin G. Klinck, letter to author, June 5, 1975.
11. The construction of the City Club pool proved to be quite a puzzle to Morgan's engineer in charge of the project. F. C. Stolte tossed and turned during a sleepless night after having spent a day trying to realize Morgan's plans for the wide-open span of concrete necessary to form the two massive arches that support the auditorium immediately above. Just about dawn he awoke with the formula absolutely clear to him. Stolte, interview with author, August 28, 1975.

6. Cottages and Mansions (pages 129–67)

1. Dorothy Stone Wolff to author, July 15, 1978.
2. These houses are illustrated in Alistair Service, *Edwardian Architecture* (Oxford: Oxford University Press, 1977), pp. 33 and 21, respectively.
3. Charles Adams Platt was a New York architect whose works were widely published. He is perhaps best known for having gotten the McCormick commission, in Lake Forest, Illinois, over competition that included Frank Lloyd Wright.
4. Mabel Urmy Seares, "Gardening Manual," *California Southland*, January 1921, p. 22.
5. Walter Steilberg, conversation with author, September 28, 1976.

7. The Hearsts and San Simeon (pages 169–215)

1. Julia Morgan to Phoebe Apperson Hearst, February 16, 1899, Bancroft Library, University of California, Berkeley.
2. The struggle between mother and son for the Pleasanton property has been documented by interviews conducted in the 1960s by Vonnie Eastham with Mrs. Hearst's ward, Anne Apperson Flint. The issue was settled when Mrs. Hearst moved in and her son moved on to New York, but that still leaves us unclear as to how much had been constructed before Julia Morgan returned from Paris.
3. Donald McLaughlin of Berkeley, who went to Pleasanton frequently as a guest from about 1900 on, recalled that Morgan extended the verandas of the main house; made additions to the music building, including a second story and a tower for Mrs. Hearst's bedroom; added another floor to the service buildings; and constructed a concrete Boys' House (Donald McLaughlin, conversations with author, 1976–80). William Randolph Hearst, Jr., recalls that the Boys' House was "several hundred feet, perhaps yards, away from the southernmost tip of the old Hacienda, as it was the intent of Grandma Hearst to give the younger group an area of their own" (letter to author, September 6, 1977).
4. Margaret Calder Hayes vividly described the Hacienda in an article recalling her visit there in 1917 ("A Weekend in the Country," *California Monthly* 90 [October 1980]: 25).
5. William Randolph Hearst, undated newspaper clipping, author's collection.
6. Bjarne Dahl, conversations with author, 1975 to present.

7. Edward Hussey, conversations with author, 1975 to about 1980.

8. Morgan's correspondence with Arthur Byne is part of the Morgan Collection.

9. Byne wrote to Morgan on January 15, 1934: "My only role in life is taking down old works of art, conserving them to the best of my ability and shipping them to America."

10. One elevator, Mr. Hearst's, linked his private quarters with the Assembly Room, while the other, in the New Wing, served the guests on upper floors. Both elevators had to be round (a bit of a problem for the Otis Co.) and were lined in carved wood, with shell and vine motifs.

11. Camille Solon, an English-French craftsman whom Morgan is said to have met at the 1915 Panama-Pacific International Exposition, created the painted-wood ceiling in the Gothic Study.

12. Marjorie Collord and Ann Rotanzi, *Castle Fare* (San Luis Obispo: Blake Printery, 1972), p. 33.

13. One Oakland firm, Rankin and Sons, was Morgan's choice for most of her plumbing work. She built a house for the Rankin family at the edge of a golf course in Oakland; not surprisingly, it was notable for its elegant bathrooms.

14. Dorothy May Boulian produced a slim volume, *Enchanted Gardens of Hearst Castle* (Cambria, Calif.: Phildor Press, 1972), which lists the flora grown on the hill, from azalea to Zantedeschia aethiopica (calla lily), plus trees from acacia to Ziziphus jujuba, as well as palms, conifers, thirty-three kinds of cypresses, and citrus and other trees in profusion. She also noted the many botanical volumes in Hearst's libraries as evidence of his ongoing interest in the landscape. Winston Frey, a professor of ornamental horticulture at Cal Poly, is preparing a monograph on the various trees at San Simeon, showing a staggering variety that rivals any arboretum in the state.

15. James Maher, during his research for his book "The American Palace" (unpublished), wrote to the author (May 20, 1975):
"It is quite clear to me now that Miss Morgan occupies a unique place in the history of American architecture for many reasons. Let me cite just one: I do not believe that any architect ever had the tremendous amount of work for domestic works from a single client that she handled for Hearst. Even if one were to lump all of his commissions for the various Vanderbilts . . . under one head, Richard Morris Hunt did not approach in his great houses the cost magnitudes that Miss Morgan handled at San Simeon alone. Nor did Horace Trumbauer in his houses for the several Wideners."

16. Bruce Porter, report to William Randolph Hearst, 1923, Morgan Collection.

8. Wyntoon and Other Hearst Projects (pages 217–39)

1. Hearst was in residence the entire summer of 1924, when he wrote to Julia Morgan (August 2, 1924): "Please come to Wyntoon. Something ought to be done about service residence and supervisors quarters, barns extended and dairy made."

Maybeck's castle for Phoebe Hearst might be expected to have influenced her son's at San Simeon more closely than it actually did. William Randolph Hearst had such a feeling for nature and for history (as did his architect) that in creating a mansion on a seaside hill, it was inevitable that his model would be Spanish or Mediterranean architecture, rather than Maybeck's appropriately Teutonic building at Wyntoon.

2. To make way for the Maybeck and Morgan castle, River House had been slated for demolition, as it occupied the site with the best view down the river. When Morgan's plans changed to the group of houses around a green, she remodeled River House for guests, and it is still used as a guesthouse today.

3. An article entitled simply "Hearst" in the October 1935 *Fortune* shows the Bear House murals (p. 45) as originally painted by Day, although without attribution to her. She always said that she didn't mind the changes Pogany had made, but she treasured her copy of the magazine and gave it to the author.

4. "The loss of your beautiful and irreplaceable collection at Wyntoon makes me sad, again and again as this object and that visualizes itself without conscious recall. I have been deeply sorry, knowing a bit what they must have been to you —but could not express it." Julia Morgan to William Randolph Hearst, February 20, 1945.

5. "Hearst," *Fortune*, p. 45.

6. Hearst gave $100,000 to the restoration program of the Mission San Antonio de Padua and offered Morgan's services, but local legend has it that the Mission Committee refused even to consider a woman architect.

7. Frank Hellenthal, contractor in charge of construction, explained that the dressing room for Marion Davies had to be grander than the one for Norma Shearer (three interviews with author, August and September 1975).

8. W. A. Swanberg, *Citizen Hearst* (New York: Bantam 1967), p. 631.

9. Drawings and many documents connected with the Medieval Museum, along with models and photographs, are in the archives of the de Young Museum, San Francisco, catalogued by Margaret Burke.

Some friends were so important to this book that they must be thanked for general as well as specific help. Bjarne Dahl, John Dizikes, Bobbie Sue Hood, Jacomena Maybeck, and Neale McGoldrick each contributed invaluably over a period of more than ten years. Christopher, Jonathan, and Kim Boutelle originally introduced me to Julia Morgan by taking me on a tour of San Simeon. Ann and Will helped push me forward. My sister, Mary Holmes, and all my family sustained me through the years of intense focus on this one subject.

It is impossible to overestimate the significance of interviews with people who knew Morgan, some of whom have not survived to see the book. Ansel Adams, Vincent Buckley, Edward H. Clark, Persis Coleman, Doris Day, Newton Drury, Frank Hellenthal, Harry Hilp, Edward Hussey, George Loorz, Hettie Belle Marcus, Gertrude Matthew, Robert McIvor, Donald McLaughlin, Morgan North, John Pellegrini, Warren Charles Perry, Victor Saville, Marian Simpson, Morgan Stedman, Walter Steilberg, Juliette Sweet, Betty Taylor, Adrien Voisin, Steve Zegar, and Louise Zook are remembered with gratitude. Of the many others who have shared their memories generously I want to thank Dr. Harold Alvarez, Dr. Frank Anker, Mrs. Kurt Anslinger, Mary Weeks Bennett, Dorothy Wormser Coblentz, Phoebe Conley, Marion Foote Conway, Mrs. Gardner Dailey, Gerard Dolmage-Heath, Fern Farnum, Marion Gorrill, Cecilia Bancroft Graham, Otto Haake, Lucy Hale, Margaret Calder Hayes, Mrs. Walter Huber, Frances Kitchen Ivy, Beth Julian, Dr. Frank Kaye, Douglas Kerr, Virginia Lawler, Harold Lyman, Elizabeth McClave, Joel McCrea, Miriam Garland McCurdy, Mary McHugh, Mrs. K. McKinnon, Polly McNaught, Sachi Hoguchu Oka, Fred Owen Pearce, Charles Pope, Mrs. Clifton Price, Alexander Rankin, Mrs. Willard Rosenquist, Emily Rued, Harold Saylor, Alexander Schilling, Edward M. Seward, Constance Spencer, Helene Stadlinger, Norma Stauffer, Florence Steen, Harold and Doris Stolte, Dr. Andre Suppo, Delores Gomez van Aiken, John Walsworth, and Gertrude Turner Warren.

Architects who have been helpful to the project include Iris Alex, Emily Bachman, Nancy Baker, Sewell Bogart, Lucia Bogotay, Jean-Paul Carlhian, John Chase, Philip Choy, Polly Cooper, Seth Curlin, William Dutcher, Joseph Esherick, Richard Fernau, Anna M. Halpin, Laura Hartman, Mui Ho, David Horn, Inge Horton, Peter Kump, Francis E. Lloyd, Warren McClure, Ronald Nagata, Wallace Neff, Thomas Potts, Mark Primack, the late Lutah Maria Riggs, Cynthia Ripley, Roy Rydell, Matt Thompson, Susana Torre, Anne Tyng, Cameron White, the late Carlton Winslow, Worley Wong, Frank Zwart, and, above all, the aforementioned Bobbie Sue Hood.

Architectural historians have also aided my efforts to track down the buildings and the records. Barbara Anderson, John Beach, Gray Brechin, Margaret Burke, Kenneth Cardwell, Richard Chafee, Robert Judson Clark, Joan Draper, Fillmore Eisenmayer, Martin Filler, David Gebhard, Daniel Gregory, Harold Kirker, Spiro Kostof, Julie Linxwiler, Richard Longstreth, Charles Marinovich, Allan Temko, Sally Woodbridge, and Georgia S. Wright are significant among those to whom I feel indebted. Robert Cox of the National Park Service helped with the Grand Canyon buildings. Melita Oden of the Saratoga Historical Museum was a valuable source for the history of her area. The late Vonnie Eastham gave me access to her research on Phoebe Apperson Hearst.

Libraries have played significant roles in my research, despite the perceived lack of material left by Morgan. The University of California system contains scattered documents, which in Berkeley were generously shared by the Bancroft Library under James Hart's direction, with the aid of archivist James Kantor, Regional Oral History Office members Willa Baum and Suzanne B. Riess, and Larry and Kathy Dinnean. Treasures in the Documents Collection of the university's College of Environmental Design were made available by Caitlin King, Stephen Tobriner, Arthur Waugh, and Margaret Wong. At the Robert E. Kennedy Library, California Polytechnic State University, San Luis Obispo, to which the Morgan estate collection went in 1980, Robert Blesse and his assistant, Dorothy Stechman, were helpful at the outset; Nancy Loe and Mary Weaver, with their *Descriptive Guide to the Julia Morgan Collection*, have established a professional archive as a center for Morgan material. Elizabeth Norris, the archivist at the National YWCA Headquarters in New York, was interested and helpful at a distance, while the nearby California Historical Society reference librarian, Maude K. Swingle, has kept an eye out for Morgan items, as did Albert Schadel of the Santa Cruz County Historical Museum. Mills College librarian emerita, Elizabeth Reynolds, and special collections librarian Anne-Marie Bouche and head librarian, Steven Pandolfo, have shared Morgan letters. Jean Pelletier and Beth Chiles of the San Bruno Library helped stir up interest in their area. The Oakland and San Francisco public libraries have special history rooms which were sources for early research, while the Berkeley Architectural Heritage Association in the persons of Anthony Bruce, Lesley Emmington (Jones), and Betty Marvin made and continue to make available information about Morgan buildings, as well as corrections of inaccurate attributions. The San Simeon monument archives have been opened to serious scholars, with first Metta Hake, then Ann Miller and Taylor Coffman, and now Robert Pavlik sharing the material they have assembled. Carol J. Everingham shared her research for the introductory volume of *The Art of San Simeon.* Many of the guides at San Simeon have been helpful and encouraging beyond the call of duty.

The Oakland Museum exhibition of January 1976, with Therese Heyman as curator, gave the first recognition to Morgan's architectural drawings. The University of California at Santa Cruz Extension, which arranged my June 1975 course on Julia Morgan, deserves special thanks, as does Joan Barry, who publicized it. The Berkeley City Club sponsored a small exhibition of drawings in 1975, as did the College of Environmental Design in 1976 and the Doe Library at Berkeley in the same year. The second Women's School of Planning and Architecture 1976 Summer School provided another opportunity at UCSC for making professionals aware of Morgan's work. The Paris meeting of the International Association of Women Architects under the leadership of Solange Herbez de la Tour carried this beyond national boundaries to the meeting at the Pompidou Center in 1978.

Permission granted me by Morgan North early in 1978 for the exclusive use of the Morgan estate material in his files was perhaps the most important single step in this research. That the privilege was short-lived as a result of his sudden death in March of that year was not only a setback in the progress of this work, and a loss to history in that his memoirs of his aunt had not been adequately recorded, but it was also a personal blow in the loss of a respected friend.

Among clients of Julia Morgan and owners or residents of Morgan buildings who contributed further valuable resources for this book are Mary Olney Bartlett, Katherine Field Caldwell, Anne Cuff, Anna Doyle Hettman, Joan Kahle, Dennis King, Mrs. R. Burnett Miller, Mr. and Mrs. W. L. Milliron, Jane Newhall, Phyllis O'Shea, Willys Peck, Mr. and Mrs. Philip Pierpont, Grace Prescott, and Irene Seitz. Friends who helped with suggestions and information include Lynn Bonfield, Bruce Cantz, Ellen Dungan, the late Vonnie Eastham, Winston Frey, the late Audrey Galli, Barbara Giffen, John H. Gregory, Lurline Hamm, Nancy Headapohl, Florence Jury, James T. Maher, Margaret McGrath, Page Smith, Margaret Sowers, Paul Vorwerk, and Janette Howard Wallace. Preliminary editors deserve my gratitude, especially Ro Lo Grippo, Mary E. Osman, Camille Rose, and Russell Schoch.

Although the quality of photographer Richard Barnes's contribution is self-evident, it is not easy to acknowledge it adequately. His technical virtuosity has been essential, of course, but so has his dedication of time and his thoughtful appreciation of both the simple and the complex that enabled his color photographs to give voice to Morgan's buildings. The architect said that her buildings would speak for her, and so they do, thanks in large part to Richard Barnes. Black and white photography by James H. Edelen also makes up a vital part of this book. Other photographs, especially slides, came from Barbara Anderson, Will Boutelle, Jonathan Dwyer, Carol J. Everingham, Richard Fernau, Winston Frey, Neale McGoldrick, Walter Niles, Victor Schiffrin, Robert Tarr, and Taylor Coffman.

Physical preparation of the manuscript and much more must be attributed to the generous spirit and special skills of Emily Bachman, Gail Rich, and Frances Rydell. Barbara Bair, Neale McGoldrick, and Alison Russell were also helpful in compiling the seemingly endless files and documentation over a period of years.

To designer Joel Avirom we owe homage for his ability to convey the architect's spirit in book form. As for Nancy Grubb, my editor, her subtle skills, her cheerful patience, and above all her enthusiasm for Julia Morgan have made the process of building the book marvelously pain-free.

Foundation support during the research for this book included grants from the Hearst Foundation, the National Endowment for the Arts, and the Sourisseau Academy. William Randolph Hearst, Jr., and the late Charles Gould were particularly sympathetic to the project from the start. Permission to examine and to quote from the Hearst-Morgan correspondence in the Hearst Warehouse Files in New York City was of major importance.

My final acknowledgment must be that there are no doubt errors and lacunae, for which I take responsibility. New information will inevitably come to light as the architecture of Julia Morgan gains increasing recognition. What has been a wonderfully varied and richly rewarding search is not yet over.

This list represents the first attempt to enumerate all of Julia Morgan's buildings, both those that exist in design only and those that were built. It is inevitably tentative and incomplete. The names of buildings and owners are original rather than current. All buildings are in California unless otherwise indicated. Entries within each year are in alphabetical order. Dates are for plans and construction (as closely as could be determined); preliminary drawings may have occurred earlier. "See also" refers the reader to other commissions for the same client. Morgan's commissions for William Randolph Hearst, too numerous to cross-reference under each entry, occurred in 1912–14, 1914, 1915, 1919–42, 1924 (2), 1924–43, 1925, 1930s (3), 1932–36, 1936 (2), 1937, 1941, and 1943–45. Her commissions for the YWCA, even more numerous, occurred in 1913–15 (2), 1913–28, 1914–15 (2), 1916–18 (2), c. 1917, 1917–18, 1918, 1919, 1919–20, 1921 (2), 1922 (2), 1923, 1924, 1925–26 (2), 1926, 1929, 1929–30, and 1930 (2).

1894–95   Professor Andrew C. Lawson house
2461 Warring Street, Berkeley
Designed by Bernard Maybeck; construction supervised by Morgan
Demolished 1906

1902   Harriet Fearing house: addition of *grand salon*
9 rue de l'Arbre sec, Fontainebleau, France
Demolished 1954

Mae Cottage (Mary E. Smith Trust Cottages)
Arbor Villa, Oakland
Demolished 1927

Frederick and Mabel Urmy Seares house
706 S. 7th Street; changed to 714 Maryland Place
University of Missouri campus
Columbia, Missouri
Job no. 1(?)
Demolished

1902–26   University of California, Berkeley
Hearst Mining Building, 1901–7; designed by John Galen Howard; Morgan worked as draftswoman, 1902–3
Greek Theater, 1903; designed by Howard; Morgan was assistant supervising architect
Girton Hall (social center for women students), 1911; job no. 318; moved to a different location on campus in the early 1940s
Unbuilt project: Phoebe Apperson Hearst Memorial Auditorium and Art Museum; designed by Morgan and Bernard Maybeck, 1923–24
Phoebe Apperson Hearst Memorial Gymnasium for Women; designed by Morgan and Maybeck, 1925–26

1903   Kindergarten and aquarium
Phoebe Apperson Hearst, client
Washington, D.C.
Not located
See also 1903–10

1903–10   Hacienda del Pozo de Verona: extensive enlarging and remodeling of A. C. Schweinfurth design (1895–98); addition of Boys' House, pools, and music room
Phoebe Apperson Hearst, client
Pleasanton
Job no. 320
Demolished by fire, 1969
See also 1903

1903–16, Mills College, Oakland
1924–26   El Campanil (bell tower), 1903–4
Margaret Carnegie Library, 1905–6
Gymnasium (by Morgan and Ira Hoover), 1909; job no. 256
Kapiolani Rest Cottage (infirmary), 1909–10; job no. 296
Ethel Moore Memorial Center (social center), 1916; job no. 426
Ming Quong Chinese Girls School, 1924–25
Geranium Cottage (behind Ming Quong), 1926; Mrs. Lynn White, client

1904   Annie Caroline Edmonds apartment building
2612–16 Regent Street, Berkeley

Alma Galbraith house
2819 Garber Street, Berkeley
Moved to 2900 Derby Street, Berkeley, 1920

Admiral Henry Glass house
2621 Bancroft Way, Berkeley
Moved to 2516 Warring Street, Berkeley, 1929

Agnes Borland Hart house
2255 Piedmont Avenue, Berkeley
House remodeled and garage added by Morgan, 1911 and 1914

Clifton H. Kroll house
Summit Avenue, Oakland
Demolished

Elsie Turner house and cottage at rear
2241 or 2247 College Avenue, Berkeley
Demolished

Mrs. Mary B. von Adelung lodging house
471 Peralta Avenue, Oakland
Demolished
Not clearly documented

1905   Samuel Breck house
Santa Rosa Avenue, Oakland
Not located

James T. Burke house
Berkeley
Not located
Job no. 179

Professor William E. Colby house
2901 Channing Way, Berkeley
Alterations by Morgan, 1911–12
Job no. 316

Jane E. Corbett house
2723 Regent Street, Berkeley

Arthur De Wint and Mary Hallock Foote house (North Star Mine house)
Grass Valley

Admiral Charles Mills Gayley house
2328 Piedmont Avenue, Berkeley
Moved and added to by Warren Perry, 1944

Louise (Mrs. C. L.) Goddard houses
2615, 2617, and 2619 Parker Street, Berkeley
Three nonidentical speculative houses; see also 1905–7 and 1908

General and Mrs. G. R. Greenleaf house
2340 Piedmont Avenue, Berkeley
Extensively remodeled by another architect after World War II

Katherine C. Henley apartment building
2516 Hillegas Street, Berkeley
Demolished

Professor Kofoid house
2616 Etna Street, Berkeley
See 1906

William Conger Morgan house
2440 Hillside Street, Berkeley

Reverend Edward L. and Bertha Parsons house
2532 Durant Street, Berkeley
Moved to 2732 Durant Street and remodeled by Morgan as student residence, 1915

Mrs. A. Sedgwick house
2903 N. Dwight Way, Berkeley

Mrs. A. A. Smith house
2310 College Avenue, Berkeley

F. A. Thomas house
883 Arlington Street, Berkeley

1905–6   Evelyn Cottage (Mary E. Smith Trust Cottages)
Arbor Villa, 3001 Park Boulevard, Oakland

1905–7   Louise (Mrs. C. L.) Goddard houses
2727 and 2731 Etna Street, Berkeley
Two speculative houses; see also 1905 and 1908

1905–17   Lakeview School
Perry and Grand streets,

Oakland
Oakland Playground
Commission, client
Lakeview School building,
1905; job no. 116
Addition to Lakeview School
building, 1910
Lakeview School Annex 1, 1915
Lakeview School Annex 2,
1916; job no. 412
Lakeview School Annex 3:
lavatory building, 1916–17
Play pergola annex, 1917
Addition to Lakeview School
building, 1917
All demolished

c. 1906   William H. and Maria E. Mills
house
306 Laurel Street, San Francisco
Job no. 163

1906   Professor Walter C. Blasdale
house
2514 College Avenue, Berkeley
Demolished

Robert Bruce house
S. Prospect Avenue, east of
Telegraph Avenue, Oakland
Demolished

Orsamus and Susan Cole house
157 Hillcrest Road, Berkeley
Extensively remodeled by
another architect after World
War II

Lewis A. Hicks house
2311 Piedmont Avenue,
Berkeley
Extensively remodeled by
another architect after World
War II

Edward L. Holmes cottage
2525 Etna Street, Berkeley (in
garden of 2523 Etna Street)

D. B. Huntley house
1031 Belle Vista Avenue,
Oakland

Professor Kofoid house
2618 Etna Street, Berkeley
See 1905

Fred Kuhle, two stores and
apartments
Grove Street, Oakland
Demolished

Mae (Mrs. B. P.) Miller house
830 McKinley Street, Oakland

Jessica Peixotto house
2225 College Avenue, Berkeley
Demolished

Dr. H. L. Tevis house and barns
Alma
Job no. 214
Demolished (now a reservoir)

1906–7   California Properties lodging
house
22nd Street, east of Grove
Street, Oakland
Demolished

Fairmont Hotel: reconstruction
California and Mason streets,
San Francisco

First Baptist Church: interior
Telegraph Avenue and 22nd
Street, Oakland

Merchants Exchange Building
Trading Room: interior
465 California Street, San
Francisco

Mrs. Estella Trask house
318 21st Street, Oakland
Demolished

Viavi Building
636–52 Pine Street, San
Francisco
Demolished 1920s

1907   Elizabeth (Mrs. Frank B.) Allen
house
405 Lee Street, Oakland

Dr. Mariana Bertola house and
office
1050 and 1052 Jackson Street,
San Francisco
Remodeled by Morgan, 1912;
job no. 368

Mrs. Angus Boggs house
1266 Washington Street, San
Francisco
Not clearly documented

Cook-Morgan-Warner
warehouse
Linden and 22nd streets,
Oakland
Demolished

Mrs. Elma C. Farnham house
Summit Avenue, Oakland
Job no. 203 or 204
Demolished in 1950s
See also 1912 and 1912–13

W. R. Griffin apartment
building
1448 Josephine Street, Berkeley
Not clearly documented

F. F. Huddard house
2350 Ellsworth Street, Berkeley
Job no. 215

Cora W. Jenkins house
120 Richmond Boulevard at
Randwick Street, Oakland

Thaddeus Joy house
2816 Derby Street, Berkeley
This is one of a pair of
speculative houses by Morgan;
the other is at 2818 Derby
Street.

Dr. and Mrs. W. H. Kellogg
house
2820 Vallejo Street, San
Francisco
Job no. 236

Edward W. Linforth house
2740 Derby Street, Berkeley
Job no. 221

Ivan M. Linforth house
2742 Derby Street, Berkeley

Mrs. Louise P. Love house
2908 Channing Way, Berkeley
Job no. 238
Demolished

Joseph J. Mason house
2726 Telegraph Avenue,
Berkeley
Job no. 231
Demolished

Charles Z. Merritt house
Claremont area, Berkeley or
Oakland
Not located
Job no. 208

Eleanor L. Moore house
2908 Channing Street, Berkeley

Rosa Morbio factory
Bluxome Street, 125 feet west of
4th Street, San Francisco
Job no. 205
Demolished

Mountain View Cemetery
Retiring Building
Piedmont Avenue, Oakland
Job no. 221 or 222
Demolished in 1950s

Charlotte Playter house
612 Mountain Avenue,
Piedmont
Job no. 209

Walter Powell house
N. Blake, 317 feet east of Dana
Street, Berkeley
Job no. 224
Moved to 2836 Derby Street,
Berkeley, 1911–12

Lucretia (Mrs. Grant) Taylor
house

14221 Saratoga-Sunnyvale Road, Saratoga

Alice Blanchard (Mrs. J. J.) Valentine house
179 Mariposa Street, Oakland
Job nos. 202, 323
Not clearly documented

Dr. Carl Walliser house
1529 Telegraph Avenue, Oakland
Demolished

1907–8   F. F. Ginn house
Thacher Road, Ojai
Job no. 232

Mr. C. H. Gray house
401 Lee Street, Oakland
Job no. 213

Mr. and Mrs. Andrew Moore house
1320 or 1324 Arch Street, Berkeley
Job no. 270

Mrs. M. D. Pierce house
1525 LeRoy Avenue, Berkeley
Job no. 233
Demolished
See also 1914–15

1907–10   Methodist Chinese Mission School (Gum Moon)
920 Washington Street at Trenton Alley, San Francisco
Job no. 234

1907–11   Professor Walter E. Magee apartment building
Berkeley
Not located
Job no. 207

1908   Mrs. W. F. Brahan house
754 14th Street, Oakland
Date not certain
Morgan's records indicate a "2nd bungalow for Mrs. Brahan, Burlingame."

Dr. G. Edwin Brinckerhoff house
324–26 El Cerrito, Piedmont
Job no. 228

Chinese Presbyterian Mission School (Donaldina Cameron House)
920 Sacramento Street, San Francisco
The name *MacDougall* appears on the building permit.

M. N. Clark house
330 Van Buren Avenue, Oakland
Demolished
Date uncertain

Warren T. and Elizabeth A. Clarke house
2317 Le Conte Avenue, Berkeley
Job no. 245
See also 1912–13

Charles Cuvellier house
369 Palm Street, Oakland
Job no. 216
Demolished

A. R. Derge house
2514 Etna Street, Berkeley
Job no. 217

S. L. Everett house
686 Mariposa Avenue, Oakland
Job no. 223

Fred Fisch storefront
311 Georgia Street, Vallejo
Job no. 239
Demolished

J. W. Flinn house
1823 University Avenue, Berkeley
Moved to 1732 Berkeley Way, Berkeley
Job no. 283

Friday Morning Club
Adams and Hoover streets, Los Angeles
Job no. 229
Not clearly documented; possibly never completed

Louise (Mrs. C. L.) Goddard house
2733 Ashby Place, Berkeley
Job no. 257
See also 1905 and 1905–7

Hamilton Methodist-Episcopal Church: alterations and completion
1525 Waller Street, San Francisco
Preliminary drawings by Bernard Maybeck
Gymnasium added by Morgan, 1920s

Kenneth Hobart house
2420 College Avenue, Berkeley
Demolished

Fred L. Hodkins house
360 Euclid Avenue, Oakland

Professor Lincoln Hutchinson house
9 Canyon Road, Berkeley
Job no. 250
Penthouse added by another architect

Kappa Alpha Theta sorority house
2723 Durant Street, Berkeley
Job no. 252
Remodeled by Morgan, c. 1930; remodeled by Gardner Dailey, c. 1950

Louise W. Katz apartment building
2556–60 Buena Vista Way, Berkeley
Job no. 240
Demolished

Professor Joseph LeConte house
19 Hillside Court, Berkeley
Job no. 271

Mrs. R. F. Mitchell cottage
2612 Dana Street, Berkeley (in garden behind 2614 Dana Street)
Job no. 267
Not clearly documented

Bertha (Mrs. G. F.) Newell house
Prospect Street, San Anselmo
Job no. 248

Dr. W. E. and Dr. Mary B. Ritter house
West Piedmont Avenue between Durant Street and Channing Way, Berkeley
Projected apartment house also referred to; never built
Job no. 254
Demolished

Addison Smith house
Piedmont
Not located
Job no. 227

Mrs. Aurora A. Stull house
3377 Pacific Avenue, San Francisco
Job no. 273
Remodeled after World War II by George Livermore

Charles Sutton house
Corner of Oakland Avenue and Moss Street, Oakland
Job no. 262

Fred C. Turner house
255 Ridgeway Street, Oakland
Job no. 255
Garage added by Morgan, 1915; job no. 454
See also 1916, 1930s, 1938–41 (3)

Herbert N. Turrell house
456 Jean Street, Oakland
Not located
Job no. 220

Mr. J. A. Vandegrift house
Fairmont Avenue, Oakland
Job no. 272
Demolished

Earl W. Wilbur house
81 Hillcrest Road, Berkeley
Job no. 241
Not clearly documented

Maynard E. Wright house
4025 Hillside Avenue, Oakland
Job no. 249
Demolished

1908–9   George L. Bouveroux house
365 Euclid Avenue, Oakland
Job no. 230
Demolished

Mrs. Angelotte J. Breck house
2003 Summit Avenue, Oakland
Job no. 247
Demolished

George Chambers house
Linda Vista Terrace, Oakland
Not located
Job no. 242

Robert Forsyth house
1946 Green Street, San
Francisco
Job no. 275
Demolished

Jesse Harrier house
6481 Benvenue Street, Oakland
Job no. 277

L. G. Harrier house
Suison
Not located

H. R. Hatfield house
2633 LeConte Avenue, Berkeley
Job no. 274

Miss Helen Hitchcock house
1010 Powell Street, San
Francisco
Job no. 251

Alfred Holman house
3531 Clay Street, San Francisco
Job no. 260

Bradford and Grace Leavitt
house
2511 Octavia Street, San
Francisco
Job no. 265

Dr. J. K. and Sarah M. McLean
house
2725 Channing Way, Berkeley
Job no. 263

Miss Estelle Miller apartment
building
Minerva C. Miller, client
1202–16 Leavenworth Street,
San Francisco
Job no. 259

Dr. Joseph and Fannie Simpson
house: alterations
363 Missouri Street, San
Francisco
Job no. 261
Not clearly documented

Mrs. M. B. Squire apartment
building
2003 Oak Street, San Francisco
Job no. 269

F. A. Thomas house
883 Arlington Street, Berkeley
Job no. 268

Vallejo Commercial Bank:
alterations
Vallejo
Job no. 218
Demolished

Adolph H. Weber house
1515 Euclid Avenue, Berkeley
Job no. 253
Demolished by fire, 1923

Miss Ray Wellman house
98 Hillcrest Avenue, Berkeley
Job no. 235

Mrs. W. H. Whiting house:
alterations
1317 Arch Street, Berkeley
Job no. 281

Professor E. J. Wickson house
2723 Bancroft Way, Berkeley
Job no. 297
Demolished

Agnes and George Wilson house
728 Capital Street, Vallejo
Job no. 206

Esther (Mrs. J. C.) Woodland and
Miss J. H. Caruthers apartment
building
1124–26 Filbert Street, San
Francisco
Job no. 264

1908–10   Professor Clifton Price
apartment building
Rear of lot at 9–17 Panoramic
Way; entrance on Orchard Lane,
Berkeley
First of two buildings by
Morgan on lot—see 1912

Saint John's Presbyterian
Church and Sunday School
College Avenue at Derby Street,
Berkeley
Job no. 237
Alterations by Morgan, 1915;
job no. 442

H. W. Thomas house
Palm Street and Bellevue
Avenue, Oakland
Not located
Alterations by Morgan, 1912–13

1908–12,   Kings Daughters Home
1930s   39th Street and Broadway,
Oakland
Main hospital and landscaped
garden; north and east wings;
job no. 225
Nurses' building; job no. 367
Male attendants' building,
1930's; job no. 774

1908–14   Gordon Blanding house:
remodeling of entrance gate;
addition of Organ House (not
documented) and of Casino
(1913–14)
450 Belvedere Road, Belvedere
(Casino)
Job no. 401
Original house designed by
Willis Polk

1908–16   Ransom and Bridges School
Hazel Lane, Piedmont
Main building, 1908; job no. 258
Dormitories and offices, 1913;
job no. 378
Laundry and maintenance
building, n.d.
Gymnasium, 1916; job no. 451
Demolished after World War II

1909   Miss Grace E. Barnard School
Ashby Avenue, Berkeley
Demolished; a house now at
1113 Delaware, Berkeley, is said
to have been moved from the
school grounds at time of
demolition.

Agnes (Mrs. Archibald) Borland
lodging house
W. Broadway, north of 1st
Street, Oakland
Demolished

Mr. and Mrs. Edward Lacey
Brayton house
Kelton Court and Hillside
Avenue, southwest corner,
Oakland
Job no. 298
Demolished
See also 1912 and 1923

Mrs. J. H. Brewer house
770 Summit Avenue, Oakland
Gardens and elevator added by
Morgan, 1915
Job no. 285
Demolished

William E. Burke house
2301 San Antonio Avenue,
Alameda
Job no. 258

Cary W. Cook house
47 Fairway Drive, San Rafael
Garage added by Morgan, 1910
Job no. 243

Miss Anna Head house
Bowditch Street, Berkeley
Job no. 291
Not located

Walter Y. Kellogg house
2232 Piedmont Avenue,
Berkeley
Job no. 276

Dr. Guy and Flora Liliencrantz
34 Craig Avenue, Piedmont
Date not documented

William Nichols house
1411 Hawthorne Terrace,
Berkeley
Job no. 266

Hart H. and Emma North house
2414 Prospect Avenue, Berkeley
Job no. 279
Demolished
See also 1910–11 and 1921

Mr. H. C. Scrutton house
2 Brown Court, Petaluma

George L. Walker house
1232 Bay Street, Alameda
Job no. 287

Miss Georgia Winteringham
house
San Rafael
Not located

1909–10 Miss Elizabeth Carson house
308 Parnassus Avenue, San
Francisco

Miss Cecilia Cronise house
2868 Vallejo Street, San
Francisco
Job no. 284

Sarah Griggs house
1626 Spruce Street, Berkeley

F. J. Laird house
2431 College Avenue, Berkeley
Job no. 292
Demolished

Ezekiel Denman McNear house
George W. McNear, client
(Ezekiel Denman was his son)
617 C Street, Petaluma
Job no. 293

George W. McNear house
27 Highland Avenue (formerly
Vernal Street), Piedmont
Job no. 392

Fred Staude house
1901 Central Avenue, Alameda
Job no. 304

H. H. Stout house
2328 Warring Street, Berkeley
Job no. 310
Demolished

Miss Jessie D. Wallace house
2261 Derby Street, Berkeley
Alterations by Morgan, 1911–12
Job no. 314

Louis and Louise Weinman
house
1315 Dayton Avenue, Alameda
Additions or alterations by
Morgan, 1912–13
Job no. 299

1909–11 Dr. Edward von Adelung house
Summit Avenue and 29th
Street, Oakland
Job no. 295
Demolished

1910 C. F. Baker house and house
behind
86 and 90 Monte Vista Avenue,
Oakland
Job no. 325
Not clearly documented

Claremont Country Club:
addition of kitchen and
remodeling
Broadway and Clifton, Oakland
Job no. 305
Demolished

Dr. Edwin A. Clay house
162 Buckley Street, Sausalito

Judge F. C. Clift apartment
building
535 Leavenworth Street, San
Francisco
Job no. 288
Not clearly documented
See also 1913

Susan (Mrs. Galen) Fisher house
3247 Kempton Road, Oakland
Job no. 280

B. D. Marx Greene house
11 Hillside Court, Berkeley
Demolished

H. C. Koempel house
Fruitvale, Oakland
Not located
Job no. 306

J. H. Pierce house
1290 Alameda, San Jose
Alterations by Morgan, 1914
Demolished

Port Costa Water Company
William Clark Barnard, client
Main Street, Port Costa
Job no. 307

Mrs. Sharp house
936 Oxford Street, Berkeley
Job no. 320

Major C. L. Tilden house:
alterations
1031 San Antonio Avenue,
Alameda
Job no. 312

Edward M. Walsh house
98 N. Linda Vista Terrace,
Oakland
Job no. 282
Demolished

Mrs. Laura P. Williams house
1324 Arch Street, Berkeley

1910–11 J. Edgar Allen house
707 D Street, Petaluma
Job no. 326

G. L. Campbell house
1425 Arch Street, Berkeley
Job no. 294

Professor H. E. Cox apartment
building
1720 Pacific Avenue, San
Francisco
Job no. 300

Philip Dibert pharmacy
117 University Avenue, Palo
Alto
Job no. 341
Demolished

Dr. David Hadden house
1400 LeRoy Avenue, Berkeley
Destroyed by fire, 1923; rebuilt
from Morgan's plans, but
possibly not by Morgan
See also 1938

Miss Julie Haste house
Not located
Job no. 329

Dr. Robert Keys house
1220 Spruce Street, Berkeley
Job no. 328

Montezuma School for Boys:
dormitory and classroom center
Bear Creek Road, Santa Cruz
Mountains, near Los Gatos

J. N. Rogers house
2924 Ashby Avenue, Berkeley
Job no. 333

U.S. Immigration Station
Hart H. North, client
Angel Island, San Francisco Bay
Not located
Three-room cottage, four-room
cottage, hospital building
addition, U.S. Appraiser's
building
Job no. 303
See also 1909 and 1921

Charles B. Wells house (Red Gate)
6076 Manchester Road, Oakland
Job no. 315

1910–12 Mr. and Mrs. Ben Reed house
535 Oakland Avenue, Oakland
Demolished
See also 1926

c. 1911 Mrs. C. N. Felton house
Redlands
Not located

1911 Louis Bartlett house
2434 Warring Street, Berkeley
Job no. 322

Allen Chickering house
11 Sierra Avenue, Piedmont
Garage added by Morgan, 1915

Mrs. Fred Clark apartment building: alterations
2320 LeConte Avenue, Berkeley
Job no. 330

Coughlin house
2019 Parker Street, Berkeley

Frank Denman house
Petaluma
Not located
Job no. 335

George L. Dillman house
Goose Valley, near Burney
Job no. 355
Demolished by fire

Mary Garlick house
2884 Jackson Street, San Francisco
Not located
Job no. 347

John L. Howard, Jr., house
2626 Harrison Street, Oakland
Job no. 348

Dr. Elizabeth Keys house: alterations
1331 Greenwich Street, San Francisco
Job no. 334

James K. Lynch house
1326 Sherman Street, Alameda
Job no. 353

Reverend Clifton Macon house
1524 29th Avenue, Oakland
Job no. 345

Mrs. L. C. Marwin house: alterations
1169 Washington Street, Oakland

Professor and Mrs. E. T. McCormac house
1404 Hawthorne Terrace, Berkeley
Job no. 337
Remodeled by Morgan, 1941; job no. 793

Charles Washington Merrill house
2307–17 Warring Street, Berkeley
Job no. 336

Mr. W. H. Smyth house: alterations
Fernwald Avenue, Berkeley
Job no. 331

Dr. Arthur H. and Lilly Wallace house
2905 Piedmont Avenue, Berkeley
Job no. 346

Mrs. Robert Watt house
36 Presidio Terrace, San Francisco
Job no. 286

P. G. Williams house
2731 Regent Street, Berkeley
Job no. 340

Seldon Williams hay and cow barns
Lisbon, near Sacramento
Demolished
See also 1928

Mrs. Lillie T. Yates house
85 Jordan Street, San Francisco
Job no. 339

1911–12 Bank of Yolo
500 Main Street, Woodland
Demolished

Dr. Sherrill Hall house
2728 Channing Way, Berkeley
Job no. 338

Henry and Lena Heller, three apartments
2263 Fulton Street, San Francisco
Job no. 356

A. and Eva Hutchinson house
2020 10th Avenue, Oakland
Job no. 352

Charles L. Lewis house
1325 Clinton Avenue, Alameda
Job no. 350

Mrs. Sarah J. Mann houses: remodeling of two Victorian houses
2222 Clay Street, San Francisco
Job no. 364

Thomas Olney house
2434 Warring Street, Berkeley
Job no. 360
See also 1912

Edwin E. Skinner house
Floribunda Avenue and County Road, Burlingame
Job no. 382
Not clearly documented

1911–13 Henry S. Howard house
2065 Oakland Avenue, Oakland
Job no. 349

1912 George F. and Juliet Rhea Berry house
518 N. Hurlingham Avenue, San Mateo
Job no. 362

Mrs. Edward Lacey Brayton house
111 Mountain Avenue, Piedmont
See also 1909 and 1923

Mrs. George J. Bucknall house: remodeling of apartments into single-family dwelling
2853 Green Street, San Francisco
Job no. 373
Demolished

Andrew Davis house
2425 College Avenue, Berkeley
Job no. 357
Demolished

Mrs. Elma C. Farnham warehouse
Broadway and Battery streets, San Francisco
Demolished
See also 1907 and 1912–13

Mr. R. A. Leet house: alterations
145 Athol Avenue, Oakland

Caleb Levensaler house
1205 Bay Street, Alameda
Job no. 359

William H. and Maria Mills house: alterations and repairs
115 Presidio Terrace, San Francisco
Job no. 370

Thomas Olney house: alterations
427 29th Street, Oakland
Job no. 360
See also 1912

Warren Olney, Jr., house: alterations
2702 Dwight Way, Berkeley
Job no. 374

Professor Clifton Price
apartment building and garage
9–17 Panoramic Way, Berkeley
Second building by Morgan on
lot—see 1908–10

F. H. Reed house
1121 Sherman Street, Alameda
Job no. 350

Dr. Charles H. Rowe house
421 Fairmont Street, Oakland
Job no. 363

Walter A. Starr house
Carrington and Union streets,
northwest corner, Piedmont
Job no. 354
Demolished
See also 1916–17

Mr. E. T. Williamson house:
remodeling
1384 S. Broadway, Chico

1912–13 Warren T. and Elizabeth A.
Clarke house
862 Arlington Street, Berkeley
Job no. 377
See also 1908

Elsie Drexler house
Mountain Home Road,
Woodside
Job no. 365

Mrs. Elma C. Farnham house
724 Kingston Street, Oakland
Not clearly documented
See also 1907 and 1912

Nurses' Settlement (residence)
19th Street and Iowa, San
Francisco
Job no. 314
Demolished

1912–14 William Randolph Hearst
house: retaining wall; house
never built
60 Atwood Street, Sausalito

1912–15 Right Reverend Bishop Louis C.
Sanford house
733 E. Peralta Way, Fresno
Job no. 343

1912–16 Amos Huggins house: alteration
of Victorian house into
apartments
2815 Kelsey Street, Berkeley
Job no. 381

1913 Richard Clark house
2833 Bancroft Way, Berkeley
Job no. 382
Alterations by Morgan, 1928

Judge F. C. Clift Hotel for
Women
642 Jones Street, San Francisco
Built for Panama-Pacific
International Exposition; not
clearly documented
See also 1910

Miss Mollie Connors house
635 Winsor, Piedmont
Not located
Job no. 283

G. Loring Cunningham house
13625 Hillway Street, Los Altos
Job no. 387

W. V. Dinsmore stores
Broadway and 24th Street,
Oakland
Demolished
See also 1914

Alfred A. Durney house
1025 Sherman Street, Alameda
Job no. 376

Unbuilt project: Mr. and Mrs.
Edward Henley house
El Cerrito

F. G. Ilsen house
339 Palm Street, Oakland
Job no. 390

T. S. Mathis house
1625 Euclid Avenue, Berkeley
Job no. 389
Demolished

Unbuilt project: Oakland
Probation Building for Juvenile
Court
Job no. 391
Drawings and cost estimates
donated by Morgan

C. H. Redington house
468 Perkins Street, Oakland
Job no. 384
Demolished late 1970s

Isabel K. Rixon house
333 Chapin Lane, Burlingame
Job no. 385

Welch house: chapel and
alterations
91 Baywood Avenue, San Mateo

Ralph White house
1841 Marin Street, Berkeley
Job no. 372

1913–14 R. B. Ayer house
246 Sea View Street, Piedmont
Alterations by Morgan, 1930

Donald Campbell house
Ashby Street, Berkeley
Not located

Nathaniel R. Crossley house
868 Cleveland Street, Oakland
Not located
Job no. 399

August F. Hockenbeamer house
1320 Arch Street, Berkeley

Mrs. H. J. Merritt apartment
house
2236 Durant Street, Berkeley

1913–15 M. F., G. E., and A. F. Atkins
(sisters)
45 and 49 Sierra Avenue,
Piedmont

Mr. L. W. Fargo house
Mill Valley
Not located
Job no. 404

Oakland YWCA
1515 Webster Street, Oakland
Pool added by Morgan, 1919
Job no. 344

San Jose YWCA
San Jose
Job no. 413
Demolished

George Tesheira house
2336 Piedmont Avenue,
Berkeley
Job no. 366

1913–28 Asilomar, YWCA Conference
Center
Pacific Grove
Outside Inn (originally
engineers' cottage), c.1913
Entrance gates, 1913
Phoebe Apperson Hearst
Administration Building, 1913;
job no. 380
10 tent houses, 1913; the last
one was demolished in 1971
Chapel, 1915; job no. 421
Guest Inn, 1915; job no. 418
Saltwater swimming pool, 1915
Warehouse, c. 1915–16
Martha and Mary Lodge,
c. 1916; job no. 449; demolished
Visitors Lodge, c. 1916
40-car garage, 1917
Hilltop Cottage, for women
employees, c. 1918
Viewpoint Cottage, c. 1918
Crocker Dining Hall and
kitchen, 1918
Concrete tennis courts, c. 1919
Softball diamond, playground,
basketball court, and volleyball
court, c. 1920
Tide Inn, for men employees,
1923

Director's cottage, 1927; demolished 1959
Pinecrest, 1927–28
Scripps Lodge, 1927–28
Merrill Hall (auditorium), 1928

1914   Apartment house
Client unknown
2712 Derby Street, Berkeley

George and Susan Bell house
2118 Marin Avenue, Berkeley
Job no. 394
Alterations by Morgan, 1922

Jere (Mrs. James T.) Burke house
2929 Russell Street, Berkeley
On Morgan list as 2911 Russell Street; street number has changed to 2929.
Job no. 388
Not clearly documented

Century Club of California; alterations and remodeling
1355 Franklin Street, San Francisco
Job no. 408

W. V. Dinsmore house
104 First Street, Pacific Grove
Job no. 409
See also 1913

Lewis H. Greene house
2808 Claremont Boulevard, Berkeley
Job no. 400

William Randolph Hearst cottage
South Rim of the Grand Canyon, Arizona
Job no. 407
Demolished c. 1950

Arthur Holman house
34 West Clay Park, San Francisco
Job no. 396

Tracey Kelly house
215 Rice Lane, Davis
Job no. 393

C. C. Moore entertainment lodge
High Street, Santa Cruz
Extensively remodeled by owner

Dr. F. W. Morse house
522 Grand Street, Oakland
Job no. 405

William Olney house
2608 Warring Street, Berkeley
Job no. 402

Santa Barbara Recreation Building
100 E. Carillo Street, Santa Barbara

Octavia Briggs Schweitzer house
69 Menlo Street, Berkeley
Not clearly documented

1914–15   Unbuilt project: Elks Club
Petaluma

Kings Daughters Exposition Resting Room
Panama-Pacific International Exposition, San Francisco
Demolished

C. H. Layson house
Arden
Not located
Job no. 422

Mrs. M. D. Pierce house
Penn Avenue and Peralta Street, Los Gatos
Job no. 433
Demolished
See also 1907–8

Theodore Columbus White house
Carmello, between 15th and 16th streets, Carmel-by-the-Sea
Job no. 410

YWCA Building: interior, with restaurant, auditorium, and resting room
Panama-Pacific International Exposition, San Francisco
Demolished

YWCA building for "Zone" employees
Panama-Pacific International Exposition, San Francisco
Demolished

1914–17   Lewis Spear house: additions and alterations
1306 Sherman Street, Alameda

c. 1915   Mrs. Maxwell Honser house
Not located

Unbuilt project: Leo Victor Korbel house
Petaluma

Modesto First Baptist Church
12th Avenue, Modesto
Demolished

1915   Mrs. Frank Andrews house: remodeling
2828 Forest Street, Berkeley

M. G. Buckley cottage
19 Block E, San Mateo Heights
Not located
Job no. 430

Mrs. M. C. Davidson house
515 Lytton Avenue, Palo Alto
Job no. 440

Elizabeth B. Eccles apartment building
1418 Larkin Street, San Francisco
Job no. 438

Representative Ralph R. Eltse house
1937 Thousand Oaks, Berkeley
Job no. 429

Examiner Building
William Randolph Hearst, client
1111 S. Broadway, Los Angeles
Job no. 386
Alterations by Morgan, 1921; job no. 565
Major alterations and annex by Morgan, 1930–31

Dr. Malcolm Goddard house
2373 Walnut Boulevard, Walnut Park, Walnut Creek
Job no. 415
Demolished (original pool still there)

Miss Sarah Dix Hamlin School
2234 Pacific Avenue, San Francisco
Demolished

Mr. E. W. Hewson house
Claremont area, Berkeley
Not located

Dr. Ruth Huffman house: alteration of Victorian house to private hospital
227 Kentucky Street, Petaluma

James L. Lombard house (Harrow Manor)
62 Farragut Street, Piedmont
Job no. 427
Gardener's cottage and garage; job no. 436

George W. McNear, Jr., house: additions
Northeast corner of Pacific Avenue (extended to Jackson) and Locust Street, San Francisco
Wedding pavilion, 1917
Demolished
Job no. 392

Dr. E. L. Mitchell and Dr. M. L. Williams house
834 Santa Barbara Road, Berkeley

Otto Reichardt house
Colma
Not located
Job no. 434

Saratoga Foothill Women's Club
Park Place, Saratoga
Job no. 419

A. J. Snow house
537 2nd Street, San Francisco
Not located

1915–16 David Atkins house:
remodeling of Victorian house
into Italianate residence
1055 Green Street, San
Francisco
Job no. 455(?)

Gertrude Bain house (The
Peppers)
430 Hot Springs Road,
Montecito, Santa Barbara

Mr. W. T. Beatty
Live Oak Meadow, Pebble
Beach
Job no. 447
Demolished

Miss Alice Gay house: repairs
196 Clarendon Street, San
Francisco
Designed by Bernard Maybeck
Job no. 463

Edwin and Jane Newhall
apartment and garage
2950 Pacific Avenue, San
Francisco
Job no. 443

Mr. and Mrs. Wadsworth house
2239 Summer Street, Berkeley

1915–17 V. Martin house
636 Hillgirt Circle, Oakland

1916 Mrs. James M. Braly house
105 S. 11th Street, San Jose
Job no. 446
Demolished

Dr. Bulson's Sanitarium
Napa
Demolished

Katherine Delmar Burke School
3025 Jackson Street, San
Francisco

Charles Fisher house
9 Hillcrest Court, Oakland
Job no. 465

Mrs. Leslie A. Glide house
160 The Uplands, Berkeley
Job no. 452

C. M. Goethe house
3731 T Street, Sacramento
Job no. 445

Kern County Sanitarium
Bakersfield
Job no. 478
Demolished

Marysville Grammar School
(Mary Covillaud School)
Job no. 453

Marysville Grammar School
pool
Job no. 513
Marysville
Demolished

Dunning and Phoebe Rideout
house
707 F Street, Marysville
Job no. 424
See also 1919

Fred C. Turner shopping center
and second-floor apartments
Piedmont Avenue and 40th
Street, Oakland
See also 1908, 1930s, 1938–41
(3)

1916–17 Helen (Mrs. Horatio) Livermore
house
1023 Vallejo Street, San
Francisco
Job no. 458
Additions by Morgan, 1927 and
1930; remodeled by Putnam
Livermore, 1981

Helen (Mrs. Horatio) Livermore
cottage (Montesol)
On Livermore ranch near
Calistoga, Route 29

Abraham Rosenberg house
3630 Jackson Street, San
Francisco
Job no. 457

Carmen Moore (Mrs. Walter A.)
Starr house
Fremont
See also 1912

1916–18 Sausalito Women's Club
120 Central Avenue, Sausalito
Job no. 470

Tulare and King Counties
Sanitarium
Springville
Job no. 477
Demolished

United Presbyterian Church
College Avenue, Oakland
Job no. 456

YWCA hostess house
Camp Fremont
Moved to 27 University
Avenue, Palo Alto, 1919

YWCA hostess house
1012 C Street, San Pedro

1916–19 General Oscar Long house
65 Hazel Lane, Piedmont

c. 1917 Beach house: remodeling
YWCA, client
Waikiki, Hawaii
Demolished 1950s

1917 Dixwell Davenport house
195 San Leandro Way, St.
Francis' Wood, San Francisco
Job no. 464

1917–18 YWCA hostess house
San Diego
Incorporated into San Diego
YWCA

1917–19 Rollo V. Watt house and garage
1 Baker Street, San Francisco
Demolished

1918 Charles N. Hexter house
527 6th Street, Marysville
Job no. 488

Oakland Post-Enquirer Building
1751 Franklin Street, Oakland
Remodeled and enlarged by
Morgan, 1928
Demolished in the 1960s

San Diego YWCA
621 C Street, San Diego
Possibly only hostess house and
pool are by Morgan
Not clearly documented

Santa Barbara County
TB Sanitarium
300 N. San Antonio Road, Santa
Barbara

1918–19 Berkeley Baptist Divinity
School
Dwight Way and Hillegas
Street, Berkeley

Calvary Presbyterian Church
Milvia and Virginia streets,
Berkeley
Job no. 522

Mrs. H. T. Dobbins house
840 Clay Street, Colusa

Mr. and Mrs. A. J. Matson house
769 Longridge Road, Oakland
Job no. 499

San Francisco Presbyterian
Orphanage, Tooker Memorial
(Sunnyhill)
San Anselmo
Demolished and rebuilt by
another architect

J. H. Stineman house
800 Walavista Avenue, Oakland
Job no. 483

1919 Dr. Edith Brownsill house
San Francisco
Not located

Miss Cowell house
San Francisco
Not located

Marysville Bank
Dunning Rideout, client
Marysville
Demolished
See also 1916

Marysville Golf Clubhouse
Plumas Lake, Marysville
Demolished

Ralph W. McCormick house
326 D Street, Marysville
Job no. 485

James Rankin house
5440 Carlton Street, Oakland

Sausalito Carnegie Library
Sausalito
Not clearly documented

2nd Church of Christ, Scientist
Spruce Street, Berkeley
Morgan may have worked with
Henry Gutterson; not clearly
documented

Vallejo YWCA
245 York Street, Vallejo
Demolished

Dr. Florence Ward Sanitarium
2700 Broadway, San Francisco
Demolished

1919–20 Mrs. Walter C. Beatie house
87 Central Street, Sausalito

Clara Huntington Perkins house
Fairview Plaza, Los Gatos

Mrs. A. B. Peterson house
(Monterey House)
Paraiso Springs Resort, Paraiso
Springs

Salt Lake City YWCA
322 E. 3rd Street, South, Salt
Lake City, Utah

Ira Wells house
Acadia and Ocean View streets,
Oakland

1919–21 High Street Presbyterian
Church
Courtland and High streets,
Oakland

1919–42 William Randolph Hearst estate
(San Simeon)
San Simeon
Cottages A (Casa del Mar), B
(Casa del Monte), C (Casa del
Sol), 1920–22
Temporary housing for workers,
1920–38
Main Building, 1922–26 (never
completed); New Wing (north
wing), 1929–39 (never
completed)
Neptune pool, 1924; enlarged,
1925 and 1935–36

Garages, 1924 on
Offices, 1924 on
Zoo and animal shelters, 1924–
35
San Simeon village warehouses,
1926–27
San Simeon village houses for
workers, 1927–29
Roman pool and tennis courts,
1927–32
Poultry farm, 1928–29
Bunkhouse, at old George
Hearst ranch, 1930
Pergola, 1936
Projects planned but never
built: Chinese Cottage, English
Cottage, Persian building, Art
Gallery and Ballroom Wing,
saltwater pool, and others

1920s   Commander John Sisson
Graham house
14474 Oak Place, Saratoga

c. 1920   Miss Margaret L. Matthews
house
1880 San Pedro Avenue or 1911
Webster Street, Berkeley
Not located

1920   Ahwahnee Sanitarium
Merced, Madera, and Stanislaus
counties, client
Ahwahnee
Demolished

Ron H. and Elizabeth Elliott
house
1 Eucalyptus Street, Berkeley

Girls' Club
17th and Howard streets, San
Francisco
Demolished

C. W. Griffin house
1621 Santa Clara Avenue,
Alameda
Job no. 524
Demolished

Dr. and Mrs. P. B. Hoffman
house
725 F Street, Marysville
Job no. 514
Remodeled by Morgan, 1923;
job no. 590

Kentfield Sanitarium
Kentfield, Marin County
Demolished

Julia (Mrs. A. E.) Kline house
364 2nd Street, Yuba City
Job no. 515

Wallace MacGregor house
1962 Yosemite (formerly San
Rafael Street), Berkeley
Job no. 520

Rear Admiral George Reiter
house
Westmoreland Drive, Saratoga
Not located
Job no. 512

Edythe Tate-Thompson house
1028 O Street, Fresno
Not located
See also 1936

Unbuilt project: Mrs. Lloyd
Wilbur house
Marysville

1920–21 Chauncey Goodrich house
(Hayfield House)
La Paloma Street, Saratoga
Job no. 508

Dr. Albert Rowe house
1 Crocker Avenue, Piedmont
Job no. 506

1921   Miss Julia Fraser house
2014 Fifth Avenue, Oakland
Demolished

Adele (Mrs. Joseph) Friedlander
houses
2030 and 2040 Gough Street,
San Francisco
Not clearly documented

L. H. Kibbe house
33 Eucalyptus Street, Berkeley
Remodeled by Morgan, 1927
Job no. 563

Dr. and Mrs. D. H. Moulton
house (Mansion House)
341 W. Mansion Avenue, Chico
Job no. 545

Hart H. North apartments (The
Beckwith Apartments)
750 12th Street, Oakland
Demolished in the late 1970s
See also 1909 and 1910–11

Novato Community House
Novato
Not clearly documented

Ocean Avenue Presbyterian
Church
32 Ocean Avenue, San
Francisco

Pasadena YWCA
78 N. Marengo Avenue,
Pasadena
Marston and van Pelt, associate
architects for main building

Potrero Hill House Community
Center
953 DeHaro Street, San
Francisco

The Residence (Fernhurst):
remodeling
YWCA, client
Honolulu, Hawaii
Demolished

San Francisco Presbyterian
Theological Seminary faculty
house
118 Bolinas Avenue, San
Anselmo
Gymnasium-theater, c. 1921
President's house, 1921
47 Seminary Avenue, San
Anselmo (on grounds of San
Francisco Presbyterian
Theological Seminary)
Job no. 523

1921–22   Reverend Robert Donaldson
house
65 San Leandro, St. Francis'
Wood, San Francisco
Job no. 562

Mrs. A. G. Eames house:
remodeling
630 W. 5th Street, Chico
Job no. 568

Emanu-el Sisterhood Residence
Page and Laguna streets, San
Francisco
Dorothy Wormser, associate
architect

J. G. Kennedy house
423 Chaucer Street, Palo Alto

c. 1922   House
50 Scenic Way, San Francisco
Not clearly documented

1922   American Legion Building
Marysville
Demolished

Berkeley YWCA
Union and Allerton streets,
Berkeley
Demolished

Ebell Rest Cottage
135 North Park View, Los
Angeles

Fresno YWCA residence
1660 M Street, Fresno

Sam H. Martin house
(Stonedene): remodeling
Suison Valley Road, Suison
Remodeled again by Morgan,
1929

Joseph Shoong house
385 Bellevue Avenue, Oakland
Job no. 574

1923   Mrs. Edward Lacey Brayton
house
Ronda and Cortez roads, Pebble
Beach
See also 1909 and 1912

Delta Zeta sorority house
2311 LeConte Avenue, Berkeley

Long Beach YWCA
1865 E. Anaheim Street, Long
Beach
Demolished in 1970s

Eliza (Mrs. Charles Bill) Morgan
house (Morgan's mother)
2404 Prospect Avenue, Berkeley
(in garden of daughter Emma
North's house)
Moved to 7779 Claremont
Avenue, Berkeley, in 1964

Sacramento Public Market
1230 J Street, Sacramento

Saratoga Federated Community
Church
Park Place, Saratoga
Job no. 575

Walter Schilling apartments:
interiors
2006 Washington Street, San
Francisco

1923–24   First Swedish Baptist Church
3rd Avenue and E. 15th Street,
Oakland

1924   Marion Davies house (Beach
House)
William Randolph Hearst,
original client, 1910
321 Beach Palisades Road
(formerly 321–415 Ocean
Front), Santa Monica
Greenhouse and pool, 1929
Demolished (staff houses
altered to private club), 1960

Marion Davies house
William Randolph Hearst,
client
North Bedford Drive, Beverly
Hills
Not clearly documented

Fresno YWCA offices
Tuolomne and L streets, Fresno

Paul Thelen house
828 Contra Costa Road,
Berkeley

Thousand Oaks Baptist Church
1821 Catalina Street, Berkeley

1924–25   Ladies Protection and Relief
Society residence (The Heritage)
3400 Laguna Street, San
Francisco

Ming Quong Chinese Girls
School
Donaldina Cameron, client
Acquired by Mills College,
Oakland, 1936

1924–43   William Randolph Hearst estate
(Wyntoon)
Near McCloud
Superintendent's and servants'
quarters, 1924
Stables and caretaker's house,
1924–25
The Chalet (servants' quarters),
1925
Bear, Cinderella, and Fairy
houses, 1932–33
Bridge House, 1933
Pool and pool houses, 1934–35
Offices (later used as dining
hall), 1935
River House: remodeled by
Morgan, 1935
Tea House, 1935; with dancing
pavilion, boat dock, facilities for
tea and picnics
The Bend: added by Morgan,
1935–41, to a house built for
Charles Stetson Wheeler by
Willis Polk; later damaged by
fires
The Gables, 1937; destroyed by
fire, 1945

c. 1925   Julia Morgan houses:
remodeling of two Victorian
houses into apartments
2229 and 2231 Divisadero
Street, San Francisco

1925   San Francisco Examiner
Building: major alterations
William Randolph Hearst,
client
5th and Market streets, San
Francisco

San Francisco Nurses'
Association building
1155 Pine Street, San Francisco
Demolished

Mrs. E. F. Shortledge house
1284 Ashmont Avenue,
Oakland

Misses Irene and Inez Smith
house
714 Grand Avenue (or possibly
1804 Central Avenue), Alameda
Not located
Job no. 622

Jules Suppo apartments, shop,
and workroom
2423–25 Polk Street, San
Francisco

Steve Zegar, child's playhouse
Mill Street, San Luis Obispo

1925–26 Margaret Baylor Inn
924 Anacalpa Street, Santa
Barbara
Job no. 584

Hollywood Studio Club
YWCA, client
1215 Lodi Place, Hollywood

YWCA Metropolitan
Headquarters
1040 Richards Street, Honolulu,
Hawaii
Job no. 610

1926 Agnes Goodwin Culver house
1411 Hawthorne Street,
Berkeley

Mr. and Mrs. Ben Reed house
200 Crocker Avenue, Piedmont
See also 1910–12

Margaret Stewart house,
guesthouse, and garage with
apartments
Benbow Valley, Garberville

University of Hawaii YWCA
University of Hawaii, Honolulu
Not clearly documented

1926–27 Miss Newell Drown house
4455 Anza Street, San Francisco

1926–30 Chapel of the Chimes,
California Crematorium
Lawrence Moore, client
4499 Piedmont Avenue,
Oakland
Job no. 631

1927 Dr. Harold Alvarez house
75 Yerba Buena, St. Francis'
Wood, San Francisco
Thaddeus Joy, associate
architect

Berkeley Day Nursery
auditorium
6th Street, between Addison
Street and University Avenue,
Berkeley

Mrs. Winifred Bonfils house
(Annie Laurie)
3320 Baker Street, San Francisco

Mrs. Robert E. Easton house
730 S. Broadway, Santa Maria

W. H. L. Hynes house
30 Crocker Avenue, Piedmont
Not clearly documented

Giulio Minetti house:
remodeling into three
apartments
2615 California Street, San
Francisco

Minerva Club (Santa Maria
Women's Club)
Lincoln and Boone streets,
Santa Maria

1927–29 Dean William Hart house:
additions of library wing,
enclosed stair tower, bath,
sleeping porch
1401 LeRoy Avenue, Berkeley

1928 Unbuilt project: Church of San
Carlos Borromeo
Monterey

Cosmopolitan Headquarters:
projection room and additions
Hollywood
Demolished

The Hearthstone
California Federation of
Women's Clubs, client
Redwood Forest Dyerville–Bull
Creek State Park, Humboldt
County

Native Daughters of the Golden
West building
500 Baker Street, San Francisco

Mr. and Mrs. T. J. Perkins house
345 Golden Gate Avenue,
Belvedere
Not documented

Dr. and Mrs. Wilkin house
Auckland, New Zealand
Plans by Morgan; construction
supervised by Edward Hussey

Seldon and Elizabeth Glide
Williams house
2821 Claremont Boulevard,
Berkeley
Job no. 648
See also 1911

1929 Mr. and Mrs. Harry Gwinn
house
14 Martha Street, Petaluma
Elevator added by Morgan, 1933

Dr. W. L. Jepson house
11 Mosswood Road, Berkeley
Job no. 687

Riverside YWCA
3245 7th Street, Riverside

1929–30 Berkeley Women's City Club
2315 Durant Street, Berkeley

The Residence
YWCA, client
940 Powell Street, San Francisco
Job no. 704

1930s Hearst Building: interior
alterations for Hearst Radio
Incorporated Studios
William Randolph Hearst,
client
3rd and Market streets, San
Francisco
Job no. 768

Hearst Globe Wireless Station
William Randolph Hearst,
client
Cahill Ridge, San Mateo
Job no. 748
Demolished

KYA Broadcasting Station
San Francisco
William Randolph Hearst,
client
Job no. 761
Demolished

Principia College women's
dormitories
Elsah, Illinois

Dr. Walter Schilling
apartments: interior design and
alteration for Else Schilling
2006 Washington Street, San
Francisco
Job no. 709

Mrs. Elsie Lee Turner house
Speculative property of Fred C.
Turner
Panoramic Way, Berkeley
Not located
See also 1908, 1916, 1938–41 (3)

1930 Chinese YWCA
965 Clay Street, San Francisco
Job no. 711

Marion Davies Foundation
Pediatric Clinic
11672 Louisiana Avenue, Los
Angeles
Job no. 706

Japanese YWCA
1830 Sutter Street, San
Francisco
Job no. 712

Mrs. Henry Marcus penthouse
apartment
1040 Lombard Street, San
Francisco
Job no. 740

August Schilling cottage
Woodside
Built on his estate for his
daughter Else
Not located
Job no. 709

1930–31 George Hearst house: extensive remodeling
401 El Cerrito, Hillsborough

1930–37 Homelani Columbarium
388 Ponahawaii Street, Hilo, Hawaii
Job no. 736

c. 1931 Town and Gown Club: alterations and repairs
2401 Dwight Way, Berkeley

1932–36 William Randolph Hearst Hacienda
Milpitas Ranch, King City-Jolon
Plus some remodeling on adjacent Mission San Antonio de Padua

1933–34 Monday Club (San Luis Obispo Women's Club)
1800 Monterey Street, San Luis Obispo

1935 A. Aguis house
210 West Street, Petaluma
Job no. 758

Dr. and Mrs. Edward Cline Bull house: extensive remodeling
2518 Union Street, San Francisco
Job no. 737

R. N. Burgess house
35 Pine Crest Street, Lakewood, Walnut Creek
Job no. 759

1936 Unbuilt project: Hotel
William Randolph Hearst, client
South Rim of the Grand Canyon, Arizona
Job no. 720

Julia Morgan house: remodeling and alterations
Cedar and Hellam streets, Monterey
Job no. 763

Edythe Tate-Thompson house and garage-studio
Scott Place, Prospect Terrace Park, Pasadena
Not located
See also 1920

VKUP Transmitting and Receiving Station, Radio Station XMTR
William Randolph Hearst, client
Redwood City
Job no. 742
Demolished

1936–38 Morehead house and guesthouse
Twin Pines, Lake Tahoe
Job no. 741

1937 Cosmopolitan bungalow for Marion Davies
MGM lot, Hollywood
Job no. 780
Not located

San Francisco Hearst Building: alterations
William Randolph Hearst, client
3rd and Market streets, San Francisco
Job no. 777

1938 Dr. David Hadden house
Euclid Avenue, Berkeley
Demolished
Job no. 766
See also 1910–11

1938–39 Mr. and Mrs. Allan M. Starr house
216 Hampton Road, Piedmont
Job no. 778

1938–41 Fred C. Turner laboratory
Bancroft Way, Berkeley
Job nos. 779 and 784(?)
Demolished
See also 1908, 1916, 1930s

Fred C. Turner medical building
Bancroft Way, Berkeley
Job no. 745
Demolished
See also 1908, 1916, 1930s

Fred C. Turner stores, offices, and Black Sheep Restaurant
2546 Bancroft Way, Berkeley
Job no. 760
See also 1908, 1916, 1930s

1939 Marion Davies house and pool
910 Benedict Canyon, Santa Monica

James N. Parsons house: alterations
Monterey
Not located

Else Schilling house
Bow Bay, Lake Tahoe
Job no. 783

1940 Unbuilt project: Mrs. A. H. Darbee Columbarium (Western Hills of Memorial City, Inc.)
Lawndale, South San Francisco
Designed with Bernard Maybeck
Job no. 782

Drs. Charles and Emma Wightman Pope house
2981 Franciscan Way, Carmel
Job no. 785

Russian Day School and Nursery
Sutter Street, between Divisadero and Broderick streets, San Francisco
Not located
Job no. 792

George F. Volkman house: alterations
2307 Broadway, San Francisco
Job no. 714
Hand-carved frieze added, 1940s; job no. 794

1941 Unbuilt project: Medieval Museum
Golden Gate Park, San Francisco
William Randolph Hearst, later City of San Francisco, clients
Job no. 786

1943–45 Unbuilt project: William Randolph Hearst Hacienda (The Clouds)
Babicora, Mexico

SELECTED BIBLIOGRAPHY

Documentary Sources

Bancroft Library, University of California, Berkeley. Includes five letters from Julia Morgan to Phoebe Apperson Hearst; some photographs; a collection of plans and drawings, most donated by Morgan's clients; Bernard Maybeck's drawings for the proposed Morgan-Maybeck columbarium commissioned by Mrs. A. H. Darbee (never built); and some drawings and plans related to Asilomar. The library's Regional Oral History Office has on file transcripts, tapes, and publications related to Suzanne B. Riess, ed., "The Julia Morgan Architectural History Project," 1976.

Documents Collection, College of Environmental Design, University of California, Berkeley. Includes correspondence and drawings from Morgan's days at the Ecole des Beaux-Arts; her drawings and specifications for the Harriet Fearing house in Fontainebleau; her diary for her 1947 trip to South America; drawings from the Forney-Stone collection; the Walter Steilberg papers; and Edward Hussey's files.

Julia Morgan Collection, Robert E. Kennedy Library, California Polytechnic State University, San Luis Obispo. Includes everything that was saved from the Morgan estate; copies of all correspondence and records related to the Hearst commissions; and most of the material left at San Simeon when the California State Department of Parks and Recreation accepted the property. *Descriptive Guide to the Julia Morgan Collection* was published in 1985.

M. H. de Young Memorial Museum, San Francisco. Includes archival material related to the monastery Santa Maria de Ovila brought from Spain, first for use at Wyntoon and then for the proposed Medieval Museum (never built).

Books

Aidala, Thomas, and Curtis Bruce. *Hearst Castle, San Simeon.* New York: Hudson Hills Press, 1981.

Andree, Herb, and Noel Young. *Santa Barbara Architecture.* Santa Barbara, Calif.: Capra Press, 1975.

Baker, Joseph E. *Past and Present of Alameda County.* Chicago: S. J. Clarke, 1914, vol. 1, opp. p. 414.

Beach, John. "The Bay Area Tradition, 1890–1915." In *Bay Area Houses,* ed. Sally B. Woodbridge. New York: Oxford University Press, 1976.

———. "Julia Morgan: An Architect from Oakland." In *Architectural Drawings by Julia Morgan,* exhibition catalog. Foreword by Therese Heyman. Chronology by Sara Holmes Boutelle. Oakland, Calif.: Oakland Museum, 1976.

Bender, Albert M. *To Remember Abraham and Max L. Rosenberg.* Photos by Ansel Adams, sketch for setting of five panels by Julia Morgan. San Francisco: Nash, 1931.

Benet, James. *A Guide to San Francisco and the Bay Region.* New York: Random House, 1963.

Bernhardi, Robert. *The Buildings of Berkeley.* Oakland, Calif.: Holmes Book Co., 1972; reprinted by Berkeley Architectural Heritage Association, 1984.

Bishton, Rodger C. *Charles M. Goethe: The Man and His Life.* Sacramento, Calif.: Sacramento State College, 1967, pp. 20, 62.

Bogart, Sewall. *Lauriston: An Architectural Biography of Herbert Edward Law.* Portola Valley, Calif.: Alpine House, 1976.

Bonfils, Winifred. *The Life and Personality of Phoebe Apperson Hearst.* San Francisco: John Henry Nash, 1928.

Boutelle, Sara Holmes. "Julia Morgan." In *Women in Architecture: A Historic and Contemporary Perspective,* ed. Susana Torre. New York: Whitney Library of Design, 1977.

———. "Julia Morgan." In *Master Builders: A Guide to Famous American Architects,* ed. Diane Maddex. Washington, D.C.: Preservation Press, National Trust for Historic Preservation, 1985.

Brand-Taylor, Elizabeth Morgan. *A History of the James Morgan Family of New London, 1607–1869.* Privately printed, n.d.

Cardwell, Kenneth H. *Bernard Maybeck: Artisan, Architect, Artist.* Santa Barbara, Calif.: Peregrine Smith, 1977.

Clark, Robert Judson, ed. *The Arts and Crafts Movement in America, 1876–1916.* Princeton, N.J.: Princeton University Press, 1972.

Clements, Robert. "Morgan, Julia, Wyntoon—1930." In Alison Sky and Michelle Stone. *Unbuilt America.* New York: Abbeville Press, 1983.

Coffman, Taylor. *Hearst Castle: The Story of William Randolph Hearst and San Simeon.* Santa Barbara, Calif.: Sequoia Books, 1985.

Delaire, E. *Les Architectes élèves de l'Ecole des Beaux-Arts.* Paris: Librairie de la Construction Moderne, 1907.

Detwiler, Justice B., et al., eds. *Who's Who in California: A Biographical Directory, 1928–29.* San Francisco: Who's Who Publishing Co., 1929.

Draper, Joan. "John Galen Howard." In *The Architect: Chapters in the History of the Profession,* ed. Spiro Kostof. New York: Oxford University Press, 1977.

Everingham, Carol J. *The Art of San Simeon.* Santa Barbara, Calif.: Haagen Printing, 1981.

Freudenheim, L. M., and E. S. Sussman. *Building with Nature: Roots of the San Francisco Bay Region Tradition.* Salt Lake City and Santa Barbara, Calif.: Peregrine Smith, 1974.

Gebhard, David, et al. *A Guide to Architecture in San Francisco and Northern California.* Santa Barbara, Calif.: Peregrine Smith, 1973.

Gebhard, David, and Robert Winter. *A Guide to Architecture in Los Angeles and Southern California.* Santa Barbara: Peregrine Smith, 1977.

Gebhard, David, and Deborah Nevins. *Two Hundred Years of American Architectural Drawings.* New York: Whitney Library of Design, 1977.

Guenther, Gary. *A Beaux-Arts Gymnasium: Julia Morgan and Bernard Maybeck.* Berkeley, Calif., 1962.

Hanchett, Byron. *In and Around the Castle.* San Luis Obispo, Calif.: Blake Publishing, 1985.

Himmelwright, C. E. *The San Francisco Earthquake and Fire, 1906.* New York: Roebling Construction Company, 1906.

Hunt, Hazel-Ann. *Asilomar, The First Fifty Years, 1913–63.* Pacific Grove: California State Park System, 1963. A booklet was compiled in 1973 as a ten-year supplement to *The First Fifty Years.*

Keep, Rosalind A. *Fourscore and Ten Years.* Oakland, Calif.: Mills College, 1946.

Kidder Smith, G. E. *The Architecture of the United States.* Vol. 3, *The Plain States and Far West.* New York: Anchor Books, 1981.

Lockwood, Charles. *Dream Palaces: Hollywood at Home.* New York: Viking Press, 1981.

Longstreth, Richard. *On the Edge of the World: Four Architects in San Francisco at the Turn of the Century.* New York: Architectural History Foundation; Cambridge, Mass., and London: MIT Press, 1983.

Marvin, Betty. *The Residential Work in Berkeley of Five Women Architects.* Berkeley, Calif.: Berkeley Architectural Heritage Association, 1984.

Miller, et al. *Pacific Grove, California.* Pacific Grove, Calif.: Pacific Grove Press, 1975.

Moore, Charles, et al. *American Domestic Vernacular Architecture: Home Sweet Home.* New York: Rizzoli, 1983.

Murray, Ken. *The Golden Days of San Simeon.* Garden City, N.Y.: Doubleday, 1971.

National Cyclopedia of American Biography. New York: James T. White and Co., 1946, vol. G, p. 151.

Older, Mrs. Fremont [Cora Miranda Baggerly]. *William Randolph Hearst, American.* New York: Appleton-Century Co., 1936.

Olmsted, Roger, and T. H. Watkins. *Here Today: San Francisco's Architectural Heritage.* San Francisco: Chronicle Books, 1975.

Partridge, Loren W. *John Galen Howard and the Berkeley Campus: Beaux-Arts Architecture in the "Athens of the West."* Berkeley, Calif.: Berkeley Architectural Heritage Association, 1978.

Pattiani, Evelyn Craig. *Piedmont, Queen of the Hills.* Piedmont, Calif.: privately printed, n.d. (on file in the Oakland Public Library).

Regnery, Dorothy F. *An Enduring Heritage: Historic Buildings of the San Francisco Peninsula.* Palo Alto, Calif.: Stanford University Press, 1980.

Richey, Elinor. *Eminent Women of the West.* Berkeley, Calif.: Howell-North Books, 1975, chap. 9.

Riess, Suzanne B., ed. "The Julia Morgan Architectural History Project." Berkeley: Bancroft Library, Regional Oral History Office, University of California, 1976, 2 vols.

St. John, Adela Rogers. *The Honeycomb.* New York: New American Library, 1970.

Seares, Mabel Urmy. *The Lyric Land of California.* Pasadena, c. 1920.

Sicherman, Barbara, et al., eds. *Notable American Women, The Modern Period: A Biographical Dictionary.* Prepared under the auspices of Radcliffe College. Cambridge, Mass.: Belknap Press of Harvard University Press, 1980.

Swanberg, W. A. *Citizen Hearst: A Biography of William Randolph Hearst.* New York: Charles Scribner's Sons, 1961.

van Pelt, John Vredenburgh. *A Discussion of Composition Especially as Applied to Architecture.* New York: Macmillan, 1902. No mention is made of Morgan, but van Pelt was a friend and fellow student at the Ecole des Beaux-Arts, and his ideas throw light on hers.

Wilson, Carol Green. *Chinatown Quest: One Hundred Years of the Donaldina Cameron House.* San Francisco: California Historical Society, 1974.

Winslow, Carleton M., Jr., and Nickola L. Frye. *The Enchanted Hill.* Hillbrae, Calif.: Celestial Arts, 1980.

Woodbridge, John, and Sally Byrne Woodbridge. *Buildings of the Bay Area: A Guide to the Architecture of the San Francisco Bay Region.* New York: Grove Press, 1960.

———. *Architecture San Francisco.* San Francisco: AIA 101 Productions, 1982.

Wright, Georgia S. "Morgan and Maybeck at Mills," unpublished exhibition catalog. Oakland, Calif.: Mills College Art Gallery, 1981.

Wright, Gwendolyn. *Building the Dream.* New York: Pantheon, 1981.

Articles and Unpublished Papers

Anderson, Judith. "Rediscovering a Forgotten Architect." *San Francisco Chronicle,* July 2, 1975, p. 21.

"April House Tour [featuring four Morgan buildings]." *Oakland Tribune,* March 27, 1966.

Architect and Engineer cites Morgan in numerous issues. October 1904, vol. 10, pp. 69–71, on Mills College. March 1907, p. 90, on Viavi building. March 1910, vol. 20, p. 34, on use of reinforced concrete at Mills College, with picture of bell tower. For articles on Morgan in *Architect and Engineer,* see also Mesic, Morrow, Steilberg, and Sumner.

Aikman, Duncan. "A Renaissance Palace in Our West." *New York Times Magazine,* July 21, 1929, pp. 10–11.

Bailey, A. "Mr. Hearst at Home." *Architectural Review* 75 (March 1934): 87–90.

"Berkeley the Beautiful." *Sunset* 18 (December 1906): 138–44.

The *Berkeley Gazette* has published articles on the Berkeley Women's City Club's thirty-fourth anniversary (November 11, 1961); on the Colby house (January 23, 1974); and on the two Panoramic Way apartment buildings (February 13, 1974).

Brewer, Henrietta. "Julia Morgan, Our Architect." *Kappa Alpha Theta Journal,* 1909, pp. 473–74.

Boutelle, Sara Holmes. "A Woman of Many Firsts." *Art* (Oakland Museum Association), January–February 1976.

———. "The Woman Who Built San Simeon." *California Monthly* 86 (April 1976): cover, 12–14, and 34.

———. "Women for Networks: Julia Morgan and Her Clients." *Heresies* 11 3 (Spring 1981): 91–94.

———. "Julia Morgan: A Synthesis of Tradition." *Architecture California* 7 (January–February 1985): 30–31.

Calais, Al. "Impeccable Pedigree May Help Protect House—Sacramento's Goethe House May Qualify as a Historic Site Because of Its Well-Known Architect." *Sacramento Bee,* November 22, 1981, p. B1.

"California's Contribution to a National Architecture." *Craftsman* 22 (August 1912): 532–60.

"Chinese YWCA Building, San Francisco, California." *Architecture* 67 (April 1933): 195–98.

Cockburn, Alexander. "California Xanadu." *House and Garden* 159 (October 1987): 222–32.

"A College Bell Tower." *Cement Age,* October 1911, p. 151.

Conley, Phebe B. "Phoebe Rideout, Philanthropist." *Marysville-Yuba City Appeal Democrat,* May 17, 1980.

Craig, Robert M. "Bernard Ralph Maybeck and the Principia: Architecture as a Philosophical Expression." *Journal of Society of Architectural Historians* 31 (October 1972): 234.

Cret, Paul-Philippe. "The Ecole des Beaux-Arts and Architectural Education." *Journal of the Society of Architectural Historians* 1 (April 1941): 3–15.

Croly, Herbert. "The California Country House." *Sunset* 18 (November 1906): 50–55.

"Editor's Report: Wm. R. Hearst, Jr.—The Enchanted Hill." *San Francisco Chronicle,* August 25, 1974, part 11, p. 1.

"EPIC-WEST to Restore Church Designed and Built by Julia Morgan." *American Preservation* 1 (December 1977–January 1978): 79.

Les Esquisses de vingt-quatre heures (Paris). Auguste Vincent, publisher. Published annually 1890–1907.

Everett, Edith. "Odd Features of California Architecture." *Keith's Magazine,* April 1910, pp. 263–65.

Failing, Patricia. "William Randolph Hearst's Enchanted Hill." *Artnews* 78 (January 1979): 53–59.

———. "She Was America's Most Successful Woman Architect—and Hardly Anybody Knows Her Name." *Artnews* 80 (January 1981): 66–71.

"Fall Stroll at Historic Mills College." *Sunset* 169 (November 1982): 5.

"First Woman Admitted to Beaux-Arts." *Daily Californian (Berkeleyan)* 12 (December 7, 1898): 1.

Gallup, Aaron. "Mills College." *Oakland Heritage Alliance News* 5 (Summer 1985): 1–5.

Gebhard, David. "Architectural Imagery, the Mission, and California." *Harvard Architectural Review* 1 (Spring 1980): 137–45.

Golkey, Ruth. "A Castle in Miniature [Seldon Williams house]." *Oakland Tribune,* February 20, 1972, Sunday Home Magazine.

Groff, Frances A. "Lovely Woman at the Exposition." *Sunset,* May 1915, pp. 881ff.

"Hearst." *Fortune* 12 (October 1935): 42–55, 123–54.

"Hearst at Home." *Fortune* 3 (May 1931): 56–58, 130.

"Highest Honors Given Woman." *San Francisco Chronicle*, May 16, 1929, p. 1.

Holmes, Nancy. "San Simeon: An American Fantasy." *Town and Country*, May 1981, pp. 164–73, 226.

Hubbard, Harold N. "Local Landmark Status Awaits YWCA Building in Pasadena." *Pasadena Star News*, November 8, 1977, pp. B–1Z.

Hubbell, Thelma L., and Gloria Lothrop. "The Friday Morning Club, An L.A. Legacy." *Southern California Quarterly* 550 (March 1968): 59–90.

Huxtable, Ada Louise. "Progressive Architecture in America: Reinforced Concrete Construction. The Work of Ernest L. Ransome, Engineer, 1884–1911." *Progressive Architecture* 38 (September 1957): 139–42.

"Is There a Bay Style?" *Architectural Record* 105 (May 1949): 92–97.

"Julia Morgan, '94, Makes Name in Architecture." *California Alumni* (U.C. Berkeley) 8 (October 23, 1915): 1.

"Julia Morgan, Omega." *Kappa Alpha Theta Journal*, 1927, pp. 170–71.

"Julia Morgan, Pioneer Architect." *YWCA News of Oakland and South Alameda* 2 (November 1975): 3–4.

Kingman, Carrie. "William E. Colby House." Paper for College of Environmental Design, University of California, Berkeley, 1975.

Lobell, J. "American Women Architects." *Artforum* 15 (Summer 1971): 31.

Lo Grippo, Ro. "Unearthing Facts on San Simeon's Creator." *San Mateo Times*, July 3, 1975.

———. "Julia Morgan's Undiscovered Work." *San Bruno Herald*, July 9, 1975.

Longstreth, Richard W. "Julia Morgan: Some Introductory Notes." *Perspecta* (Yale University) 15 (1975): 74–86. Reprinted as *Julia Morgan, Architect*. Berkeley: Berkeley Architectural Heritage Association, 1977 and 1986, with 12 additional photographs.

Maclay, Mira. "Berkeley Women's City Club." *Arts and Architecture* 39 (June 1931): 25–29.

Mead, Marcia. "Women's Versatility in Arts Enriches Field of Architecture." *Christian Science Monitor*, November 27, 1931, p. 5.

"Merchants of Frisco." *Architect* 122 (October 1976): 46–47. Discusses restoration of the Merchants Exchange Building Trading Room—architecture by Willis Polk, interior design by Julia Morgan.

Mesic, Julian. "Berkeley Women's City Club." *Architect and Engineer* 105 (April 1931): 24–47.

Mili, Gjon (photographer). "A Unique Tour of San Simeon." *Life* 43 (August 29, 1957): 68–79. This article, which did not mention Morgan, prompted Allan Temko's letter to the editor about her, *Life* 43 (September 16, 1957): 10.

"The Minerva Club of Santa Maria." *Western Architecture* 32 (November 1923): 126–28.

Molten, P. L. "Asilomar." *Architectural Review* 157 (January 1975): 123–24.

Morrow, Irving F. *Architect and Engineer* 47 (October 1916): 51, 62. Photographs of Morgan's work.

———. "Reflections on Houses." *Architect and Engineer* 63 (April 1923): 51–55.

North, Flora D. "She Built for the Ages." *Kappa Alpha Theta Journal*, Spring 1967, pp. 9–11.

"Noted Architect Julia Morgan Dies after Long Illness." *San Francisco Chronicle*, February 3, 1957, p. 3.

Obituary. *American Institute of Architects Journal* 28, pt. 1 (May 1957): 28.

Obituary. *California Monthly*, May 1957.

Olson, Lynne. "The Unlikely Creator of Hearst's San Simeon." *Smithsonian* 16 (December 1985): 60–73.

Osman, Mary E. "Julia Morgan of California: A Passion for Quality and Anonymity." *American Institute of Architects Journal* 65 (June 1976): 44–48.

Perry, Frank. "St. Francis' Wood." *Building Review* 22 (August 1922): plate 14.

"The PPIE in Its Glorious Prime." *Overland Monthly* 65 (1915): 289.

"Refectory of La Cuesta Encantada, Estate of William Randolph Hearst, San Simeon, California." *American Architect and Architecture* 145 (September 1934): 37–42.

Reynolds, Flora Elizabeth. "Coming Full Circle: The Story of the Mills Library." *Mills College Quarterly*, February 1977, pp. 5–11.

Robbins, Millie. "San Simeon's Architect." *San Francisco Chronicle*, January 16, 1963, p. 15.

Rochlin, Harriet. "Distinguished Generation of Women Architects in California." *American Institute of Architects Journal* 66 (August 1977): 38–39.

Scharlach, Bernice. "Julia Morgan's Buildings Grow Old Gracefully." *Courier* (California Historical Society), April 1975.

———. "The Legacy of Julia Morgan." *San Francisco Chronicle*, August 24, 1975, California Living section, pp. 24–27, 29–31.

Schuyler, Montgomery. "The Work of Napoleon LeBrun and Sons." *Architectural Record*, May 1910, p. 365.

Seares, Mabel Urmy. "Some Types of Shingle Houses." *House Beautiful* 29 (February 1911): 89–90.

———. "A Community Approaches Its Ideal." *California Arts and Architecture* 38 (June 1930): 19–21, 1970, 1972.

Steilberg, Walter. "Some Examples of the Work of Julia Morgan." *Architect and Engineer* 55 (November 1918): 38–107.

Sumner, Charles K. "Some Aspects of School Architecture." *Architect and Engineer* 64 (March 1921): 46–67.

"Superintending the Building of Prof. Lawson's House." *Daily Californian (Berkeleyan)* 6 (October 28, 1895): 4.

Thompson, Elisabeth Kendall. "The Early Domestic Architecture of the San Francisco Bay Region." *Journal of the Society of Architectural Historians* 10 (October 1951): 15–21.

Tinnemann, Sister Ethel M. "The Mary R. Smith's Trust Cottages." *Oakland Heritage Alliance News*, Winter 1985, pp. 1–4.

Tyler, Charlotte. "An Annotated Bibliography of Julia Morgan, California Architect." Paper for College of Environmental Design library, University of California, Berkeley, 1964.

van Slambrouck, Paul. "A Business Landmark Restored: The Merchants Exchange Trading Hall Reopens Its Doors after Years of Neglect and Near Extinction." *San Francisco Business* 11 (January 1976): cover, 20–23.

van Zanten, David. "Le Système des Beaux-Arts." *Architecture d'aujourd'hui* 182 (November–December 1975): 97–106.

"Women in Architecture: The New Professional: Historic Beginnings." *Progressive Architecture* 58 (March 1977): 42–57.

Woodbridge, Sally. "Preservation: St. John's." *Architectural Forum* 139 (September 1973): 18.

———. "Historic Architecture: Wyntoon." *Architectural Digest*, January 1988, pp. 97–103, 156.

Woodring, Peggy. Unpublished monograph on Julia Morgan prepared for *Architecture Plus* and delivered as lecture at Berkeley City Club, October 20, 1975.

Wright, Hamilton M. "The World's Exposition." *Overland Monthly* 65 (January 1915): 57–64.

"YWCA Building, Honolulu, Hawaii, Views and Plans." *Architecture* 57 (March 1928): 151–54.

INDEX

PHOTOGRAPHY CREDITS

Unless otherwise indicated, all color photographs are by Richard Barnes. Other photographers and sources of photographic material are as follows:

Architect and Engineer, November 1918: 64 (top, photo by Walter Steilberg), 67 (top, photo by Walter Steilberg); April 1931: 124 (left).

Douglas Arthur: 14 (right).

Bancroft Library, University of California, Berkeley: 52, 53, 83, 91, 169.

Richard Barnes: 9 (bottom), 50, 72 (top), 74 (bottom), 97 (right), 134 (top), 175 (top right).

Berkeley Architectural Heritage Association: 72.

Courtesy Sewell Bogart, from his book *Lauriston* (Portola Valley, Calif.: Alpine House Publications, 1976): 79.

Margaret Burke: 118, 218 (center).

Lauren Carter, Santa Cruz: 153 (bottom).

Courtesy Castlewood Country Club: 172, 173.

Courtesy Dorothy Wormser Coblentz: 46 (top).

Taylor Coffman: 201 (bottom left).

Bjarne Dahl: 80 (top left and bottom left), 108 (top).

Dapprich Photo, Los Angeles: 12, 185.

Courtesy Mrs. Dean: 138.

Document Collection, College of Environmental Design, University of California, Berkeley: 34–36, 38, 56, 70, 218 (bottom).

James H. Edelen: 9 (top), 15 (left, bottom center, and right), 58, 62, 63, 65 (bottom), 67 (bottom), 68, 69, 74 (top), 75, 88 (top), 92, 107, 120, 137 (bottom), 140, 142–45, 147, 148, 152 (top and center), 153 (top), 167, 174, 220–22, 223 (left), 224, 225 (top left and bottom), 228 (top).

Fern Hicks Farnum: 155.

Richard Fernau: 208 (top).

Plans drawn by Fernau & Hartman, Berkeley: 134–36.

Foote Collection: 129, 131.

Courtesy Winston Frey: 181, 203 (bottom right).

Lucy Hale: 242.

Russell D. Hardy, Courtesy Lyndon/Buchanan Associates, Berkeley: 106.

Hearst Collection, New York: 236 (bottom).

Mrs. Walter Hettman Collection, San Francisco: 60 (top).

Courtesy Hollywood Studio Club, 113, 114.

Courtesy John E. Jordan: 139.

Courtesy Betty Lewis: 57.

George Loorz: 230 (center and bottom).

Courtesy Jacomena Maybeck, Berkeley: 48.

Courtesy Susan Cole McCarthy: 132, 133.

Neale McGoldrick: 13 (top), 108 (bottom), 109, 112, 180 (top), 234 (top).

Ray Miller: 115 (top).

National Board YWCA Archives: 88 (bottom), 93, 100, 101 (tracing by Chris Macy), 102–5.

Courtesy Elizabeth Reynolds Collection: 60 (bottom).

Courtesy Milicent Rossi: 201 (bottom right).

Courtesy San Francisco YWCA: 115 (bottom, photo by Hassman-Myers, San Francisco), 116, 117.

Irene Seitz: 154.

Kidder Smith: 193 (left).

Drawn by Michael Sotero: 146, 158, 159, 237 (redrawn from tracing by author of original in Hearst Collection, New York).

Special Collections, University Archives, Cal Poly, San Luis Obispo: 18–21, 22 (Morgan Collection in Berkeley before it was housed at Cal Poly), 30, 31, 40, 54, 78 (bottom, from *Trial by Fire*, insurance document), 127 (right, photo by Newton Drury), 152 (bottom), 156 (right), 175 (top left), 176, 178 (photo by Walter Steilberg), 179 (bottom, photo by Dorothy Wormser), 182, 187–88 (on loan from Hearst Collection, New York), 202, 203 (bottom left), 212, 217, 232, 233, 234 (bottom), 235.

Courtesy Allan Starr: 137 (top).

Walter Steilberg: 14 (top left and bottom left), 61, 64 (top left and bottom left), 238.

Courtesy Walter Steilberg: 65 (top), 189 (photo by Philip Negus Frasse).

Courtesy Dolly Sturges: 82.

Ticor Title Insurance (Los Angeles) Collection of Historical Photographs, California Historical Society: 175 (bottom).

Vano Photography: 43.